Starting with Shakespeare

Starting with Shakespeare

Successfully Introducing Shakespeare to Children

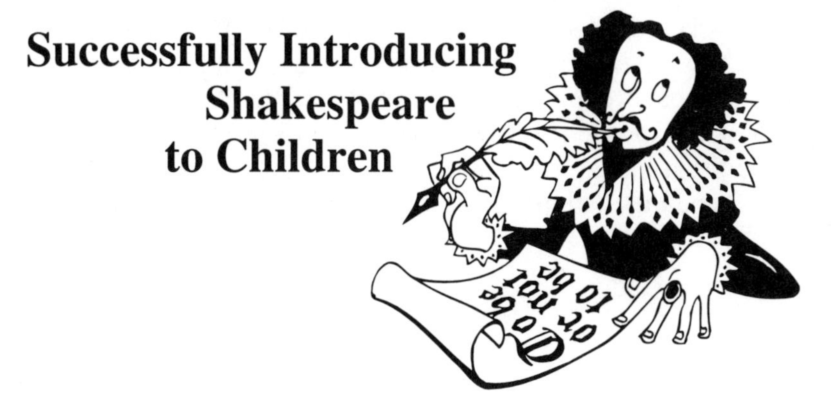

Pauline Nelson
Todd Daubert

Illustrated by
Jason Shwartz

2000
Teacher Ideas Press
A Division of
Libraries Unlimited, Inc.
Englewood, Colorado

To everyone who had to study Shakespeare and hated it! You always knew there should be a better way—and now there is!

TEACHER IDEAS PRESS
A Division of
Libraries Unlimited, Inc.
P.O. Box 6633
Englewood, CO 80155-6633
1-800-237-6124
www.lu.com/tip

Library of Congress Cataloging-in-Publication Data

Nelson, Pauline.
Starting with Shakespeare : successfully introducing Shakespeare to children / by Pauline Nelson, Todd Daubert ; illustrated by Jason Shwartz.
xv, 217 p. 22x28 cm.
Includes bibliographical references and index.
ISBN 1-56308-753-7
1. Shakespeare, William, 1564-1616--Study and teaching (Elementary) 2. English drama--Study and teaching (Elementary) 3. Drama in education. I. Daubert, Todd. II. Shwartz, Jason. III. Title.
PR2987.N45 1999
822.3′3--DC21 99-38709
CIP

Contents

Oh for a muse of fire, that would ascend the brightest heaven of invention.
(*Henry V*, Prologue)

Introduction: Lighting the Fire ix

Part One: Setting the Stage

Fuel for the Fire 3
- The Bard's Bare-Bones Bio 3
- The Bard's Better Bio 3
- The Bard's Best Bio 3
- The Bard's Beefy Bio 4
- The Bard's Beefy Bio—Second Helpings! 5

Spontaneous Combustion 6
- Playing with the Bard 6

Fanning the Flames 10
- The Hook 10
- The Line 12
- The Sinker 15

How Not to Get Burned 16
- Learning from Shakespearience 16
- Shakespeare Work Rubric 18
- Shakespeare Behavior Rubric 18

Part Two: The Plays

Hamlet 21
- What You Should Know about *Hamlet* 23
- Who's Who 23
  - The Major Characters 23
  - The Major Minor Characters 24
  - The Minor Minor Characters 25
- What's What 25
  - Background Information 25
  - Scene by Scene 25
- What's Happening 26
  - The Story 26
  - Kidspeak and Shakespeak 27
- Will's Words—Selections for Recitation 31

Hamlet (*cont.*)
Lights, Camera, Action 43
Movie Making 43
The Tragedy of Hamlet, Prince of Denmark 46
Don't Just Sit There! 50
Language Arts 50
Social Studies 55
Art 56
Math 57
Science 58
Hot Stuff 59
Notes 59
Annotated Bibliography and Resources 60

Macbeth 61
What You Should Know About *Macbeth* 63
Who's Who 63
The Major Characters 63
The Major Minor Characters 64
The Minor Minor Characters 64
What's What 65
Background Information 65
Scene by Scene 66
What's Happening 67
The Story 67
Kidspeak and Shakespeak 68
Will's Words—Selections for Recitation 75
Lights, Camera, Action 87
Movie Making 87
Macbeth 91
Don't Just Sit There! 96
Language Arts 96
Social Studies 102
Art 104
Math 105
Science 106
Creative Thinking 106
Hot Stuff 107
Notes 107
Annotated Bibliography and Resources 107

A Midsummer Night's Dream 109
What You Should Know About *A Midsummer Night's Dream* 111
Who's Who 111
The Major Characters 111
The Minor Characters 114

What's What 115
Background Information 115
What's Happening 117
The Story 117
Kidspeak and Shakespeak 119
Will's Words—Selections for Recitation 126
Lights, Camera, Action 138
Movie Making 138
A Midsummer Night's Dream 141
Don't Just Sit There! 149
Language Arts 149
Social Studies/Geography/History 152
Math/Science 153
Hot Stuff 154
Notes 154
Annotated Bibliography and Resources 155

Romeo and Juliet 157
What You Should Know About *Romeo and Juliet* 159
Who's Who 159
The Major Characters 159
The Major Minor Characters 160
The Minor Minor Characters 161
What's What 163
Background Information 163
What's Happening 164
The Story 164
Kidspeak and Shakespeak 166
Will's Words—Selections for Recitation 175
Lights, Camera, Action 191
Movie Making 191
The Most Excellent and Lamentable Tragedy of Romeo and Juliet 194
Don't Just Sit There! 203
Language Arts 203
Social Studies/Geography/History 206
Math/Science 207
Hot Stuff 209
Notes 209
Annotated Bibliography and Resources 209
Conclusion 211
Parent Responses 211
Student Responses 214

Index 217

Introduction

Lighting the Fire

Fearless minds climb sooner unto crowns.
(Henry VI, 4.7)

So, you want to introduce the Bard to elementary school students. We know exactly how you are feeling right now! We have stood where you are—ready to put a toe in the water, but wondering if piranhas lurk just below the surface. You are probably thinking, "There must be danger if I am the only one down by the water!" Well, you are in luck, because you are now reading the quintessential guide on how to not only get into the water painlessly but also how to explore the depths and resurface without experiencing a bad case of the bends! In other words, this book will give you the tools you need to present Shakespeare to young children successfully—no hassles, no headaches—no kidding!

Is not the truth the truth?
(Henry IV, 2.4)

We assume that you are not a member of The Royal Shakespeare Company, and that you have not recently written a thesis titled *The Life and Times of William Shakespeare, and the Effect His Birth Order Had on the Neuroses of Lady Macbeth.* We further assume that, even though you work with young children, you are of normal intelligence—although some say that choosing a career in teaching does bring this assumption into question! (*We* wouldn't say this, of course, because we are teachers, too!) Having established the preceding assumptions, we can state with a fair degree of accuracy that, like most of us, you

- know that Shakespeare lived in England a long time ago;
- can name two or three of his plays;
- couldn't tell the whole plot of any one play but could creatively combine plots of two or more to create a play Shakespeare *should* have written;
- did Shakespeare at school—but are still interested in his plays, despite the whole experience;
- would not choose *Shakespeare* on "Jeopardy," even if the only other category left was *Coelenterata.*

However, in spite of being normal and stressed by the demands of school and home, you are willing to go where few elementary teachers have gone before. *Great!* You won't be sorry! We hope our experiences and ideas will make it easier for you.

Why Shakespeare?

For more than 400 years, Shakespeare has been considered one of the world's greatest playwrights and poets. Shakespeare's plays are a treasure-house of rich language, and they reveal to students the source of many of our modern expressions (e.g., "The world's mine oyster," *The Merry Wives of Windsor*). The plots are timeless, chronicling high comedy and heart-wrenching tragedy, and are still relevant today. The characters portray traits all too human and experience dilemmas no less relevant today than when created so many centuries ago. Is it possible that anyone would even consider ignoring such a genius?

Why Shakespeare in Elementary School?

Students need to be rescued from the DDT—Dumbing-Down Trend! Educators need to provide their schools' curricula with challenge and variety as well as with a strong commitment to teaching basic skills. The stories, characters, and language of William Shakespeare meet the needs of students and the dictates of the curriculum by providing

- challenge and variety,
- a unique vehicle for instruction in the basic skills of language arts,
- a focal point for a stimulating interdisciplinary unit.

Shakespeare can be made relevant to the lives of young students. Experience has shown us that, with flair and enthusiasm, elementary students will understand the story line of a play, begin to appreciate the language, and become excited and eager to learn more!

Through the study of Shakespeare's plays, young children will learn to

- recall significant details,
- use literary terminology accurately,
- recognize, compare, and contrast recurrent themes between plays,
- demonstrate an understanding of Shakespeare's use of words and figurative language,
- make personal, literary, historical, and multicultural connections,
- increase his or her vocabulary,
- sharpen listening and speaking skills,
- become motivated to learn more.

Teachers with the vision and the courage to try something new always have to suffer the slings and arrows of doubting—and usually very vocal—colleagues! You will find the following section useful when dealing with the questions, doubts, sneers, and, we hope, interest from those who choose to stand on the shore watching you set off on an incredible adventure!

Top 20 Answers to the Question "Why on Earth Would You Want to Teach Shakespeare to Children?"

1. His stories are as good as those of the Brothers Grimm—and a lot better than some of the stories out there today.
2. Children enjoy the challenge.
3. Children enjoy the stories and are motivated to learn.
4. Shakespeare empowers the child—puts the child in a position of teaching their parents something that is valued.
5. Parents are impressed, and they begin to revive their faith in public education.
6. It demystifies Shakespeare and makes more formal study easier later.
7. Teachers use all kinds of topics as starting places for thematic units—Shakespeare is a top-quality starting place.
8. Study of the plays provides a source of rich, picturesque language through riddles and puns.
9. The characters in Shakespeare's plays are timeless.
10. The study of Shakespeare reveals the history of the language.
11. Studying Shakespeare with children frees Shakespeare from the high-brow ties that have sanctified the plays and taken all the fun out of them.
12. Studying Shakespeare's plays provides children with examples of what high-quality writing sounds like.
13. The language of Shakespeare pops up all the time in phrases and sayings.
14. Children enjoy top-quality work.
15. Children will rise to your expectations. Raise standards—expect more.
16. The study of Shakespeare's plays can initiate learning in many areas of the curriculum—history, geography, and language skills.
17. This is something the teacher can get enthusiastic about, too!
18. Studying the plays opens a whole new world for many students.
19. The plays provide a springboard for discussion and debate around issues that are as relevant today as they were more than 400 years ago.
20. The pendulum tends to swing in an extreme arc in education, and we should be cautious about disregarding our literary heritage merely because it is Eurocentric when Eurocentricism is not currently politically correct.

If the skeptics fail to be convinced at this point, just ask them how many answers they can give to the question "*Why not?*"

We owe it to young students to present to them the amazing, remarkable, astounding plays of Shakespeare, and to present them in a way that will leave the students craving more. The time has come to stop underestimating the capabilities of young children and to begin expecting the moon. Who knows, we might reach the stars!

The skies are painted with unnumberd sparks
They are all fire and every one doth shine.
(Julius Caesar, 3.1)

Educator's interpretation:

The schools are full of inspired learners
They are all enthusiastic and every one doth shine!

Been There, Done That! (Advice from the Front Lines)

Secrets to Successfully Introducing Elementary Students to a Shakespeare Play

1. Post this quote and hang it where it can inspire you and make you smile when things get a little challenging!

   Though this be madness,
   yet there is method in't.
   (Hamlet, 2.2)

2. You have to want to do it! You have to approach the experience with a positive attitude—and a strong stomach! You will live to tell the tale—and to do it again!

3. Choose a play that you likc—or have at least heard of! Become an expert on the story line and characters by reading the Kidspeak story, watching the movie version, or—if you're daring—read the play.

4. You never get a second chance to make a first impression, so when you decide to introduce the Bard, go for broke! Grab the students' interest, get them hooked, and reel them in—before they realize they have heard somebody say Shakespeare is hard, and boring, too!

5. Never forget—this is supposed to be *fun!* In Shakespeare's time, attending the theater was a lively, interactive experience! If it were possible to transport the audience of the Globe Theatre to modern times, they would be more at home in Madison Square Garden than in an opera house.

How This Book Is Organized

When we introduce Shakespeare to our students, the first step we take is to prepare ourselves. It is important that we know the characters, background, and story line before we can expect our students to learn it. We have organized this book to assist you in your preparation for each play. You will find that the preparation process for each play looks the same. We have found that when we emphasize the process of preparation, it remains the same even as each play's content changes. Below is a description of each step in the process—characters, background, story line, activities, and resources.

Who's Who

If you are a Shakespeare "purist," no doubt you will notice the absence of some of the characters in our versions of his plays. Our intent is not to slight the play or to deprive the students or to imply that we can do a better job than Shakespeare. Instead, we are interested in making the story and characters both manageable and understandable. We would like to introduce you to only the essential characters from the play accompanied by some of their most memorable lines.

What's What

The background information we provide is not essential to the understanding of each play, so feel free to skip to The Story. The background information is very interesting, however, and you will be able to impress your students and colleagues if you keep these little-known anecdotes at your fingertips!

What's Happening

The colloquial, Kidspeak version of the play will be blended with pertinent quotes in Shakespeak. We hope that the blending of the two will make Shakespeare's language more natural and understandable to you and your students. Don't be afraid to introduce young students to the text from the play—Shakespeak. The strangeness of the language is often appealing to children, and when they are familiar with the story they can relate more easily to the difficult and different language.

Don't Just Sit There!

Integrated Activities

Performing Shakespeare has traditionally been the best way both to experience and to learn the plays. Shakespeare also crosses boundaries of culture and generation. After 400 years, people can still relate to the human experiences in the stories. In the classroom, we have found that because Shakespeare's plays cross curriculum boundaries, too, students are able to relate to the characters and stories at various levels. Students can apply what they learn from the plays not only to drama but to writing, social studies, geography, history, art, science, and math. Taking an integrated approach with the play provides for greater depth of understanding, appreciation, and enjoyment.

Selections for Recitation

Today, memorizing poetry or text from plays is not usually included in the modern elementary school curriculum, as it has been in the past. Because of the irrelevance and undue length of the pieces chosen, memorizing came to be regarded as a less-than-useful classroom practice. This is unfortunate. If poetry or text is chosen appropriately, memorizing serves several useful purposes. It

- develops memory skills
- encourages discovery of memory "tricks"—mnemonics
- encourages self-discipline
- promotes self-confidence
- develops good oral presentation skills
- helps increase vocabulary
- gives students who have weak fine motor skills an opportunity to be successful
- promotes enjoyment of the text

I cannot but remember such things were,
That were most precious to me.
(Macbeth, 4.3)

To maximize the benefits of this exercise, we must do more than just hand out text and tell the students to go and learn it. It is vital for students to understand the text they are learning so that they can recite the piece with conviction and feeling. Having students recite something without any understanding of what they are saying is a complete waste of time. The only thing the student will have learned from the experience is that he or she has genes similar to those of a parrot! The exercise should be a learning experience that will enhance and expand students' skills in reading, writing, listening, and speaking.

Experience has shown us that students become motivated to memorize text when we add some friendly competition into the mix. We hold an in-class "Shakespeare Contest." This is a competitive event we have created to determine the best recitation from the play we are studying. Usually, we set a six-line minimum; costumes are encouraged but not required. If you arc not a lover of competition, you can organize a "Shakespeare Performance"; here students memorize text to entertain each other, peers, and parents.

Here's how to motivate memorization:

1. Explain the concept of the "Shakespeare Contest" or the "Shakespeare Performance" to your students and set a tentative date for the event; this establishes a time frame and provides an incentive to *get busy*.
2. Read through the selections we have included.
3. Have your students select the pieces they want to memorize.

4. It is entirely up to you if you wish to restrict choices to the text here or to allow a wider choice. If you do allow a wider choice, you will have to write the word definitions and the simple English (Kidspeak) versions for each additional piece.

5. When your students have made their selections, meet with each text group to go through the text, word definitions (Say What??), and Kidspeak version to ensure that students clearly understand the meaning of the text.

6. Encourage students in the same text group to work together and to experiment with different approaches to the same piece.

7. Allow students to illustrate their interpretation of the scene their text is from.

8. Celebrate success (one line at a time).

Each of the reproducible pages contains approximately eight lines from the play that are likely to appeal to students; several of them are famous quotes from the play. Each quote also plays a prominent part in the "movie" that your class might create. Encourage your students to illustrate their scene. It is amazing how much easier it is to memorize when the text is visualized.

Lights, Camera, Action: Making the Movie

We can already hear what you must be saying: "I can see getting elementary students to understand a complex story with complex characters; I can even see them memorizing a few lines to impress their parents, but you must be crazy if you think it's possible to perform the entire play with these kids, let alone make a movie out of it. I'm a teacher, not Steven Spielberg." The truth is, if you have done everything to light your students' "fires," they will beg you to let them perform the play.

At this point, it will be useful for you to remember the words on *The Hitchhiker's Guide to the Galaxy* by Douglas Adams: "Don't Panic!" Making a movie of the play is much easier than performing it live. All you need is a camcorder, a few props, some costumes, simple sets, and enthusiastic actors.

Resources

Far be it for us to consider ourselves the final word, the be all and end all, or the experts on the Bard. At the end of each play we have provided an annotated bibliography of what we consider the best picture books, reference books, and videotapes, for each play.

Part One

Setting the Stage

Fuel for the Fire

I can easier teach twenty what were good to be done,
than to be one of the twenty to follow my own teaching.
(*The Merchant of Venice,* 1.2)

What do you want to know about Shakespeare? Answer: Enough to appear smarter than your students! You have a choice of the bare-bones version to the well-padded beefy version, plus a couple in between. Read what you need!

The Bard's Bare-Bones Bio

- Born: 1564, probably on April 23
- Died: 1616 on April 23

The Bard's Better Bio

To the above information add the following:

- Born in Stratford-on-Avon, England.
- Married Anne Hathaway when he was 18 and she was 26.
- Went to London; stayed for about 25 years to act and write. He wrote 37 plays and, while some of them are dogs, several are quite amazing! The bottom line is that he was good at what he did and he made money at it!
- Returned to Stratford in 1611, a wealthy man. No record exists of his cause of death, but it is not beyond the realm of possibility that Anne Hathaway—having managed very nicely without him for 25 years—could not get used to having him under foot day in and day out and took matters into her own hands! (This is not the traditionally held theory!)

The Bard's Best Bio

To the above information add the following:

- William Shakespeare's father, John, was a glove maker and dealer in wool and grain. As his business grew he gained greater and greater status in Stratford, until he eventually gained, then lost, the position of high bailiff—which is the modern equivalent of a mayor.
- Shakespeare's mother, Mary Arden, came from an important Catholic family, but because Catholics were persecuted during Elizabethan times, it is likely that Shakespeare was raised an Anglican.
- It would be interesting to know whether Shakespeare was an exceptional student from day one or whether his writing skills were late blooming, but there are no records of his even having attended school!

- Most of his biographers agree that before becoming a playwright he followed in his father's footsteps and made gloves and dealt in a few commodities.
- He married Anne Hathaway in 1582 and their daughter, Susanna, was born six months later. Two years later, the family increased by two when twins were born, Judith and Hamnet. Sadly, Hamnet died in 1596, at age 11.
- Nothing is recorded about Shakespeare from 1585 to 1592, but it is speculated that he turned his hand to several jobs during this time, including moneylending, tutoring, soldiering, and the law. This may account for the detailed knowledge of various occupations revealed in his plays.
- No one knows the exact date of his move to London, but it is believed to have been initiated by a brush with the law! The story goes that Shakespeare was caught poaching on Sir Thomas Lucy's estate. After being prosecuted, he retaliated by writing an insulting poem about Sir Thomas; this forced him to leave Stratford in a hurry and head for London. The first official mention of his actually being in London was in an insulting pamphlet, written by a rival playwright, in 1592.
- In 1594, the acting company known as The Lord Chamberlain's Men is formed and Shakespeare served with them as an actor and playwright.
- In 1603, Shakespeare's company was given a royal patent and was renamed The King's Men; the company performed regularly at the court of James I.
- Around 1610, Shakespeare left London, a wealthy man, and returned to his family in Stratford, where he stayed until his death in 1616—on his birthday. The following is written on a plaque on his grave:

> Good friend, for Jesus sake forbear
> To dig the dust enclosed here.
> Blessed be the man that spares these stones
> And cursed be he that moves my bones.

Not exactly inspired verse—but interesting!

The Bard's Beefy Bio

To the preceding information add the following—if you really want to!

There are some facts about Shakespeare that many choose to ignore because they tend to tarnish the myth of the creative genius and family man of highest moral fiber. Without a doubt, most—but not all—of his plays support the label "creative genius," but what is known about his life may make us dubious about the label "family man of highest moral fiber." He did not hang around the house much! His understanding of "family man" seemed to be that absence makes the heart grow fonder. It is also difficult to justify the label "highest moral fiber" when the facts of his private life are examined. To say the least, premarital sex, homoerotism, and extramarital affairs with persons of doubtful reputation does not fit the Bard's traditional image, yet these are the lesser-publicized facts of his life. If his private life left something to be desired, his public life was not all sweetness and light, either. Although his genius for writing cannot be denied, he was not of the starving artist mentality. Indeed, he was a businessman and a shrewd investor. He liked money and never forgot a debt—even if it meant taking someone to court over a trivial amount of money. A bisexual moneylender who dabbled in real estate is not how many people imagine the Bard, but it's probably close to the truth (Epstein 1993).[2]

Let's not end on a sour note! It important to remember—"The play's the thing" (*Hamlet*, 2.2). The plays of Shakespeare are our focus, and they are incredible, momentous, moving, noble, amusing, inspiring, and unforgettable!

The Bard's Beefy Bio—Second Helpings!

If you are not already stuffed with information, add the following.

Shakespeare wrote 36 plays, 154 sonnets, and two narrative poems. The following are the dates his plays are thought to have been written:

1588–93 *The Comedy of Errors**
1588–94 *Love's Labour's Lost*
1590–91 *1 Henry VI*
1591–92 *2 Henry VI*
1592–94 *3 Henry VI*
1593–94 *Richard III*
1593–95 *Titus Andronicus*
1594–96 *A Midsummer Night's Dream* *
1594–1595 *Romeo and Juliet*
1594–96 *The Taming of the Shrew* *
1595 *Richard II*
1596–97 *King John*
1596–97 *The Merchant of Venice* *
1597 *1 Henry IV*
1597–98 *2 Henry IV*
1597–1601 *The Merry Wives of Windsor*
1598–1600 *Much Ado About Nothing*
1598–99 *Henry V*
1599 *Julius Caesar*
1599–1600 *As You Like It*
1599–1600 *Twelfth Night* *
1600–01 *Hamlet* *
1601–02 *Troilus and Cressida*
1602–04 *All's Well That Ends Well*
1603–04 *Othello*
1604 *Measure for Measure*
1605–06 *King Lear*
1605–06 *Macbeth* *
1605–08 *Timon of Athens*
1606–07 *Antony and Cleopatra*
1607–09 *Coriolanus*
1608–09 *Pericles*
1609–10 *Cymbeline*
1610–11 *The Winter's Tale*
1611 *The Tempest*
1612–13 *Henry VIII*

*Indicates plays that are close to our hearts and lend themselves to adaptation for elementary students without too much difficulty.

Spontaneous Combustion

Playing with the Bard

General Activities for Shakespeare's Language, Life, and Times

Reading about Shakespeare's mysterious and controversial life and times is one thing; however, experiencing him through integrated activities is quite another. What follows are activities for introducing students to the life and times of the Bard.

Thee's and Thou's

Why did Shakespeare write using such strange words? Did people actually talk like that? Research Old English and see how the words you use today sounded back then.

Now That's Good Handwriting!

Pens and pencils, typewriters, and word processors: These are the ways we write today, but how were words written 400 years ago? How does a quill pen work? Can you learn the art of calligraphy?

First Impressions Are Everything

The first letters of most important pieces of writing were written in a fancy way. This is called *illuminated manuscript.* Can you find examples of this type of art? Can you make your own?

Do You Have the Time?

When it is lunchtime where you live, what is happening in France? When you go to bed, what is happening in Italy? Investigate the different time zones of the world, and see if you can make a clock that will help you answer these questions.

Where, Oh Where?

Shakespeare wrote stories of people from many lands, but did he have a favorite place? Find out where some of his plays took place and mark them on a map. What can you discover?

The Black Death

In England, the disease called *the plague* often got so bad that the theater had to shut down. What was it? How could you get it? Research this disease and discover the answers for yourself. Look for information on how the nursery rhyme "Ring o' Rosies" is connected to the plague.

London—Then and Now

What was life really like 400 years ago? What did people wear? What did they eat? How were children treated? Investigate Elizabethan England and create a Venn diagram showing the similarities and differences between then and now.

Life Line

Use the information you have about Shakespeare's life and create a time line. Create another time line of the plays that he wrote. Compare the two time lines; notice anything interesting?

Going Global

What was the Globe Theatre? What did it look like? What would it have been like to see a play there? Theater in Shakespeare's time was very different from what it is today. Find out just how different.

To Visit or Not to Visit? That Is the Question

Plan a Shakespearean theme park. Select five plays to focus on and design rides appropriate to the story line of each play.

What Do You Want?

Which of our modern-day inventions do you think would have amazed the Elizabethans the most? Why? Which invention would have been the most useful? Organize a debate around this topic.

Meet the Minds

Create a talk show, with your class as the interactive audience, with the following guests: Shakespeare, Elizabeth I, Mary Queen of Scots, and Sir Walter Raleigh.

This = That

Mathematical symbols were first introduced during the Renaissance. Before the Renaissance, the lack of equals and plus (= or +) signs made math very difficult! Can you solve this problem?

4 3 11 4 4 12 6 6 = 3 (4-3+11/4.4+12-6/6=3)

Write some signless problems and exchange them with classmates to solve.

Show Me a Sign

In Elizabethan times, houses were not numbered. Painted signs were used to designate particular houses. Paint a sign that you would like to have hanging outside your house. It can be an animal or tree, or it can tell something about the occupants of your house.

Sailing! Sailing! Over the Ocean Blue!

Sailing ships were very important during Elizabethan times. They were the means of transportation for the many explorers of the time, and naval ships defended the country from would-be invaders. Draw a sailing ship in full sail and add labels for the names of things you know. Then look up sailing ships in a visual dictionary. You will be amazed by the number of things named on the sailing ships!

Discovery Zones

The following are famous explorers from 1500 to 1600.

Balboa
Ponce de León
Magellan
Cortés
Francis Drake

Choose two from the list and compare their travels. Who went the farthest? Who found the most interesting place? Who was most successful?

And the survey said . . .

What do your friends and family know about Shakespeare? Take a survey to find out. Here are some questions to get you started:

Have you heard of William Shakespeare?
Do you know what he is famous for?
Did you study Shakespeare at school?
Did you like Shakespeare then?
Have you ever seen a Shakespeare play?
Can you name two of his plays?
Can you tell the plot of any of his plays?
Do you like his plays now?

Lets Boogie!

Elizabethans were very fond of dancing as a form of entertainment. They had many different types of dances with names such as the *measure*, which was slow and stately; the *pavan,* which was danced slowly in a line like a procession; the *galliard,* which was quick and lively; and the *capriol*, which was lively and required the dancers to jump!

Find some Elizabethan music and create a dance; give your dance a name and perform it for the class—get them all to join in, too!

Not Tenpin!

Bowls was a popular outdoor game in Shakespeare's time. In fact, it is still very popular in England today. Bowls is played on a lawn with heavy balls called *woods*. The object of the game is to roll your ball across the lawn and have it stop as close as possible to a small white ball called a *jack*.

Find balls to use for woods and a jack and, after a little practice, organize a bowls tournament.

True or False?

The Elizabethans had many misconceptions about the world. Rewrite the following and correct the false statements:

The planet Earth is at the center of the universe. It is the most important planet and all the others rotate around it in circular orbits. There are seven planets circling the Earth and they are the moon, Mercury, Mars, Jupiter, Saturn, Sol (the sun), and Venus. As the planets circle the Earth they make musical sounds, and when they are in line the music is in harmony. The planets influence events and the people on Earth. You should always consult an astrologer before making any major decisions in your life, just to be sure the planets are in a favorable alignment.

Box It Up

In a shoe box, create a diorama of one of the following:

- the Globe Theatre
- an Elizabethan house
- a sailing ship
- your favorite scene from your favorite play

Double Jeopardy

With some friends, brainstorm lots of questions about Shakespeare, his life and times, and his plays. Then—and this is the hard part!—find the answers to all the questions! Use the information you have gathered to create a Shakespearean quiz show.

Fanning the Flames

Screw your courage to the sticking place
And we'll not fail.
(Macbeth, 1.7)

Introducing Shakespeare to children follows the hook, line, and sinker philosophy of teaching!

Hook—a tantalizing mention of a great story waiting to be told
Line—the introduction of the characters
Sinker—an enthusiastic telling of the story

The Hook

Getting Their Interest

By this point, you will want to know all you can about Shakespeare and the background information of the play. You should also be very familiar with the characters and the plot. It is a good idea, even though you will feel a bit silly, to practice telling the story several times in front of a mirror, or to a devoted dumb animal, until you feel confident enough to face the real thing—telling the story to your students.

Even though you are now an expert and, we hope, an enthusiast, it would be a big mistake to walk into your room one day and say, "Boys and girls, I am going to tell you a story." Boring! If the resulting groans don't extinguish your fire, they will certainly dampen any sparks that may be ready to ignite in your students. This is the time to be devious and circumspect! Several approaches are sneaky enough to snag unwitting students and hook them onto Shakespeare before they can even say *Macbeth*! If you can restrain your own enthusiasm—and we assume you *are* feeling enthusiastic!—you might want to try one of the following indirect approaches to introducing the play.

The "Reluctant" Hook

Hook the students with this:

> "I have read this really great play. It was so exciting—all about fairies and fighting and magic and stuff but (look sad and sympathetic) it might be a bit hard for you to understand and I don't know if I should tell you about it, even though it is a very exciting and funny story! What do you think?"

Take no bets that they will say it's too hard for their simple brains and want to read something along the lines of *Dick and Jane*! The more you vacillate and look reluctant the more frenzied they will become. Play this approach right and they will soon be collecting money to bribe you to tell them!

The "Appeal to the Ego" Hook

Try this:

> "I am going to tell you a story called *Macbeth,* and it is from a play written by a man named William Shakespeare. Now, everyone will say this is too tough for itty-bitty little ____ -graders (fill in your grade level). People expect you to be learning about ____________________ (fill in the blank with any easy piece of literature, from *Goldilocks and the Three Bears* to *Little House in the Big Woods,* depending on the grade level). But I know how smart you guys really are, and I know you can handle Shakespeare—even though you are not supposed to be able to understand his plays until high school and college!"

The "Outright Lie" Hook

You need your most innocent expression for this one! Affect a casual, conversational tone as you say this:

> "Since we have a little extra time here, boys and girls, let me tell you about the play my daughter (son, nephew, niece, Great Aunt Martha, or whomever) is studying in college."

This is reminiscent of the appeal-to-the-ego approach in as much that you are flattering your students by assuming they are capable of understanding a play that is studied in college!

The "Enthusiastic" Hook

This is the relatively honest approach:

No legacy is so rich as honesty.
(All's Well That Ends Well, 3.5)

Honesty coupled to beauty is to have
honey a sauce to sugar.
(As You Like It, 3.3)

Share your enthusiasm about Shakespeare and the plays. If you let your students feel your excitement and pleasure, they will be hooked. The hook can be baited just a little by staging this revelation:

> "Girls and boys, we are going to skip the planned movie on 'Toenail Decorating in Different Cultures' because I want to tell you about a very exciting play I have been reading."

To a noneducator, the very mention of "hooks," and distortions of the truth, would cause eyebrows to raise and a barrage of loud, self-righteous "tuts!" to issue. However, educators know that the hook's the thing! The art of teaching is complicated and delicate, and what may look like lying and cheating to the layperson is actually a fine educator's ability to motivate learners by stimulating their curiosity and arousing their desires to learn. We will stoop to *any* level to bring culture to the masses! It is our duty!

The Line

Getting Their Interest in the Play

When you have hooked your students' interest, the "line" is the next step. This is the introduction to the characters. Although you may be eager to jump right into the story, it is vital that you introduce the characters first. Experience has shown us that telling the story "cold turkey" leads to confusion over who's who, not to mention what's what.

Here are some ways to bring the characters to life:

Bare Bones

Write a character's name on the chalkboard and discuss each one (using the *Who's Who* section of the book) as you add them to the list. This is not the most creative approach, but it can be effective if you are the actor type and give an "impromptu" rendering of each character with enthusiasm and without inhibition!

Flesh and Bones

This is a variation using dolls, puppets, or pictures.
You will need

- dolls—as outrageous looking as possible (e.g., a G. I. Joe for Hamlet, etc.). The weirder the dolls, the more interested the audience will be and the more memorable the characters will become.

  or

- puppets—same criteria as for the dolls. The puppets can be the hand type or simple paper figures cut from a catalog or an old book and glued onto Popsicle sticks.

  or

- pictures (in frames would be a nice touch!) of people. Again, they should be as interesting as possible to keep the audience hooked, for example, the president could be presented as Macbeth; however, it would be wise to use discretion when pairing real people with fictitious characters (especially when choosing Bottom). We are not responsible for any libel actions against you resulting from using these ideas!

The Bolt of Lightning

You will need

- eight 4"x12" pieces of card with the name of a character on each. Attach a piece of yarn or string to each card so that it can hang around the neck of a volunteer;
- eight small cards, with words for each character written on them. The words are a response to a planned question you are going to ask during your description of the character. Doing this helps make the introductions more interactive and entertaining for the students.

This is a very effective way of introducing the characters because it actively involves the students, and it is a lot of fun! You should have a clear picture of each of the characters from their *Who's Who* descriptions. Review this section, and make note cards if necessary to help with your presentation.

Here's how our presentation would go:

1. Explain to the students that you are going to introduce the main characters of the play and ask for a volunteer to "be" a character.
2. Dress the volunteer for the part using donated hats or dress-up clothes for the costume (optional).
3. Hang one of the character cards card around his neck, e.g., "Puck" from *A Midsummer Night's Dream*, and have him stand in front of the class.

4. You then describe that character as you point to the student and refer to him as the character you are describing. Make your introduction of the character as entertaining as possible. Use a lighthearted, conversational tone and have fun. If you enjoy what you are doing, it increases the chances that your students will enjoy it, too!

   Here is an example of what may be said when introducing Puck:

   > Lurking in the darkness, with his eyes wide open, searching for trouble is a very special fairy named Robin Goodfellow. You can call him Puck. If there is ever any trouble after the sun goes down, you can bet that it was caused by Puck. Doesn't he look like a troublemaker? Well, on this particular evening, deep in the forest, Puck was scheming with his king and master, Oberon. You can imagine the mischief Puck could cause. Using his magic, Puck turned a poor actor into an ass (donkey), and made two boys fall in love with the same girl, all on the same night. "Didn't you feel a little bit bad about all the trouble you caused?" Student responds, "No way, and to tell you the truth, I can't wait to see what happens tomorrow night." Before you go wandering into the forest at night, remember Puck may be watching, and who knows what he may do?

It's Alive!

This approach to presenting the characters is the most ambitious and may be the most memorable. You will need eight people (in costume would be great—but not necessary).

Your panel of eight guests will be introduced and, if they know the play, can tell about themselves. If they are up to it, they could even answer questions from the audience—and you could be the talk-show host!

We have seen teachers ask parents to come in to portray the different characters. If you do this, it is important that your volunteers know the play and their roles very well. Even if you can only get a few volunteers to portray the four lovers, or the three fairies, it will be worth the preparation.

Select the method of presenting the characters that most appeals to you. No matter which one you select, give it your best shot. You don't get a second chance to make a good first impression, and if you don't use the best "line," it will break and you will lose the "hook"!

The Sinker

Preparing for Stories and Activities

Because we have studied many different ways of retelling this play, and have introduced the story to many different students, we would like to share with you our version of Shakespeare's plays. Through experience, we have found it much more effective to "tell" the story rather than "read" it. The story can be told in sections over several days or all at one time, depending on the play and the age and attention span of the students. You can also choose to introduce activities while the story unfolds. This would span several days and definitely not be presented all in one sitting! You would tell part of the story, pause for an activity or two, and then continue the story. As an alternative, you may prefer to present the games and activities after telling the story. The telling of the story and integration of the activities is entirely up to you. What works for you is the way to go!

The integrated activities can be managed in any of the following flexible ways:

1. Whole Class—Activities can be selected to be accomplished as a whole class either individually or in small cooperative groups. An end product could be a class book or cooperative presentation. It would be effective to use some of the activities as a whole class while you present the characters and story line.
2. Independent Work—Students could be assigned an activity, or they could choose one as an independent project. If you have three or four activities to choose from, students will form into natural groups for you to work with during the project time. By limiting the number of activities to choose from, you also increase the chance of students using each other for assistance, motivation, and challenge.
3. Centers—Choose some of your favorite activities and set them up as centers around your classroom to be completed independently. Upon completion of each activity, students turn in what they have accomplished. The management of this is similar to the independent work approach because individual students are free to choose activities from around the room. Preparation and the creation of an inviting center for students to work in are key to the success of this approach.

How Not to Get Burned

Learning from Shakespearience

Making the Rules

While students are working on any of the various integrated activities, you will have a chance to do any or all of the following:

1. You will have time to work with individuals or cooperative groups as they work on the activities. This way you will be able to monitor the quality of the work and extend it when necessary.
2. You will have time to work with individual students who are interested in performing sections of the play. With everyone else "on task," you will be able to devote your full attention to your budding thespians.
3. If you choose to do a full or even a partial performance of the play (videotaped or not), then you will need time to work with small groups of actors. By having engaging activities for the rest of the class, you will be able to focus your attention on directing the play.

If your attention is focused elsewhere, how can you ensure that the rest of your class stays engaged and produces high-quality work?

We like to ask our students, "If school were like a baseball game, could you play without knowing the rules?" After receiving a resounding "No," we explain that just as there are rules in a sports game that you are expected to follow in order to WIN, there are expectations (rules) in school that you need to know in order to WIN. The expectations for the work session need to be stated for the students in order for them to know how they are progressing with their behavior and work.

We have written rubrics (rules) with students for many activities from independent reading time to cleaning the classroom, and the results have always been the same. When children knew exactly what was expected, they performed to exceed that expectation. Here's how it works:

1. Decide on a name for three levels of expectation. Here are some examples:
   - low, average, high (this is rather boring)
   - basic, proficient, advanced (this is what we use in our school district)
   - not good enough, just right, superb (now this is more like it)
2. The words you choose are not as important as the attitude that accompanies them. Almost all children want to be high, advanced, or superb.
3. You set the average, proficient, or just right expectations. For your grade level and your group of children, your expectations for work and behavior must be very specific and observable. For example, in third grade three proficient behavior expectations would be to:

- Speak in a low voice when asking a question or sharing information with someone else.
- Walk around the classroom when you change activities.
- Return all materials after using them.

Three proficient work expectations would be:

- Follow all directions for each activity.
- All handwriting must be neat and easily read.
- All written work must contain complete sentences.

4. With the whole class, brainstorm descriptions for a basic and an advanced expectation. For example, your students may decide that an advanced or superb descriptor for the "complete sentences" expectation would be "all written work must be in paragraph form and contain five sentences each." The basic or not good enough descriptor may be "all written work is not sentences."
5. The students have fun setting the standards for high and low achievement while they are internalizing the expectations.
6. After all the descriptors for behavior and work have been made, assign some students to make a large poster of each rubric for easy viewing.
7. Begin each work session by reviewing the rubrics. You may even want to ask each student where he or she would rate him or herself on each rubric, or ask for examples of superb work to show the class before setting out to work.

After the "rules of the game" have been made and posted, the students begin to ask questions like "Does this look proficient or advanced?" and "What do I need to do to make this superb?" As a teacher, you can use the rubrics to give specific direction for children to take during their work time. You can say things like "Your voice is basic right now; what can you do to change that?" and "It's wonderful to see so many superb workers in this room!"

We have included two examples of rubrics that we use in our classrooms to set the expectations for behavior and work; using rubrics frees us to work with individuals and small groups. Feel free to use our sample rubrics as your guide when writing a personalized rubric for your classroom.

Shakespeare Work Rubric

Not good enough work is

- not following activity directions
- handwriting that is sloppy and hard to read
- sentences that are incomplete

Just right work is

- following most of the activity directions
- handwriting that is sometimes hard to read
- sentences that are sometimes incomplete

Superb work is

- following all directions for all activities
- all handwriting is neat and easy to read
- all sentences are complete with capitals and periods

Shakespeare Behavior Rubric

Not good enough behavior is

- speaking in a loud, distracting voice
- moving too quickly around the room
- not returning materials after using them

Just right behavior is

- speaking in a low voice most of the time
- walking from activity to activity most of the time
- returning most of the materials after using them

Superb behavior is

- speaking quietly with others all of the time
- walking carefully around the room all of the time
- returning all of the materials after using them

Part Two

Hamlet

What You Should Know About *Hamlet*

Who's Who

When presenting Shakespeare to young children, we believe it is necessary to simplify the plays by removing nonessential (in our opinion!) characters whose presence would contribute little to the students' understanding of the fundamental story line—but would contribute much to their confusion! If your particular favorite minor character has been axed, please keep in mind that it was for a good cause.

"Let us from point to point this story know,
to make the even truth in pleasure flow."
(All's Well That Ends Well, 5.3)

The Major Characters

Hamlet

Hamlet is the son of the recently deceased king of Denmark, who was also called Hamlet. He is, therefore, a prince and is heir to the throne of Denmark. Hamlet is a Great Dane! Whether he is house-trained or not is questionable! His strong personality, tantrums, and mood swings cause lots of problems around the house—or in this case, around the castle of Elsinore. He is the James Dean of Denmark: rebellious, misunderstood, and scornful of the adult establishment. The perfect teen idol!

Gertrude (GER-trood)

She is Hamlet's mother and is married—rather hastily—to her dead husband's brother. Gertrude may not be the villain of this piece, but her distinct lack of sensitivity and timing caused many of Hamlet's problems. That she remarried as quickly as she did suggests many things about her character, not least of which is a strong drive to look out for number one—whatever the cost to her nearest and dearest.

Claudius (CLAW-dee-us)

He is:

- the new king of Denmark;
- the husband (and brother-in-law) of Gertrude;
- the stepfather (and uncle) of Hamlet;
- the brother (and murderer) of the dead king.

What a guy! Talk about being all things to all people!

Ophelia (oh-FEEL-ya)

Ophelia is everything you would not want your daughter to be. She is a wimp who is willing to be Hamlet's doormat. She is a pleaser to the extreme. Being a good daughter is one thing, but Ophelia is so obsessed with doing everything she is told that she is like the legendary "Candle in the Wind" (Elton John), getting blown in all directions by whomever happens to breeze by. Consequently, candles being what they are, she gets snuffed out. Actually, her suicide is about the only thing she does of her own volition—not the best way to establish one's independence!

Laertes (lay-ERT-eez)

Laertes is Ophelia's brother and is filled from top to toe with good qualities. He is an obedient son, a caring brother, a good friend, and a loyal subject. Unfortunately, he is also a bit naïve, and finds himself in the unenviable position of pointing a poisoned sword at Hamlet—not to mention his being on the receiving end, too! Some days it doesn't pay to get out of bed!

The Major Minor Characters

The Ghost

Hamlet's father comes back from the dead—in full armor!—to demand that Hamlet avenge his death. Hamlet, who is having a tough enough time adjusting to his changing family circumstances, is just about pushed over the edge by the appearance, revelations, and demands of his father:

> If thou didst ever thy dear father love
> Revenge his foul and most unnatural death.
> **(1.5)**

The appearance of his father's ghost was the motivating straw that broke the back of Hamlet's reason.

Polonius (pol-OH-nee-us)

Polonius is the father of Ophelia and Laertes and is one of the king's ministers. He is rather long-winded but mostly harmless. However, his love of intrigue and spying leads to his getting Hamlet's sword in the "arras"—and, as everyone knows, that is a very unpleasant place to be stabbed!

Horatio (hor-RAY-shee-oh)

Horatio is a nice guy and Hamlet's old school pal. He is Hamlet's most trusted and loyal friend throughout the play, and usually manages to remain calm, cool, and collected under the severe strain of Hamlet's friendship.

The Minor Minor Characters

Rozencrantz and Guildenstern (ROSEN-crans and GILDEN-stern)

Hamlet's answer to Tweedledum and Tweedledee—but meaner! They are childhood friends of Hamlet—and with friends like these, no wonder he is having problems!

What's What

Background Information

As with several of Shakespeare's stories, the plot of *Hamlet* was "borrowed" from a preexisting story about an early king of Denmark. In the original story, Amleth's father, the king of Denmark, is killed by his brother, who later marries his widow; the story revolves around Amleth's quest for revenge.[1] This, and many events in the story, is mirrored almost exactly in Shakespeare's version. The major difference between *Amleth* and *Hamlet* is that the former has a happy ending and the latter ends in a virtual bloodbath! It would be interesting to debate Shakespeare's reasons for such a drastic alteration of the original story. However, if he acted true to his mercenary nature, it is fair to assume that he changed the end of the original story for purely commercial reasons. An exciting fight would be sure to attract theatergoers—and their money!

The play *Hamlet* has an interesting history. There is a problem regarding exactly what parts of the play were actually written by Shakespeare! Three versions of the play exist, from which all later editions are taken:

- *The First Quarto* (2,154 lines) published in 1601. It is called the bad quarto and is thought to be an unauthorized version—stolen, and sold, by actors.
- *The Second Quarto* (3,674 lines) published in 1604. This is thought to have been released by Shakespeare to establish the correct version.
- *The First Folio* (3,535 lines) published in 1623. This is thought to be the "final copy," the way Shakespeare wanted the play to be performed for maximum effect on stage. However, because the folio was compiled seven years after Shakespeare's death and contains an additional 83 lines that do not appear in the Second Quarto, there is plenty of food for thought!

Scene by Scene

Act 1

Scene 1—Elsinore Castle in Denmark. The guards report to Horatio that they saw a ghost.
Scene 2—The court is meeting in the great hall of the castle.
Scene 3—A room in Polonius's house.
Scene 4—Hamlet sees the ghost.
Scene 5—Hamlet talks with the ghost, then plays it cool with his friends.

Act 2

Scene 1—A room in Polonius's house.
Scene 2—Polonius tattles to Hamlet's mom and dad.

Act 3

Scene 1—Polonius and Claudius spy on Hamlet in the castle.
Scene 2—The actors perform the play.
Scene 3—Hamlet finds Claudius praying and decides not to kill him just yet.
Scene 4—Hamlet accidentally kills Polonius in Gertrude's room.

Act 4

Scene 1—Claudius plans to get Hamlet out of his hair by sending him away.
Scene 2—Hamlet talks to his former friends Rosencrantz and Guildenstern.
Scene 3—Claudius sends Hamlet to England.
Scene 4—The sea coast near Elsinore.
Scene 5—Ophelia has gone mad. Her brother, Laertes, arrives.
Scene 6—Laertes gets a letter from Hamlet.
Scene 7—Claudius hatches a plot against Hamlet and tells lies to Laertes.

Act 5

Scene 1—Hamlet comes home. Ophelia is dead.
Scene 2—Hamlet duels with Laertes. All the main characters die, except Horatio.

What's Happening

The Story

As described in the introductory section, introducing Shakespeare to children follows the hook, line, and sinker approach to teaching!

Activities and games for presenting the hook (a tantalizing mention of a great story waiting to be told), and the line (the introduction of the characters), can be found in the introduction and should be presented to the students before continuing the story.

We have sprinkled popular lines from the actual play throughout the story. These verses correspond with the reproducible verses in the section of this book called Will's Words. You may wish to offer the verses for memorizing and reciting to your class as you tell the story. Even better, you may want to have your students perform short scenes from the story as you tell it. We find that, by placing Shakespeare's words and actions into the mouths and bodies of the children, they understand and appreciate the play more completely.

Let's Talk

We have found great success in increasing our students' connection to the play by providing frequent opportunities to discuss, debate, and just plain talk about it. Let's Talk can be done in a variety of ways:

1. Student-led discussion. Intriguing questions can be posed to the whole class; however, instead of you (the teacher) selecting the speaker, allow the student who is speaking to choose the next speaker.

2. Let's not talk. After asking a question to the whole class, give the students "sticky notes" to write their responses on. Place the students' responses on the chalkboard and, as a whole class, group the "sticky notes" into categories and summarize the results.

3. Small group discussion. Following your question, organize students in groups of two to four. Each group selects a leader and a recorder. The leader chooses who speaks, and the recorder writes down what is said. At the end of the discussion, the recorder reports what was said to the rest of the class.

4. Debate. You will need a podium (music stand) and a controversial dilemma. After posing the dilemma to the students, allow them to choose sides and move to either side of the podium. Once in place, students will take turns explaining why their points of view are correct. When each side has had a turn to state its position, give students a chance to change sides. This will continue until there is a strong majority or you run out of time.

Look for the Let's Talk symbols for discussion and debate topics. These topics are very flexible and may be used in two ways:

1. in natural breaks during your telling of the story;

2. after the entire story has been told, as a way of reviewing and solidifying the story in the students' minds.

The Sinker

The enthusiastic telling of the story.

Our Version

For information on some of the many excellent read-aloud versions of *Hamlet* see the Annotated Bibliography; it is worth shopping around to find the version that suits your style. The following is the version that suits our style—our version!

Read it (or loosely recite from memory) with gusto and enthusiasm—without inhibition!

Kidspeak and Shakespeak

The following story of *Hamlet* is written in plain English, Kidspeak, and at certain points in the story actual text from the play is included (Shakespeak)! Don't be afraid to introduce young students to Shakespeak. The strangeness of the language is often appealing to children; when they are familiar with the story, they can relate more easily to the difficult language.

The following is only one way to retell the story of *Hamlet*. You should infuse it with your personality and enthusiasm. That way it will be more fun for you, and more fun for the students: "Here we go! Get ready to study Shakespeare!! Even though you are such itty-bitty kindies (first, second, and third graders)! Get your brains in gear, 'cause here it comes! This is a really cool story all about . . . "

The Tragedy of Hamlet, Prince of Denmark

All is not well in Denmark; in fact, hardly anything is well. From Hamlet's point of view, if it could go wrong, it has. His father, whom he loved dearly, died two months ago. It came as a shock to Hamlet, but a greater shock followed. His mother, Gertrude, has married again *and*—of all people!—she has married her dead husband's brother, Claudius! Hamlet is having a very hard time dealing with this: "**Good Hamlet cast thy nighted colour off, and let thine eye look like a friend on Denmark. Do not forever with thy vailed lids seek for thy noble father in the dust**."

Discuss how children feel when parents divorce.

Hamlet has a funny feeling about the whole thing but he just can't pin anything down. The appearance of his father's ghost pins it down in no time flat! Apparently the ghost has appeared a couple of times to the guards of Elsinore Castle while they were on the night watch: "**Two nights together had these gentlemen, Marcellus and Barnardo, on their watch in the dead waste and middle of the night, been thus encountered. A figure like your father**." It loomed up out of nowhere, but refused to speak. The guards decide to pass the problem on to Hamlet because it was his father, and after hearing their story Hamlet agrees to go the battlements, with his friend Horatio, to see what is going on.

Sure enough, there is a ghost and this time it speaks. The ghost tells Hamlet that it is the spirit of his dead father and that it has come back to urge Hamlet to avenge his murder. Not just his death—his *murder!* "**I am thy father's spirit, doomed for a certain time to walk the night, and for the day confined to fast in fires, till the foul crimes done in my days of nature are burnt and purged away**." It tells Hamlet that the murderer is none other than his own brother, Claudius. This is the same Claudius who wasted no time in getting the recently bereaved and very beautiful Gertrude to say "I do"!

Debate the existence of ghosts. Discuss how wise it is for Hamlet to believe what he hears from the ghost. Debate whether or not Gertrude knew that Claudius murdered her first husband.

This revelation upsets Hamlet, but validates the uneasy feeling he has been having since the marriage of his mother. He decides, just to be on the safe side, to gather a little evidence—just so that people can't accuse him of making the whole thing up to pay his uncle back for rushing his mother to the altar. Just for the record, Claudius doesn't seem to be that bad for a murderer. He is very affectionate toward Gertrude, and he is also very efficient when dealing with affairs of state. He loses no time in sending ambassadors with a very clear message to the pushy king of Norway, who has his sights set on Denmark—and not just for a friendly visit!

Debate whether or not a murderer can have good qualities.

Just to confuse matters and to keep Claudius off guard, Hamlet acts as if he is mad. He seems to have a natural talent for madness and is very convincing! Claudius is worried and he asks Hamlet's old friends, Rosencrantz and Guildenstern, to keep an eye on him. Someone else has been keeping an eye on Hamlet—Ophelia, his former lady-love. She is very worried about him because they had been having a meaningful relationship at one point, but now he seems to have fallen out of love and into madness. That would worry anyone!

When Claudius and Polonius, Ophelia's father, secretly watch the former lovers together, Hamlet's treatment of Ophelia convinces them that Hamlet has definitely lost his mind.

Discuss parents' spying on their children. Debate whether parents have the right to invade their children's privacy if they are worried about their behavior.

Claudius believes that Hamlet's madness is not caused by unrequited love for Ophelia, and he strongly suspects that the cause of his madness is the knowledge of the true circumstances of his father's death. Claudius decides that, because Hamlet can't shape up, he will have to be shipped out.

Things are getting pretty grim around Elsinore. All the fun seems have gone out of life. Luckily, a group of traveling actors arrive on the scene ready, willing, and able to put a little zip into the dreary lives of our main characters. The arrival of the actors perks Hamlet up and gives him a very devious idea: "**I'll have these players play something like the murder of my father before mine uncle. I'll observe his looks, I'll tent him to the quick**." He persuades the actors to perform a play about the murder of a king by his brother—a plot that is very familiar to more than one person in the royal family! Hamlet plans to watch closely his uncle's reaction to the performance; he knows that Claudius will give himself away if he is guilty. His plan works. Claudius becomes more and more uncomfortable during the play and, just as the actors reach the part where the villain murders the good guy, Claudius orders them to stop. This is all just a little too close to the truth for comfort! Claudius's reaction confirms Hamlet's suspicions. Now he knows the truth—and Claudius knows he knows, and Hamlet knows he knows he knows, and Claudius knows he knows he knows he knows . . . and so on! If things were tense before, you can imagine what it is like now!

Discuss Hamlet's plan for discovering his uncle's guilt. Can you think of a better way?

While visiting his mother's room, Hamlet hears a noise behind a curtain. Thinking that it is his uncle, and that this is a great chance to get rid of him, Hamlet runs his sword through the curtain—and the person hiding there. Oops! No evil uncle, just poor old nosy—and now dead—Polonius. "**Thou wretched, rash, intruding fool, farewell. I took thee for thy better**." This faux pas gives Claudius a valid reason for ordering Hamlet out of the country, accompanied by a couple of fine fellows who are being paid to make sure he doesn't come back.

Debate whether Hamlet should have been charged with murder.

The death of Polonius is also the last straw for Ophelia. Her screws are loose, and anyone can see the wheel is spinning but the hamster is dead! When she is found floating belly up it's almost a relief to everyone that she is finally out of her misery: "**Till that her garments, heavy with their drink, pulled the poor wretch from her melodious lay to muddy death**." Her brother Laertes is not relieved, however. He has come home for the funeral of his father and now finds that his mad sister has kicked the bucket, too. Claudius wastes no time in placing the blame for both deaths on Hamlet, firing up Laertes's hatred for his onetime best bud.

Discuss how Laertes is feeling about Hamlet at this point. Has your best friend ever done something you found hard to forgive? What could your best friend do that you could never forgive?

Meanwhile, Hamlet, after a skirmish with pirates and a small problem regarding a letter ordering his execution, has returned safely from England. He is devastated by the news of Ophelia's death, because he really did love her, deep down. He tries to be nice to Laertes and offers his condolences, but Laertes wants none of it. All he wants is Hamlet's blood, and Claudius is very happy to arrange things so that Laertes will get what he wants. Claudius persuades Laertes to participate in an exhibition sword fight with Hamlet. The plan is that Laertes will use a poisoned sword; one cut with it will kill Hamlet, satisfying Laertes's need for revenge—and Claudius's need to get Hamlet out of the way, permanently!

Discuss how Claudius is using Laertes. Debate whether or not Claudius is guilty of murder because he planned it, even though he did not commit the actual act of murder.

Hamlet is reluctant to fight his former friend, but Laertes won't be dissuaded and so the fight is on. This is supposed to be a friendly exhibition match, but it doesn't take Hamlet long to realize that Laertes is in earnest—deadly earnest! Claudius is taking no chances. He has a cup of poisoned wine at his side, which he intends to give to Hamlet. The duel is fast and furious. Hamlet wounds Laertes twice and then is wounded himself—with the poisoned sword. It the scuffle, they drop their swords and, when the fight resumes, they each have the other's sword. During the fight, the queen, Gertrude, sips from the poisoned cup and, when Hamlet wounds Laertes with the poisoned sword, the queen sinks slowly in the west and dies.

Discuss how Claudius must feel when his plan misfires. Debate whether or not he really cared about Gertrude.

With his dying breath, Laertes confesses to the poisoned sword and tells Hamlet that it was all Claudius's idea: "**Hamlet, thou art slain; No medicine in the world can do thee good; In thee there is not half an hour of life—The treacherous instrument is in thy hand**." The dying Hamlet wounds the king with the poisoned sword and then forces him to drink the poisoned wine, just for good measure!

Debate whether or not Hamlet was justified in taking the law into his own hands and killing his uncle.

As if there aren't enough dead bodies at this point, Horatio, Hamlet's friend, offers to drink the poison, too, but Hamlet tells him he must live to tell the truth of what has happened: "**Horatio, I am dead. Thou livest; report me and my cause aright to the unsatisfied**."

At this point, Fortinbras, a Norwegian prince, arrives and, with his dying breath, Hamlet gives him the throne of Denmark, thus proving what we always knew—timing is everything!

Hamlet is called a "revenge tragedy." Discuss the idea of revenge. Debate the statement, "An eye for an eye, a tooth for a tooth."

Will's Words—Selections for Recitation

Gertrude (to Hamlet)

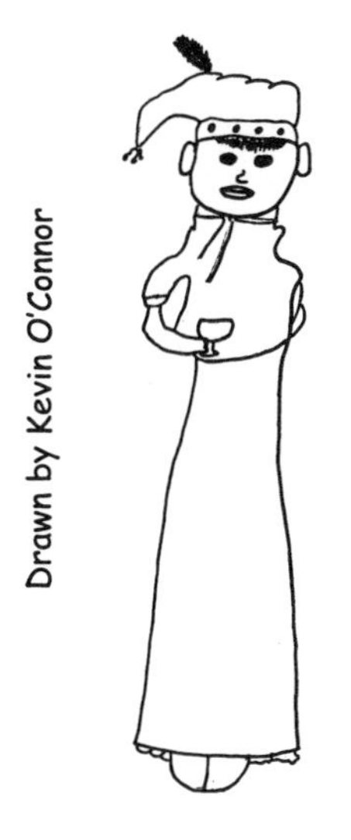
Drawn by Kevin O'Connor

Good Hamlet cast thy nighted colour off,
And let thine eye look like a friend on Denmark.
Do not forever with thy vailed lids
Seek for thy noble father in the dust.
Thou knowest 'tis common, all that lives must die,
Passing through nature to eternity.

(Act 1, Scene 2)

Say What??

Gertrude—pronounced GER-trood
thy nighted colour—your dark and gloomy colored clothes
Denmark—this refers to the king, Claudius
vailed lids—downcast eyes

Kidspeak

Gertrude, Hamlet's mother, is trying to coax him into a better mood. She tells him that it is time to stop mourning the death of his father and that he should be friends with Claudius, her new husband. Everyone must die and Hamlet has to accept that.

NAME:____________________________________

Hamlet (to himself; this is called a soliloquy)

Drawn by Danielle Warly

O that this too too solid flesh would melt,
Thaw and resolve itself into a dew,
Or that the Everlasting had not fixed
His canon against self-slaughter. O God,
God,
How weary, stale, flat and unprofitable
Seem to me all the uses of this world!

(Act 1, Scene 2)

Say What??

soliloquy—a speech given by a character who is alone onstage
resolve itself—turn into
dew—moisture
Everlasting—God
canon—rule or law
self-slaughter—suicide
all the uses of this world—everything in the world

Kidspeak

Hamlet is feeling a bit low—actually he is feeling lower than a snake's belly at this point! Let's face it, this is major depression! He wishes he could just melt away because nothing in the world interests him. He would kill himself if it were not against God's law. This boy needs help!

NAME:____

Horatio (to Hamlet)

Two nights together had these gentlemen,
Marcellus and Barnardo, on their watch
In the dead waste and middle of the night,
Been thus encountered. A figure like your
father,
Armed at point exactly, cap-a-pe,
Appears before them and with solid march
Goes slow and stately by them.

(Act 1, Scene 2)

Say What??

Horatio—pronounced hor-RAY-shee-oh
two nights together—two nights in a row
on their watch—on guard
encountered—met
at point—perfect in every detail
cap-a-pe—from head to toe

Kidspeak

For two nights in a row the soldiers have seen a ghostly figure. It is dressed from head to toe in armor, perfect in every detail, and it marches slowly past them. S-P-O-O-K-Y!

NAME:____

Ophelia (to Laertes)

I shall the effect of this good lesson keep
As watchman to my heart. But good my brother,
Do not as some ungracious pastors do,
Show me the steep and thorny way to heaven,
While like a puffed and reckless libertine
Himself the primrose path of dalliance treads,
And recks not his own rede.

(Act 1, Scene 3)

Say What??

Ophelia—pronounced oh-FEEL-ya
libertine—someone who lacks morals
dalliance—time wasting
recks not his own rede—does not take his own advice

Kidspeak

Laertes, Ophelia's brother, has just given her some advice about getting too involved with Hamlet. He says she should be good and be careful that she does not get a bad reputation. She says she will follow his advice, but she hopes he will take his own advice and just not set up lots of rules for her, yet impose none on himself and has a wonderful time.

NAME:____

Ghost (to Hamlet)

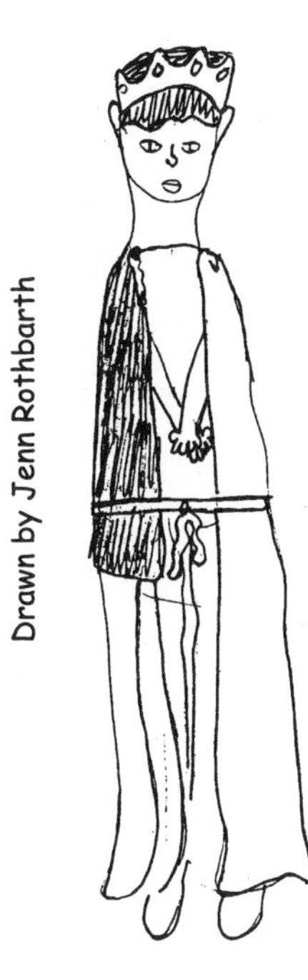

I am thy father's spirit,
Doomed for a certain time to walk the night,
And for the day confined to fast in fires,
Till the foul crimes done in my days of nature
Are burnt and purged away. But for that I am forbid
To tell the secrets of my prison house,
I could a tale unfold whose lightest word
Would harrow up thy soul, freeze thy young blood. . .

(Act 1, Scene 3)

Say What??

fast—not eat
my days of nature—my lifetime
harrow—rip

Kidspeak

King Hamlet is not a happy camper! He tells his son that he is not having a great time in the next life. He has to walk around all night and burn all day, and if that is not bad enough, he doesn't get to eat anything either! He says he is not allowed to tell more than that but if he could . . . well, he could tell things that would curl Hamlet's toes! Do you get the feeling this ghost is a whiner?!

NAME:____

Polonius (to Laertes)

Drawn by Danielle Warly

Neither a borrower or a lender be,
For loan oft loses both itself and friend,
And borrowing dulls the edge of husbandry.
This above, to thine own self be true,
And it must follow, as night the day,
Thou canst not then be false to any man.

(Act 1, Scene 3)

Say What??

Polonius—pronounced pol-OH-nee-us
husbandry—good, thrifty housekeeping

Kidspeak

Polonius gives good advice to his son in this speech. He tells him not borrow to or lend money because when you lend money you often lose the money and the friendship of the person you lent it to, and borrowing money makes you lazy about working. He tells Laertes to be true to himself, not to betray the things he believes in; he will then be an honorable and trustworthy man.

NAME: ____

Hamlet (to himself, about the actors who have arrived at court)

I'll have these players
Play something like the murder of my father
Before mine uncle. I'll observe his looks,
I'll tent him to the quick. If a do blench,
I know my course.

(Act 2, Scene 2)

Say What??

tent—probe
quick—the most sensitive part
If a do blench—If he goes pale
I know my course—I will know what to do next

Kidspeak

Hamlet has a plan to show his uncle's guilt. He wants the traveling actors to perform a play that shows the murder of a king by his brother. If Claudius reacts in shock to the performance, Hamlet will take this as a sure sign of guilt and will take his revenge.

This speech ends with these famous lines:

The play's the thing
Wherein I'll catch the conscience of the king.

(Act 2, Scene 2)

NAME:____

Hamlet (to himself)

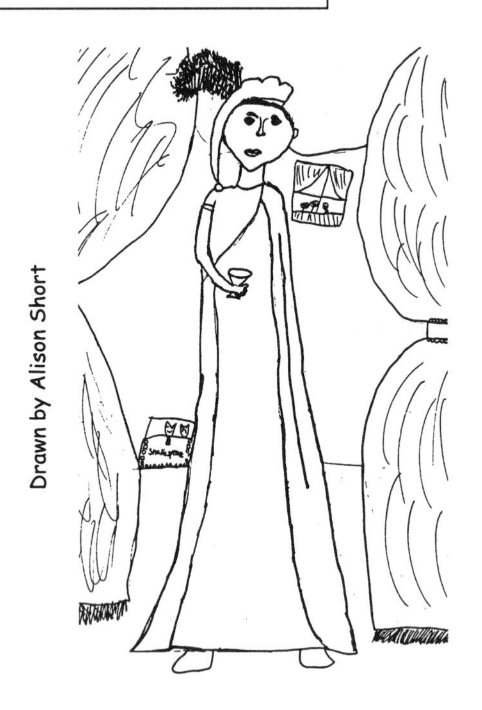

Drawn by Alison Short

To be, or not to be, that is the question.
Whether 'tis nobler in the mind to suffer
The slings and arrows of outrageous fortune,
Or to take up arms against a sea of troubles,
And by opposing end them. To die, to sleep.
No more; and by a sleep to say we end
The heartache and the thousand natural shocks
That flesh is heir to—'tis a consummation
Devoutly to be wished.

(Act 3, Scene 1)

Say What??

soliloquy—a speech given by a character who is alone onstage
natural shocks—illnesses or accidents
consummation—the ultimate end

Kidspeak

Hamlet's spirits are so low at this point that he cannot decide whether to live or die. Should he be noble and good and accept his fate, or should he fight against the cruel world and try to change things? He tells himself that dying is just like being asleep (—pssst, Hamlet! Read my lips—*Dead people do not wake up!* Think again!) He thinks that if he is dead, he will be freed from all his problems. There is one small problem with suicide as a problem-solving strategy—*You're dead!*

NAME:____________________________________

Hamlet (to Ophelia)

Drawn by Megan Keppler

If thou dost marry, I'll give thee this plague for
thy dowry: be thou as chaste as ice, as pure as
snow, thou shalt not escape calumny. Get thee to a
nunnery, go: farewell. Or if thou wilt needs
marry, marry a fool; for wise men know well enough
what monsters you make of them. To a nunnery go,
and quickly too. Farewell.

(Act 3, Scene 1)

Say What??

Ophelia—pronounced oh-FEEL-ya
dowry—money and valuables that a girl brought to her new husband
chaste—pure
calumny—malicious lies
nunnery—convent

Kidspeak

Hamlet is giving poor Ophelia a real "tongue lashing." His verbal attack on her is very cruel. He is wishing bad things for her and tells her to get to a convent. He is acting like a cruel madman with the girl he is supposed to be in love with.

NAME:____________________________________

Hamlet (to Horatio, about a skull in the graveyard)

Let me see. (He takes the skull.) Alas, poor Yorick! I knew him, Horatio, a fellow of infinite jest, of most excellent fancy, he hath borne me on his back a thousand times; and now how abhorred in my imagination it is! My gorge rises at it. Here hung those lips that I have kissed I know not how oft. Where be your gibes now? Your gambols, your songs, your flashes of merriment, that were wont to set the table on a roar? Not one now, to mock your own grinning?

(Act 5, Scene 1)

Say What??

Horatio—pronounced hor-RAY-shee-oh
infinite—without end
jest—good humor
abhorred—hated
gorge—stomach
gibes—teasing words
gambols—to skip about playfully

Kidspeak

Seeing the skull of the old jester, whom he had known so well, is very upsetting to Hamlet. He recalls how Yorick was once so full of fun, entertaining people, and now all that is left is a revolting skull. What is even more depressing is the thought that this is the fate awaiting everyone, from the rich and famous on down. Bummer!

NAME:______________________________

Laertes (to Hamlet, after he is hit by Laertes in the duel)

It is here Hamlet. Hamlet, thou art slain;
No medicine in the world can do thee good.
In thee there is not half an hour of life.
The treacherous instrument is in thy hand,
Unbated and envenomed. The foul practice
Hath turned itself on me; lo, here I lie,
Never to rise again.

(Act 5, Scene 2)

Say What??

Laertes—pronounced lay-ERT-eez
slain—killed
unbated—sharp
envenomed—poisonous
foul practice—wicked plan

Kidspeak

Laertes explains, with his dying breath, that the sword is poisoned and, just as he is dying, so will Hamlet. The sword belonged to Laertes but Hamlet picked it up after he was hit by Laertes and the swords were dropped. The plan to kill Hamlet with the poisoned sword worked, but at the cost of Laertes's life.

NAME:____

Hamlet (to Horatio)

Oh, I die, Horatio!
The potent poison quite o'ercrows my spirit.
I cannot live to hear the news from England,
But I do prophesy th' election lights
On Fortinbras; he hath my dying voice.
So tell him, with th' occurrents, more and less,
Which have solicited—the rest is silence.

(Act 5, Scene 2)

Say What??

potent—strong
o'ercrows—triumphs over
lights—rests
voice—vote
occurrents—happenings
solicited—brought about

Kidspeak

The poison is taking effect and Hamlet knows that he is dying. He hears noise close by. It is Fortinbras, prince of Norway, arriving with the English ambassadors. Hamlet knows death is very near and that he won't live to hear the news from England. Because he guesses that Fortinbras will be chosen as king, he says that Fortinbras has his vote for the job. Hamlet asks Horatio to tell what happened and why.

"—the rest is silence" is usually spoken by the actor, but it is possible that this was originally a stage direction and that Hamlet's speech ended with the unfinished sentence, "So tell him, with th' occurrents, more and less, which have solicited . . ."

NAME:____________________________________

Lights, Camera, Action

Movie Making

Please don't skip this section!! Movie making with elementary students will not drive you to an early retirement! Putting on a live performance is guaranteed to drive you up the nearest wall in no time flat, but, through the miracle of technology—in the shape of a camcorder—you will help your students experience the excitement of performing—and you *will* live to tell the tale!

You are about to discover how simple the movie-making process can be. All you need is a camcorder, props, simple costumes, a "castle" wall, some actors, and a little self-confidence! The question is how to get everything with a minimum of effort on your part. (You must save your energies for the creative process!)

1. Camcorder. If your school doesn't have one, send home a begging letter liberally sprinkled with veiled references as to how guilty the parents should feel if a camcorder is not forthcoming! Be sure to familiarize yourself with the camcorder before the actual filming. Nothing kills enthusiasm faster than a fumbler who misses an award-winning performance through technical ineptitude!

2. Costumes. The costumes for this production are very simple to put together. Because this is a modern production, the actors wear their regular clothes—spruced up a little if you so desire. If several actors play the major roles, be aware of continuity so that the audience won't be completely baffled!

3. Props. We include the list of props at the beginning of the script, which follows this section. Dropping a few hints about what is needed usually results in instant props! (Remember: Crowns can be found in abundance at certain local hamburger joints named after royal personages!) Have your students make a large sign (that says "HAMLET") for the camera to focus on as an introduction to the movie. For added effect, they could also make a mural, a map of Denmark, or some other visual.

4. Sets. The best thing about a camcorder, apart from its ability to edit out the disasters instantly, is its mobility. You can shoot in a variety of locations. The "in-house" scenes require homey places—maybe the teachers' lounge?

   Your enthusiastic students will be overflowing with ideas for locations with atmosphere. Let them have lots of input so they feel ownership of, and responsibility for, the performance. Remember, to have control, you must give control.

5. Actors. This is the hardest part of all because everyone wants the BIG parts, and it is up to you to choose who does what. Here is an almost painless way:

   - Have students list several parts they would like to play. This gives you some leeway.
   - Have the students write down why they want to be a certain character.
   - If all else fails, flip a coin. Remember, auctioning off parts to the highest bidders is not an option!

6. Tips:

   - Slip written dialogue into books, or tape them onto props to aid the memories of nervous actors!
   - Manufacture extra parts by including lots of servants and soldiers so that as many students as possible are included. Shakespeare wouldn't mind—the play's the thing!
   - Your movie will take on a very professional look if you have an introduction consisting of a title, visuals, and even mood music!
   - Give the following script outline to the actors and let them pad their own scenes with improvisation. The key to successful improvisation is a thorough understanding of the play!
   - Hold lots of practice sessions prior to film day—and for the sake of your sanity, don't try to film all the scenes in one day!
   - Show credits at the end of the movie—film all the students who played Hamlet holding a large sign that says "Hamlet." All the King Claudiuses hold his name; all Queen Gertrudes hold her name, and so on.

Now that you have everything you need, *go make a movie!*

Cast of Characters

*Hamlet

*Claudius (Hamlet's uncle and stepfather)

*Gertrude (Hamlet's mother)

*Ophelia (Hamlet's neighbor and sometimes girl friend) (optional)

*Laertes (Ophelia's brother)

*Horatio (Hamlet's best friend)

Friends and neighbors

Narrators (The number of narrators can vary from only one to as many as the teacher is brave enough to include!)

*These characters are portrayed by different students in each scene. Continuity is maintained through costumes and props that identify the characters, regardless of the actor. This allows more students to participate—and also eliminates the stress of one student having to learn a lot of lines!

Props

- television
- fake swords
- pop can
- tape recorder—to provide sound for the scenes that Hamlet is supposed to be watching on television

Management Notes

This version of the play brings the action to the here and now. By modernizing the play, we are able to make Hamlet's problems seem a little more relevant to the students. If they see Hamlet in modern dress—sneakers, baseball cap turned back-to-front, etc., they may be able to identify more easily with his difficulties: the sudden remarriage of his mother, the death of his father, his confusion about living and dying, rebellion and loyalty, and the additional problems his relationship with his girlfriend, Ophelia, brings. Perhaps some of the students have had to deal with feelings similar to those experienced by Hamlet and have also been asked to ". . . cast thy nighted colour off." This Hamlet is still the same character, but his appearance in modern clothes enables the students to identify with him more easily.

The story is told by the narrator(s) who introduces each scene to the audience. The narrator should talk to the audience intimately, as if he were talking to a group of buddies, telling them the latest gossip about a mutual friend. A student who is confident and loaded with personality and wit may be a "challenge" in the classroom, but would be great in this role!

The sections titled Quality Quotes appear at relevant points in the text and enable students who want to recite the "real" lines to do so.

The stage directions are intended to guide the students as they improvise each scene.

The Tragedy of Hamlet, Prince of Denmark

Introduction

Narrator is sitting reading a newspaper. (*Tip: Lines can be written in the newspaper as a prompt.*) If you are using several narrators, have them all reading, or lounging, so that they all interact with the audience—as if they are greeting a long-lost pal.

Narrator (*looking up, warmly*)**:** Hey! How are you! Long time no see. I heard you were here and I was hoping to run into you. I knew you would look up your old pals! (*shaking newspaper, narrator says ruefully*) Here's one old pal you won't be seeing. Hamlet. Have you seen this? (*holding paper toward audience*) No? You mean you haven't heard the news? Really? Well sit down, you are in for a shock, man. Hamlet is dead! Can you believe it? Me either. I knew he was having some problems but I had no idea things were this bad. It's all here in the paper; well, not all of it, just how it ended. You knew about Hamlet's home life, I suppose? No? Well, I guess it's no secret now. Hamlet was having major problems after his old man died and his mom couldn't wait a month before tying the knot again with Hamlet's uncle! Yeah! His dad's brother! Can you believe it? Hamlet couldn't either, and between you and me, I think it really messed with his mind.

Act 1, Scene 1

Claudius and Gertrude are getting ready to go out. Hamlet comes in and they have an argument because they say Hamlet is too moody and gloomy.

“ Quality Quotes:

Gertrude: Good Hamlet cast thy nighted colour off,
And let thine eye look like a friend on Denmark.
Do not forever with thy vailed lids
Seek for thy noble father in the dust.

Hamlet: O that this too too solid flesh would melt,
Thaw and resolve itself into a dew,
Or that the Everlasting had not fixed
His canon against self-slaughter. O God, God,
How weary, stale, flat and unprofitable
Seem to me all the uses of this world!

Act 1, Scene 2

Hamlet turns on the television and sits down to watch. (*Tip: Have television facing away from audience so they cannot see blank screen. Hamlet should switch on the tape player while acting as if turning on the television.*) Suddenly, the screen “shows” his dead father, and he is speaking to Hamlet. Hamlet retells what his father is saying about being murdered and seeking revenge because the audience cannot see the screen—and there's nothing on it anyway!

“ Quality Quotes

Ghost (*to Hamlet*)**:** I am thy father’s spirit,
Doomed for a certain time to walk the night,
And for the day confined to fast in fires,
Till the foul crimes done in my days of nature
Are burnt and purged away.

Narrator (*to audience*)**:** Hamlet was not really surprised by the news the ghost told him. He had thought all along that his uncle, step-daddy Claudius, had had more than a little to do with his father’s death. Do you think he saw his dead dad on the box? (*pause*) Who knows, (*shrug*) maybe the dead dude really did show up on *Prime Time Live*—or, in his case, *Prime Time Dead!* It doesn’t really matter because Hamlet *believed* he saw him, and the seed of revenge was planted.

Hamlet got pretty low around this time. He even considered putting an end to it all—permanently, if you catch my drift! I passed him one day and he was talking to himself about whether it was better to live or die. He was losing it, man!

Act 2, Scene 1

Hamlet is walking alone and talking to himself about life and death. (*Tip: Filming this outdoors would provide a pleasant change of scene.*)

“ Quality Quotes

Hamlet: To be, or not to be, that is the question.
Whether ’tis nobler in the mind to suffer
The slings and arrows of outrageous fortune,
Or to take up arms against a sea of troubles,
And by opposing end them. To die, to sleep.
No more; and by a sleep to say we end
The heartache and the thousand natural shocks
That flesh is heir to—’tis a consummation
Devoutly to be wished.

Narrator (*sadly, with hand on heart*)**:** Gets you right here, doesn’t it? Or is it here?! (*puts hand on the side of his neck*) Anyway, Hamlet decides to get Claudius for killing his dad, but he wants to make sure Claudius did it—and not the butler! Ha! Ha! Get it? No? Oh, well! (*passes hand over head and makes airplane sound, indicating the joke went over the heads of the audience*) Anyway, like I said, Hamlet wanted to be sure, and one evening while scanning the *TV Guide*, the idea comes to him.

Act 2, Scene 2

Hamlet sees in the *TV Guide* that there is a show coming on about a man who killed his brother and then married his brother’s wife. He invites his mother and Claudius to come and watch it with him. By watching Claudius’s reaction, he now knows the truth, and Claudius knows he knows.

“ Quality Quotes

Hamlet: I'll have these players
Play something like the murder of my father
Before mine uncle. I'll observe his looks,
I'll tent him to the quick. If a do blench,
I know my course.

Narrator: Hey! Do you remember that cute chick Ophelia? The one with the (*indicates hair*) and the (*indicates body*) and the big dumb jock of a brother who would annihilate anyone who looked at her? Well, guess what—she's dead, too! I kid you not, things have been pretty grim around here lately!

I never did get all the details about it, but it appears a tiff with Hamlet pushed her over the edge—and into the deep end of her parents' swimming pool one dark night. Sad, they had just had it cleaned and filled for the summer! But I'm getting ahead of myself.

Optional Scene

A meeting between Hamlet and Ophelia. She wants to know why he is acting so cool toward her and he wants her to quit nagging him because he has a lot on his mind these days. They argue and part.

“ Quality Quotes

Hamlet: If thou dost marry, I'll give thee this plague for thy dowry: be thou as chaste as ice, as pure as snow, thou shalt not escape calumny. Get thee to a nunnery, go. Farewell. Or if thou wilt needs marry, marry a fool; for wise men know well enough what monsters you make of them. To a nunnery go, and quickly too. Farewell.

Ophelia: And I of ladies most deject and wretched,
That sucked the honey of his music vows,
Now see that noble and most sovereign reason,
Like sweet bells jangles, out of time and harsh;
That unmatched form and feature of blown youth
Blasted with ecstasy. Oh woe is me
To have seen what I have seen, see what I see.

Narrator: Well, as the *Titanic* said to the iceberg, something's got to give. Claudius knows that Hamlet is on a short fuse right now, and that it's just a matter of time until the crunch comes, so he decides to get the first, and—he hopes!—the only, lick in! He cooks up a plan with Laertes, Ophelia's brother, to fix Hamlet once and for all, cook his goose, settle his hash, or—in the lingo of today—lay a smack on him!

Hamlet and Laertes both belong to the school fencing team, and Claudius's plan is for Laertes to cut Hamlet with a poisoned sword during an upcoming exhibition. Laertes blames Hamlet for the death of his sister and so is more than willing to do the dirty deed. Claudius decides, as added insurance, to poison a can of pop and finish off Hamlet that way if Laertes can't do the job.

Act 3, Scene 1

Claudius and Laertes meet outside the gym and Claudius gives Laertes the poisoned sword. They go into the gym and the exhibition begins.

During this scene the following things happen:

- Gertrude drinks the poisoned pop.
- Laertes cuts Hamlet with the poisoned sword.
- Both drop their swords and inadvertently pick up each other's swords.
- Hamlet wounds Laertes.
- Gertrude dies.
- Laertes dies.
- Hamlet kills Claudius, then dies himself.

Quality Quotes

Laertes: It is here Hamlet. Hamlet, thou art slain;
No medicine in the world can do thee good.
In thee there is not half an hour of life.
The treacherous instrument is in thy hand,
Unbated and envenomed. The foul practice
Hath turned itself on me; lo, here I lie,
Never to rise again.

Hamlet: Oh, I die, Horatio!
The potent poison quite o'ercrows my spirit.
I cannot live to hear the news from England,
But I do prophesy th' election lights
On Fortinbras; he hath my dying voice.
So tell him, with th' occurrents, more and less,
Which have solicited—the rest is silence.

Narrator: Sad, huh? It says here (*indicating newspaper*) that the police came and took statements from the crowd. Some guy called Horatio, apparently a good friend—probably the only friend!—of Hamlet, told them what Hamlet had found out about his father's death. His testimony did clear Hamlet's name to a degree, but hey, what good did that do? When you're dead—guess what?— you're dead. "The undiscovered country from whose bourn, no traveler returns." Deep, huh? Well, (*gets up to leave*) it's been a blast. Actually, it's been pretty depressing, but it was good to see you. Maybe next time you drop by, things will have perked up a bit around here! On the other hand—maybe not! See ya!

This version is missing some interesting scenes—Polonius's murder, Ophelia's mad scene, the graveyard-and-skull scene. These could be inserted with a little creative thought, using the narrator-and-actor format. Add more scenes if you wish, or abridge it further, and tailor your production to fit your time frame—and energy level! Whatever you choose to perform, we guarantee your students will amaze you with their enthusiasm, commitment, and ability!

Don't Just Sit There!

Knowledge, the wing wherewith we fly to heaven.
(*Henry VI*, 4.7)

The following activities are intended to bring the play into all curriculum areas and thus enhance students' understanding and interest. The teacher may select several activities to deepen students' understanding of a certain aspect of the play, or only one or two, merely as fun breaks during rehearsals. On a grander scale, the teacher may decide to use *Hamlet* as the core of a thematic study. In brief, the thematic, or project, approach to learning involves an extended study of a topic that crosses all curricula areas. The benefits of this approach lie in the total immersion of students in the topic and in the learning that occurs from connections students make between their lives and experiences and the topic. For a more detailed look at thematic learning and the aims of this approach, we highly recommend *Engaging Children's Minds: The Project Approach* by Lillian Katz and Sylvia Chard.[2]

We have grouped the activities by curriculum subjects, beginning with language arts, and we strongly encourage teachers to adapt, expand, or condense the activities to meet the needs and interests of their students.

We have described the first two activities in detail to provide as complete a picture as possible of the process of classroom application. Following these two activities are lots of "bare bones" that you can discard or fatten up for classroom consumption! Enjoy!

Language Arts

Mind Like a Steel Trap!

- Level: kindergarten and up
- Time: 15 minutes
- Grouping: whole class
- Supplies: none
- Preparation: Have the students sit in a circle and, as a brief warm-up, ask them to think about Hamlet. Ask some questions to stimulate creative thinking and help the students focus on the character: What kind of person was Hamlet? What worried him? What kind of life did he lead? Keep this fairly brief, especially with younger students, so that they don't get tired of sitting. When the warm-up is complete, explain the game.
- Procedure: The first person says the following: "Hamlet was . . ." and fills in the missing words to complete the sentence. The second person repeats what person one said and then adds another adjective. The sentence is repeated by everyone in the circle, getting longer as it goes. If a student cannot repeat the previous sentence or supply an "add-on" the student is out. "Out" can mean

moving out of the circle until that round is over, or it can mean leaving that circle and going to join in another one. The latter format is better for K–2 students, as being "out" is tough when you are young! The game is over when three students in a row cannot repeat the sentence. Hint: The teacher, or a capable and willing student, should write down the adjectives used as the game progresses so that any disagreements about what has been said can be promptly settled. This is a cumulative memory game. If you have a large class, or very young students, you may want to divide the class into two or more circles to make the game a little easier.

Extensions: Use other characters from the play. Use different sentence starters: "Hamlet should have . . ."; "Hamlet needed . . ."; "If I were Hamlet, I would . . ."

The second activity is more creative and also a little more involved and, therefore, requires more preparation. It will be worth it; you might even want to assign a student the task of videotaping the final performances—for posterity!

Can We Talk?

- Level: kindergarten and up
- Time: 45–60 minutes
- Grouping: whole class in cooperative groups of five or six students
- Supplies: pencils and paper for note taking, if needed

Preparation: It is a good idea to divide the class into small groups with paper and pencils ready before you explain the tasks. Explaining the tasks first, and *then* getting supplies and forming groups tends to disrupt the flow, and someone will always forget what to do by the time he or she gets organized to do it! Once the groups are settled, tell the students that each group is going to produce a talk show. They must decide if there is to be one or two hosts; the rest of the group will play the guests, characters from *Hamlet*. Give the groups three minutes to decide how many hosts they will have and which characters will be guests. When this is done, announce that they have a further ten minutes to brainstorm a list of questions for the talk show host(s) to ask the guests. The groups should compose probing questions to encourage lively conversations among the guests. While the students are working, circulate and encourage creativity and humor. When the ten minutes are up, assign three minutes to decide who gets which part! The good thing about this format is that everyone gets a part, so it should not be too difficult to come to a consensus. It is rather fun, when requiring the students to decide who does what, to add the stipulation that no one can speak until the decisions have been made! You will see some very expressive, and frustrated, students!

Procedure: Disperse the groups to practice their talk shows. Circulate, encouraging them to polish their performances and make the show as real as possible. Allow 10–15 minutes for rehearsal and then assemble all the groups for the Grand Performances. Each group performs its talk show and encourages the class to participate with questions and comments for the guests—just like the real thing!

Bard's-Eye View

How different would this story be if it were told by Horatio, or Gertrude, or a servant in the court? Write a new version of this play from a different point of view.

Then What?

Design a flowchart that shows the sequence of events in the play. Create and insert other options into the chart to produce alternate outcomes. The finished chart should look like a plan for a Choose Your Own Adventure story, with different options leading to various outcomes.

Oh, Ophelia!

Write a letter, as Ophelia, to Dear Abby; tell her about the problems you are having with your lover, Hamlet, and ask for advice.

Write Dear Abby's response to Ophelia, giving her advice on the issues she mentioned.

News, Hot Off the Press!

You are the ace reporter from the local newspaper and you got the scoop on the goings on at the castle of Elsinore.

Create an eye-catching headline and an exciting account of the action! Remember: Inquiring minds want to know!

Excuse Me, But . . .

Write two questions you would love to ask the following characters: Hamlet, Gertrude, Claudius, and the ghost.

Dear Diary

Staple several pages together and attach a cover to make a diary; decorate it to make it look "royal"! This is Hamlet's diary, and he wrote in it from the day before his father died until the day he (Hamlet) died. Fill in the entries as if you were Hamlet. Be creative and convincing!

Off to the Movies

After watching two movie versions of the play, compare and contrast the performances given by the actors who portrayed Hamlet.

Oscar Time

Watch a movie version of *Hamlet*; then draw a Venn diagram to compare and contrast the movie version and a "real" version of the play.

What Would Have Happened If . . .

- Hamlet had been a woman?
- The ghost had never appeared?
- Ophelia had been more assertive?
- This had happened today?

A Picture Is Worth a Thousand Words

Select your favorite scene and describe what happened in "Kidspeak"—ordinary language! Imagine that you are explaining the scene to a younger child; be sure to keep it simple. Practice the retelling of the story until you feel confident enough to do a presentation for another class.

And They All Lived Happily Ever After!

Rewrite the ending of the play so that everyone lives happily ever after—with all the problems solved!

Rap It Up

Tell the story of Hamlet in the form of a poem. Set it to a beat and you'll have a rap!

Smaller Rap!

If the thought of rapping the whole play seems overwhelming, do only one scene. Maybe you could get some friends together and do a scene each—*then* you will Rap It Up!

A Scene to Be Seen

Create cooperative groups to give impromptu performances of scenes from the play. To get the groups started, write the scenes on strips of paper; the one picked is the one performed.

Split Personality

If you were an actor, which character would you like to portray in the play? Explain your choice.

If you actually had to live your life as one of the people in the story, who would you choose to be? Explain your choice.

Spiderman?

Draw an idea web. Write a character's name in the center and surround the name with adjectives that describe that person.

He Was a Great Dane!

With a group of friends, collect items for a *Hamlet* display in a corner of the classroom. Be creative—even if it is a little dishonest! You could have the skull of poor Yorick, the poison Claudius used, the dueling swords, etc.

The Wedding of the Year

Gertrude and Claudius's wedding is not described in the play. Research weddings to discover all you can about the ceremony, then write an account of the wedding of Hamlet's mother and uncle as it would probably have taken place. Your writing could take the form of a newspaper article or even as an additional scene for the play.

Mix and Match

If you could remove one character from the play, other than the title character, to change the outcome of the story, who would that be? Explain your selection.

Or . . . If you could add one more character to the play to change the outcome of the story, who would that be? Explain your selection.

Super Sleuth

Imagine that you are a private detective and Prince Hamlet has hired you to investigate the murder of his father. Write a series of reports to him telling about the clues you have found and the progress you are making in the investigation.

Letter Perfect

Choose a character in the play to write a letter to. Who would it be and why? Would you give advice, a warning, or a "good telling off" for his or her behavior?? Write the letter and share it with a friend. Did the friend agree with your choice? Would he or she have said the things you said?

Inquiring Minds Want to Knoweth

How do you think Hamlet's father died? You are the ace crime reporter for the local newspaper. Write an account of Hamlet's father's final hours based on an exclusive interview you had with one of his servants.

The World's a Stage

Let's use our imaginations to change the last scene a little.When the sword fight scene is over, no one is left alive to tell the tale—and no witnesses to the events.

You are the local law-and-order person, and when you arrive on the scene you have to use your keen powers of observation to deduce the chain of events that led to the carnage you see before you. Record your observations, state the conclusions you reach, and explain what evidence you have to support your theory.

Odd Man Out

Hamlet wanted to be a hero. Compile a list of 20 attributes a hero or heroine should possess. How many of these did Hamlet possess? How many heroes can you list, real and/or fictional?

From Ode to New

Translate Hamlet's famous soliloquy, "To be, or not to be" into modern-day speech.

Ding!

Tell the story on tape and make a matching book. When it is time for the reader/ listener to turn the page, give a cue sound—like "Ding!"

Board with *Hamlet*

Create a board game based on the play *Hamlet.* Design the board and the game pieces and write the rules and instructions for playing. Play the game with a friend and note his or her comments and suggestions.

Don't Get Cross

Design a crossword puzzle that will challenge your friends' knowledge of the play. Include characters' names, places, feelings, and key words from the text.

This Is CMN

You are the anchor person on the famous CMN news program and you have to deliver the latest report in the breaking story of the murder and mayhem at Elsinore.

Write a suitably exciting script for your news presentation and perform it for the class.

Here Comes the Judge

You will need to present the case of *Hamlet vs. Claudius.* Have each character prepare his case in private so that they give nothing away to the other side. Can Hamlet prove that Claudius is guilty of murder? Or will Claudius finally clear his name?

Exciting News?

Imagine that you are either Gertrude or Claudius and that you are feeling a bit nervous about your recent marriage. You are concerned about how Hamlet is going to react to the news. Carefully plan what you want to say to Hamlet, and write him a letter about your marriage.

Social Studies

Jet Setter?

Hamlet was sent to England by Claudius. How far apart are these countries? If you were Hamlet's travel agent, how would you get him to England and back in those days; how would you do it if Hamlet were alive today?

Right to Remain Silent

In the play, Hamlet dies, along with a good many other people! What if he had not died, but ended up on trial for murder? You are a judge, and Hamlet has been tried in your court! What verdict would you reach?

Write a speech stating the verdict you reached, why you reached this verdict, and the sentence you would impose if you found him guilty!

Sad, but True

The murder of a political figure is called an *assassination.* The murder of King Hamlet was an assassination. Many world leaders have been assassinated. Research three assassinations and write a paragraph about each, explaining what took place, the motives behind it, and the outcome.

Everything in Its Place

Draw a map of Denmark; then put the following places on it:

- Copenhagen
- Skagerrak
- Kattegat
- Alborg
- Skagen

It Tickled Your Fancy!

Has the play *Hamlet* sparked your interest in Denmark? Would you like to know more about this ancient country and its inhabitants? With a little detective work you should be able to track down a Dane to interview. Prepare your questions before the interview; this will allow you to be time efficient.

Making a Den-mark on the World!

Do your part to boost Denmark's tourist trade by designing a brochure that will show some of the wonderful things to be seen and done there.

Art

Let's Give Them a Hand

Create a puppet of your favorite character; get together with a friend and put on a puppet show!

Mark the Spot

Design and make a bookmark showing your favorite character. On the back, write some lines your character said in the play.

A Poster-it Note

Imagine that your class is performing *Hamlet* and that you have been assigned the job of publicity. Design a poster that will grab the attention of the public and make them want to come to the show. Remember to include details about when and where. Perhaps, when they see your poster, the class will be inspired to put on the show!

Genius at Work

Using pieces of thin card and metal or wood, and some thread, make a mobile showing the main characters from the play *Hamlet*. If you like a challenge, try to make your mobile visually represent the characters' relationships to each other; for example, Claudius should be positioned farthest from Hamlet. Who should be closest to him?

Puzzling Pictures

On a piece of white card, draw your favorite scene from *Hamlet*. Then carefully cut it into jigsaw puzzle pieces. Put the pieces in an envelope and let your friends solve the puzzle—and admire your artistic talent!

Creative Castles

Castles were designed to give the inhabitants the maximum amount of protection while providing a home for the lord and his family, their servants, soldiers, and craftsmen, as well as the villagers when danger threatened. Do some castle research and learn all you can about the interior design and requirements for a castle "on the cutting edge"; then either design your own castle or draw Elsinore, as you think it would have looked, inside and out.

Math

Glad You Asked!

- Design a survey to discover which character in the play people enjoy the most.
- Design a survey to discover which character in the play people think is the meanest.
- Design a survey to discover which character in the play people think would make the best friend.
- Design a survey to discover which character in the play people think could have been left out.

Graph the results of each survey.

A Rose by Any Other Word

Write 10 different titles for the play. Then survey your classmates to find out which one they prefer.

And the Survey Says . . .

Create a list of no more than five statements (to keep it manageable), and beside each statement draw columns with the headings Agree, Disagree, and Undecided at the top. Survey your friends for their responses to your statements; then analyze the results.

Sample statements:

- Hamlet handled his problems very well.
- Ophelia was too wimpy.

Beyond Compare

Write your name in the right circle of a Venn diagram and write Hamlet's name in the left circle. How are you like Hamlet? Write these attributes in the center section. Write attributes that are unique to you in the right circle. Write attributes that are unique to Hamlet in the left circle.

Venn Are You Safe?

When is something a poison, and when is it not? Make a Venn diagram to show items that are always poisonous, sometimes poisonous, and never poisonous. Write a sentence describing what you discover.

Playing a Part

Make a list of the characters you consider to be important in the play, and then try to solve these fraction challenges:

What fraction of the important characters in *Hamlet*

- die?
- are women?
- go insane?
- did you like?
- got what they deserved?

What's Happenin' When?

How much time passes during the play *Hamlet*? Create a time line that shows when certain events in the play occurred. Write sentences that tell how much time has elapsed or how much time is left until the end.

Science

Say What?

Hamlet's father was killed by having poison poured into his ear. Research whether or not this is possible. Draw a diagram of an ear, label the parts, and describe what would happen if poison were introduced into an ear.

Hamlet PG-13

A filmstrip is a series of pictures created on a strip of film (or, in this case, paper!) that tell a story in logical sequence. Here's how to make one.

You will need:

- a long strip of paper, about three inches wide
- one cup of cooking oil in a pan
- markers and/or colored pencils
- two sponges

What to do:

- Draw lines across the paper to divide the strip into two-inch sections.
- Draw a picture in each section to tell the story of *Hamlet.*
- Put the film strip in the oil and let it soak for 15–20 seconds before lifting it out carefully and pulling it gently through your fingers to remove the excess oil. Then run it between two sponges to absorb more oil.
- Hang the strip up to dry. The oil will make your film strip glossy and translucent—just like the real thing!
- Display it on a window.

I Spy

What hi-tech piece of equipment would have been most useful to Hamlet in his efforts to find out who murdered his father? Would it be a video camera to film events, a bugging device to listen in on private conversations, or maybe an electronic game so that he could have some fun and forget his problems!

Brrrrr!

Cryogenics is a branch of physics that explores the concept of storing things at extremely low temperatures. Scientists are investigating the possibility of freezing people who die and storing them until cures for their fatal illnesses are found. The frozen bodies would then be thawed, revived, and cured. Research the topic of cryogenics and write a report on its current stage of development. If Hamlet had been frozen when he died, and could be revived today, what changes would he see in the world?

Poison Patrol

King Claudius was very sneaky with poison. You may think there are no poisons in your house, but there are. Keep you and your family safe by drawing a map of your house and counting, with an adult, the number of poisons you find in each room. Are all the poisons out of the reach of children? Make a Poison Patrol poster listing rules to keep kids safe and include the poison control phone number.

Don't Break My Heart

Ophelia went mad and then died for love of Hamlet. Many people attribute love with the heart. Is there really a connection? Research the function of the human heart and write a report complete with a diagram explaining how it works.

Hot Stuff

Notes

1. Cambridge School, *Shakespeare,* ed. Richard Andrews and Rex Gibson (Cambridge, England: Cambridge University Press, 1994).

2. Lillian Katz and Sylvia Chard, *Engaging Children's Minds: The Project Approach* (Norwood, NJ: Ablex, 1989).

Annotated Bibliography and Resources

Following is a list of great books, and other resources, that provide inspiration, information—and fuel for the fire!

One final suggestion: Having maps—ancient and modern—of Denmark and its neighbors will give the play a new dimension. Comparing old and new maps reveals changes in a country's borders and provides stimulus for further social studies investigations.

Garfield, Leon. *Hamlet*. Shakespeare the Animated Tales Series. London, England: Heinemann Young Books, 1992.

We have found that Leon Garfield's books are always good. This one can accompany the Animated Tales video and tells the story in "Kidspeak," with a sprinkling of text, and is eerily illustrated with scenes from the HBO video.

———. *Shakespeare Stories*. Boston: Houghton Mifflin, 1985.

There are 12 stories in this volume, including *Macbeth*, *Hamlet*, *A Midsummer Night's Dream*, and *Romeo and Juliet*. They are well written and are a great way to get a handle on the story lines before tackling the plays.

———. *Shakespeare Stories II*. Boston: Houghton Mifflin, 1994.

Among the nine stories in this volume are *Julius Caesar*, *Much Ado About Nothing*, and *The Winter's Tale*. As with the first book, the stories are well written and a great introduction to the plays.

Shakespeare. *Hamlet*. Cambridge School Shakespeare Series, ed. Richard Andrews and Rex Gibson. Cambridge, England: Cambridge University Press, 1994.

This is the full text and is a useful reference for the teacher, as well as for those students who get so fired up that they want more, more, more! The pages on the right contain text, and the facing pages are full of ideas and suggestions for enhancing students' understanding of what is happening at that particular point in the play.

Shakespeare. *Hamlet*. Shakespeare for Everyone Series, ed. Jennifer Mulherin. Morristown, NJ: Silver Burdett Press, 1988.

A must for those enthusiastic students!

Shakespeare. *Hamlet for Young People*. Shakespeare for Young People Series, ed. Diane Davidson, bk. 7. Fair Oaks, CA: Swan Books, 1997.

This series is an excellent resource for teachers and is user-friendly for students.

Shakespeare the Animated Tales: Hamlet. Produced and directed by Dave Edwards. 30 min. Random House. Videocassette.

The video gives an abridged version of the play, but keeps the main story lines intact. Quotes and "Kidspeak" are interspersed for ease of understanding. The animation is very well done, illustrating well the brooding atmosphere of Elsinore.

Macbeth

What You Should Know About *Macbeth*

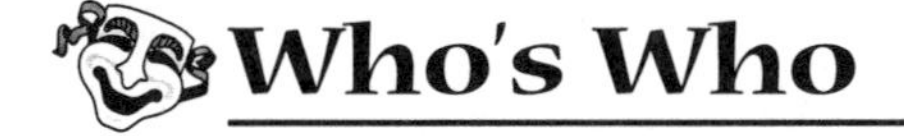

Who's Who

When presenting Shakespeare to young children, we believe it is necessary to simplify the plays by removing nonessential (in our opinion!) characters whose presence would contribute little to the students' understanding of the fundamental story line—but would contribute much to their confusion! If your particular favorite minor character has been axed, please keep in mind that it was for a good cause.

> *"Let us from point to point this story know, to make*
> *the even truth in pleasure flow"*
> *(All's Well That Ends Well, 5.3).*

The Major Characters

King Duncan

Wise, good, noble, and king of Scotland. Elder-statesman type: tailor-made for Sean Connery! He is murdered by Macbeth and his wife when he visits their castle.

Macbeth (also called Thane of Glamis and Thane of Cawdor)

A brave and, for a while, noble man who has everything: a good job, as a general in the army of King Duncan, and a clever and, for an even shorter while, loving wife. He is also suffering from what could be called the Oliver Twist complex—he wants more, and he is willing to do what it takes (even commit murder) to get it.

Lady Macbeth

The wife of Macbeth. She is ruthlessly ambitious and she encourages her husband to murder King Duncan. She is the type of crafty and conniving heroine that would be right at home plotting and scheming on a prime-time "soap"!

Banquo

A friend of Macbeth and fellow officer. He is a nice guy, one of the boys, a loyal pal who would stand by Macbeth through thick and thin. As a reward for possessing all these virtues, and for being named father of the year, he is murdered, on Macbeth's orders. He does not go quietly, however. His bloody ghost has the nerve to come to the dinner party Macbeth is giving.

Macduff

A Scottish nobleman (born by Caesarian section!—hint! hint! wink! wink!) who suspects Macbeth of the murder of King Duncan. While he is in England, his family is killed, and he doesn't need three guesses to figure out who did it! He returns to Scotland, in great haste and bad temper, for a Big Mac!

The Three Witches

The predictions of these three "secret, black and midnight hags" (4.1) provide the catalyst that changes Macbeth's ambition into a murderous obsession.

The Major Minor Characters

Malcolm

He is the eldest son of King Duncan, and a bit of a wimp. He wasted no time at all in leaving when the body of his father was found. Foot-long screws could not have kept his courage on the sticking place! (This is a snide reference to a comment Lady M. made to the Big M. when he was getting cold feet about the murder: "Screw your courage to the sticking place, and we'll not fail" [1.7].)

Donalbain

This is King Duncan's younger son who, like his brother, lost no time in protecting his own hide after the murder of his father by hotfooting it away from the scene of the crime. Justifying their hasty departure, of course! "Where we are, there's daggers in men's smiles" (2.3).

Fleance

He has no claim to fame other than he is the son of Banquo—and seemed like quite a nice guy. Because Fleance did manage to escape the murderers sent by the Big Mac, we can assume that he *did* go on to father the kings of Scotland, which makes him a rather major minor character.

The Minor Minor Characters

Lady Macduff

She is the rather boring, but devoted, wife of Macduff and loving mother of his children. She appears only briefly in the play in order to get bumped off, that is, murdered. Her murder, by you-know-who, is the last straw, as far as Macduff is concerned, and her death leads to the face-off—then head-off!—at the end of the play.

What's What

Background Information

Shakespeare found this story where he had already "borrowed" several other ideas: in *The History of Scotland* by Raphael Holinshed. He made some dramatic—startling and theatrical—changes to the truth to make sure it was appealing and to ensure the story line was politically correct, and not offensive to the new monarch and potential patron, King James I!

In truth, King Duncan was a rather feeble young man, not the respected old statesman portrayed in the play, and Banquo helped Macbeth murder him! King James I had inherited the throne of Scotland through his ancestors, Banquo and Fleance; therefore, it would have been very tacky, and even dangerous, to suggest the king's ancestors committed regicide! So, in Shakespeare's version, Banquo was noble, brave, loyal, and pure as the driven snow. He was an innocent victim of the evil, depraved Macbeth who, rumor has it, was the person least related to King James I in the whole of Scotland!

Shakespeare also took a huge liberty with Macbeth's reign, which was actually about 17 years (1040–1057), and condensed it to less than a year. Macbeth really met his end, not at the hands of Macduff, but in a battle against the army of Malcolm, King Duncan's son.

Being a shrewd businessman, as well as a literary genius, Shakespeare capitalized on the king's interest in witches. Because the king had recently written a book on the subject, Shakespeare put three witches into his new play. Also, knowing the king's preference for shorter plays, Shakespeare kept *Macbeth* "king-sized"! It is by far the shortest of Shakespear's tragedies, all of which are about half as long again as *Macbeth*. This play does not meander; it sticks to one theme and story line, unlike the other tragedies.

Although the play is set in eleventh-century Scotland, the players probably spoke with English accents and most likely wore Jacobean dress. Costumes were often bought second hand or donated to the company by patrons, and the same ones were used in all the company's productions. The players relied more on the script and imagination of the audience to set the scene, rather than on elaborate costumes. The colors of the costumes were very important because they provided clues for the audience about the nature of each character. Macbeth probably wore a dark costume, symbolizing evil, covered with a red cloak, representing blood. King Duncan's costume was probably white, symbolizing purity and nobility.

According to some accounts, the play was first performed in August 1606 at Hampton Court, a palace near London, for King James I and his brother-in-law, King Christian of Denmark. The special effects—disappearing witches and apparitions from a cauldron—suggest that the play was performed indoors, where stage machinery was more readily available. However, others claim the first performance occurred outside, in the spring of 1611, when a Dr. Simon Forman saw it at the Globe Theatre and took detailed notes about the production. The exact date of the first production is not as significant as our not yet having seen the last performance of this great tragedy.

Scene by Scene

Macbeth takes place in Scotland, where battles between lords were common and the king had to keep them in check. The lords loyal to the king help him keep the peace.

Act 1

Scene 1—The three witches are on the moors discussing when they will meet again.

Scene 2—King Duncan and his followers. A bloody sergeant arrives and tells them all about the battle. He says that Macbeth and Banquo were very brave but the Thane (Lord) of Cawdor is a traitor. The king orders the Thane of Cawdor to be killed and says that Macbeth should have his title.

Scene 3—The three witches are doing their thing. Enter Macbeth and Banquo. They call Macbeth Thane of Cawdor and tell him he will be king. They say Banquo's children will be kings. Macbeth and Banquo don't really believe any of it until a messenger arrives and tells Macbeth that the king has made him Thane of Cawdor. Then they think, "Wow! If this is true, the witches could be right about all of it!"

Scene 4—King Duncan greets Macbeth and Banquo.

Scene 5—Lady Macbeth reads Macbeth's letter. She gets a message that the king is coming that night, and she gets the idea of bumping him off. Macbeth arrives. She tells him of her plan.

Scene 6—King Duncan arrives.

Scene 7—Macbeth is trying to talk himself into committing the murder. Lady M. arrives and Macbeth says he doesn't want to do it. She says he is weak and a coward and makes fun of him. Finally, he agrees to do it.

Act 2

Scene 1—Banquo and his son Fleance talk. In comes Macbeth. Banquo and Fleance leave and Macbeth talks to himself about the planned murder. Off he goes to commit the murder.

Scene 2—Lady Macbeth and Macbeth after the murder. He is jittery; she is trying to cheer him up. Someone knocks at the gate.

Scene 3—The porter opens the gate—this is a comic-relief scene—Macduff and Lennox arrive. Macbeth comes in and acts innocent. The murder is discovered. King Duncan's sons, Donaldbain and Malcolm, decide to run before the same thing happens to them.

Scene 4— Macduff talks about Macbeth with Ross and an old man.

Act 3

Scene 1—Banquo talk to Macbeth and leaves. Macbeth tells the murderers to kill Banquo

Scene 2—Lady Macbeth and Macbeth talk about playing it cool at the banquet.

Scene 3—Banquo is murdered; his son escapes.

Scene 4—At the banquet, the murderers come to see Macbeth. Macbeth thinks he sees Banquo at the table; Lady Macbeth tries to smooth things over.

Scene 5—The three witches talk to Hecate—their boss!

Scene 6—Two lords discuss how high and mighty Macbeth is getting. They don't like it.

Act 4

Scene 1—The three witches and Hecate are still hanging out together when Macbeth arrives for more info about what is to come. They tell him to watch out for Macduff. They say he will be okay until Great Birnam Wood comes to Dunsinane, and that he cannot be harmed by any of woman born. They disappear and Lennox comes in.

Scene 2—Macduff's wife is angry because Macduff left her unprotected. Murderers from Macbeth come in and kill her and her son.

Scene 3—Macduff and Malcolm (King Duncan's son) talk for a l-o-n-g time about Macbeth. They say he has become greedy and treacherous—mad, even. Macduff receives the news that his wife and son are dead.

Act 5

Scene 1—Maid tells doctor about the weird goings on of Lady Macbeth—sleepwalking and depression.

Scene 2—Macduff and the troops get ready to sneak up on Macbeth.

Scene 3—Macbeth is a bit nuts by now. Raves about being safe because everyone is of woman born—and the woods don't move, etc. Macbeth discusses Lady Macbeth.

Scene 4—Malcolm and friends in the woods.

Scene 5—Macbeth is told that Lady Macbeth is dead; then he is told that the woods are moving.

Scene 6—Macduff and Co. march to Macbeth's castle carrying branches to disguise their numbers.

Scene 7—Macbeth kills a young man who comes into the castle, then Macduff arrives. Macbeth and Macduff have a row and fight; Macbeth is killed. Malcolm and buddies enter and talk about the battle. Macduff comes in with Macbeth's head and hails Malcolm as king of Scotland.

What's Happening

The Story

As described in the introductory section, introducing Shakespeare to children follows the hook, line, and sinker approach to teaching!

Activities and games for presenting the hook (a tantalizing mention of a great story waiting to be told) and the line (the introduction of the characters) can be found in the introduction and should be presented to the students before continuing with the story.

We have sprinkled popular lines from the actual play throughout the story. These verses correspond with the reproducible verses in the section of this book called *Will's Words*. You may wish to offer the verses for memorizing and reciting to your class as you tell the story. Even better, you may want to have your students perform short scenes from the story as you tell it. We find that, by placing Shakespeare's words and actions into the mouths and bodies of the children, they understand and appreciate the play more completely.

Let's Talk

We have found great success in increasing our students' connection to the play by providing frequent opportunities to discuss, debate, and just plain talk about it. Let's Talk can be done in a variety of ways:

1. Student-led discussion. Intriguing questions can be posed to the whole class; however, instead of you selecting the speaker, let the student who is speaking choose the next speaker.
2. Let's not talk. After posing a question to the whole class, give the students "sticky notes" to write their responses on. Place students' responses on the chalkboard and, as a whole class, group the "sticky notes" into categories and summarize the results.
3. Small group discussion. Following your question, organize students in groups of two to four. Each group selects a leader and a recorder. The leader will choose who speaks, and the recorder will write down what each person says. At the end of the discussion, the recorder will report the proceedings to the rest of the class.
4. Debate. You will need a podium (music stand) and a controversial dilemma. After posing the dilemma to the students, allow them to choose sides and move to each side of the podium. Once in place, students will take turns explaining the reasons their points of view are right. When each side has stated its position, students change sides. This will continue until a strong majority prevails or you run out of time.

Look for the Let's Talk symbols for discussion and debate topics. They are located at relevant points in the story and may be used in two ways:

1. in natural breaks during your telling of the story;
2. after the entire story has been told, as a way of reviewing and solidifying the story in students' minds.

The Sinker

The enthusiastic telling of the story.

Our Version

For information on some of the many excellent read-aloud versions of Macbeth, see the Annotated Bibliography; it is worth shopping around to find the version that suits your style. The following is the version that suits *our* style—our version!

Read it (or, preferably, loosely recite from memory) with gusto and enthusiasm—without inhibition!

Kidspeak and Shakespeak

The following story of *Macbeth* is written in plain English, Kidspeak, and at certain points in the story actual text from the play is included, Shakespeak! Don't be afraid to introduce young students to Shakespeak. The strangeness of the language is often appealing to children, and when they are familiar with the story, they can relate more easily to the difficult language.

The following is only one way to retell the story of *Macbeth*. You should infuse it with your personality and enthusiasm: "Here we go! Get ready to study Shakespeare!! Even though you are such itty-bitty kindies (first, second, and third graders)! Get your brains in gear 'cause here it comes! This is a really cool story all about blood and guts, witches and war. You'll love it!"

Macbeth

According to the story, this all happened a long time ago in a country called Scotland. (Ask: Is anyone here from Scotland? know where it is? heard of it? know anything about it?) The king of Scotland, King Duncan, is having problems with some of the lords (thanes) who are rebelling against him, even though he is a really nice king, gives lots of parties, hands out money and land to his thanes, and so on. However, the king has some very tough thanes on his side, and one of them is named Macbeth, Thane of Glamis. He is the king's cousin and would lay down his life for the king—if he really *had* to!

Duncan learns that Macbeth has been even braver than usual and he decides to give him an extra title, Thane of Cawdor, because the guy who is Thane of Cawdor has turned into a dirty, low-down creep and has betrayed the king. He is going to be executed soon and, of course, won't be needing his title! "**No more that Thane of Cawdor shall deceive our bosom interest. Go pronounce his present death and with his former title greet Macbeth.**"

Meanwhile, the wonderful, totally awesome, brave, fearless, etc., etc., Macbeth, and his best bud Banquo, are strutting their stuff on their way to see the king. They are going to give him the latest good news about the battle, how they really kicked you-know-what! Halfway across this really spooky, gloomy, misty moor, they meet three weird women who have been lurking there waiting for them. These three witchy weirdoes are so ugly, and so icky, that the two big manly thanes, even though they are so brave, are a bit nervous. Banquo is suspicious that the ugly women might actually be men because they have so much hair on their faces! "**. . . you should be women, and yet your beards forbid me to interpret that you are so.**"

Discuss the reactions of Macbeth and Banquo to their encounter with the witches. Debate foretelling the future.

Yuck! While Macbeth and Banquo are trying to decide whether to stay, or turn tail and run, the first witch says, "Hello, there, Thane of Glamis!" This gets Macbeth's attention! How does she know who he is? "**All hail Macbeth! Hail to thee, Thane of Glamis.**"

Then the second witch turns on the charm and says, "Hi! Thane of Cawdor!" Now, Macbeth hasn't heard the good news yet from King Duncan about his extra title, so he is confused and thinks, "Why is she calling me Thane of Cawdor? What does she know that I don't? Hmmmm!" "**All hail Macbeth! Hail to thee, Thane of Cawdor.**"

And then—and this is what really knocks Macbeth's socks off—the third witch greets him with this: "**All hail, Macbeth! That shalt be King hereafter.**" When he figures out what she is saying, Macbeth is all ears and ready to hear more! (What did the third witch mean?)

Not to be left out, Banquo asks for a tidbit of the future. The witches turn their charm on him, and give him their good news/bad news routine. They say:

1. He is lesser than Macbeth (bad news!) but will be greater than Macbeth (good news!).
2. He is not as happy as Macbeth (bad news!) but will be happier! (good news!).
3. He is not a king (bad news!) but his children will be kings! (*really* good news!) **"Thou shalt get kings, though thou be none: So, all hail, Macbeth and Banquo!"**

Macbeth's ears are flapping during these predictions for Banquo, and he isn't too thrilled about what he heard. It sounds as though some good times are heading Banquo's way, but Macbeth wants all the good stuff for himself. The witches told him he would be king, so what's the deal with Banquo's brats getting his throne?? He doesn't like the sound of that.

Macbeth is jealous of the prophesies told to Banquo, his best friend. Have you ever resented or been jealous of some good luck that befell a friend? Discuss friendship and how friends feel about one another.

Macbeth has just about convinced himself that the women are as nutty as they look when a messenger pants up and hails him as—you've guessed it!—Thane of Cawdor: "**We are sent to give thee from our royal master thanks; . . . He bade me from him, call thee Thane of Cawdor**." Well, fancy that! That was just what the weird women predicted! Who would have thought it?

Macbeth and Banquo are amazed, and immediately jump to the conclusion that if one of the witches' prophesies is true, all of them must be true. They are so excited they have to try really hard not to laugh and cheer and celebrate like football players in the end zone: "**If chance will have me King, why, chance may crown me**."

They manage to look humble, sincere, and loyal as they come face-to-face with that nice old fella, King Duncan. "**Stars hide your fires! Let not light see my black and deep desires**." Macbeth is eyeing the crown for size, and Banquo thinks how proud he will be of his sons when they become royal. The king suspects nothing and greets them both like long-lost pals.

Somehow, Macbeth finds the time to drop a note to his wife telling her all about the witches on the heath and the things they said. Then the king suggests that they all go to Macbeth's castle for the night. How convenient!

Discuss loyalty. How is it possible for a virtuous man to be corrupted so quickly? What would you have done in Macbeth's place?

Not long after they arrive at the castle, Lady Macbeth, who is a charming hostess, has the king settled in so that she can have a word or two or three with her husband. Not one to beat around the bush, she wastes no time in suggesting that they give the witches' prophesies a helping hand by bumping off King Duncan while he is their guest. This is a rather tacky suggestion, as killing guests is usually frowned upon, and Macbeth is not too keen on doing it: "**He's here in double trust: First as I am his kinsman and his subject strong both against the deed; then, as his host, who should against his murderer shut the door, not bear the knife myself**."

But once Lady M. has a bee in her bonnet—or a flea in her ear—or a crown in her future—she can't or won't let it go. She bullies and nags until Macbeth does the dirty deed: "**We fail? but screw your courage to the sticking-place, and we'll not fail**."

Discuss Lady Macbeth. What could have made Macbeth fall in love will a woman who is so cold-blooded and single-minded? Debate whether or not Macbeth would have committed the murder anyway, even if his wife had not pushed him into it.

He stabs the sleeping king; then Lady Macbeth, the brains of the family, wipes the knives on the clothes of the sleeping servants so they will get the blame. Crafty! "**If he do bleed, I'll gild the faces of the grooms withal; for it must seem their guilt**." When the murder is discovered, Macbeth and his lovely wife act as though they are shocked and no one—except perhaps a man called Macduff (remember that name)—suspects a thing. The plan works and it looks as if they are home free.

Everything is just peachy for a while, but then a strange thing happens: Macbeth and his wife discover that the murder is on their minds, and it is slowly driving them nuts. "**Thou hast it now: King, Cawdor, Glamis, all, as the weird women promis'd: and, I fear, thou play'dst most foully for 't**."

Have you ever suffered from a guilty conscience? Describe how you felt and how you dealt with it.

They keep thinking about it, worrying about it, even dreaming about it. They need something to take their minds off their dirty deed. What about a party! There is no use being king if you can't party hearty, so they plan a great feast and invite anyone who's anyone. Among the guests is Banquo, who has really been getting on Macbeth's nerves lately simply by being there. Macbeth convinces himself that, if Banquo was out of the way, permanently, all his worries would be over. "**Our fears in Banquo stick deep, and in his royalty of nature reigns that which would be feared**."

Macbeth sends two murderers to kill Banquo and Banquo's son. The kid has to die, too, because the witches said Banquo's sons would be kings, and just the thought of that happening really gets up Macbeth's nose! "**For Banquo's issue have I fil'd my mind; for them the gracious Duncan have I murder'd**."

The murderers come back after doing the dirty deed, and arrive just as the party is starting. They tell Macbeth that Banquo is a dead duck but that his son escaped. Ah, well, you win some, you loose some. When Macbeth goes back to the table to join the party, guess who is sitting at the table as large as life? Yes, the dead duck, Banquo! Macbeth can't believe his eyes, and he shouldn't! No one else sees Banquo for the simple reason he isn't there. Macbeth is loosing his grip. He starts talking to Banquo, saying such things as "Don't look at me like that, you nasty person! I didn't do it, and you can't prove I did!" "**Thou canst not say I did it; never shake thy gory locks at me**."

Debate whether or not Macbeth is mad or evil.

Lady Macbeth tries to shut her husband up and calm things down, but all the fun has gone out of the party: "**Sit, worthy friends: my lord is often thus, and hath been from his youth: pray you, keep seat; the fit is momentary; upon a thought he will be well again**." Things are quiet for a while. Then Macbeth starts up again and Lady Macbeth sends the guests home with some feeble story about Macbeth's having had a bad day: "**I pray you speak not; he grows worse and worse. Question enrages him. At once good night: stand not upon the order of your going, but go at once**."

Things are not going so well for the new king and queen. They were happier in the good old days when they were just Lord and Lady Macbeth.

Macbeth and his wife appear to regret what they have done. Do you think they would turn the clock back if they could? Is there anything they can do at this point to help matters?

Seeing the dead Banquo's ghost made Macbeth feel so jumpy that he decides to go back to the psychic friends network. The witches are on the heath and cooking up some mischief in their cauldron. They put some very interesting things into their brew: fillet of snake, newt's eye, and frog's toes, to name but a few! Yummy! "**Double, double, toil and trouble; fire burn and cauldron bubble. Fillet of a fenny snake, in the cauldron boil and bake; eye of newt, and toe of frog, wool of bat and tongue of dog, adder's fork, and blind-worm's sting, lizard's leg, and howlet's wing, for a charm of powerful trouble, like a hell-broth boil and bubble**." They are expecting a guest and they want to have everything just right! "**By the pricking of my thumbs, something wicked this way comes**."

Macbeth strolls up to them trying to play it cool and be as friendly as possible. "**How now, you secret, black, and midnight hags. What is't you do?**"

He asks for some more helpful hints about what the future holds for him, and the witches ask him if he wants to hear the news from them or from their masters. Macbeth opts for the horse's mouth version, and the witches conjure up strange apparitions from their cauldron. The first one tells Macbeth to beware of Macduff. Being a tough guy, Macbeth isn't too worried about Macduff.

The second apparition tells him that he cannot be harmed by anyone who was born of a woman. This is great news! Who is not born of a woman? Macbeth begins to experience the beginnings of a Superman complex!

The third apparition puts the icing on his cake. It tells him that he will not be defeated until Birnam Wood (a local beauty spot famous for having lots of trees) comes to high Dunsinane Hill. Now, even Macbeth, who has seen witches and bloody ghosts, cannot believe that trees will pull themselves out of the ground and run down the road to Dunsinane. This must mean he will never be defeated: "**Be lion-mettl'd, proud, and take no care who chafes, who frets, or where conspirers are: Macbeth shall never vanquish'd be until Great Birnam Wood to high Dunsinane Hill shall come against him**."

Discuss how Macbeth must be feeling after such good news. Debate whether it was wise of him to go back to the witches.

When Macbeth leaves the witches, he is feeling 10 feet tall and thinking about a career in basketball! Words like invincible, indomitable, invulnerable, and "hot stuff" are running around in his head.

Maybe it's because he is so full of his own importance at this point that he makes a really dumb move. When a messenger tells him that Macduff has gone to England, Macbeth decides to have the very unimportant, and boring, Lady Macduff killed—and the baby Macduffs, too. "**The castle of Macduff I will surprise; seize upon Fife; give to the edge of the sword his wife, his babes, and all unfortunate souls that trace him in his line. No boasting like a fool; This deed I'll do before this purpose cool.**"

Discuss Macbeth's possible motives for killing Macduff's family.

Killing the Macduffs seems to serve no purpose at all, except to show us that Macbeth is finding it easier and easier to kill. This is not good, and it is also a big mistake. If there is one thing guaranteed to tick a husband off, it's the murder of his family! When

Macduff hears the sad news, he is really mad, and he wants Macbeth's blood in the worst possible way! He packs his bags, gets his army together, and hightails it to Scotland as fast as the poor roads and lack of transportation will allow. **"Oh I could play the woman with mine eyes, and braggart with my tongue. But, gentle heavens, cut short all intermission, front to front bring thou this fiend of Scotland and myself; within my sword length set him; if he 'scape, Heaven forgive him too!"**

Back in Scotland, Mr. and Mrs. Macbeth are not enjoying the lifestyle of the rich and famous. Lady M. can't sleep, and when she does manage to cop a few Zs, she sleepwalks, reliving the murder of the King: **"Out, damned spot! Out I say! What, will these hands ne'er be clean? Here's the smell of the blood still: all the perfumes of Arabia will not sweeten this little hand**." Macbeth adopts the "deal with it" attitude toward his wife because he has problems of his own.

Does Macbeth still love his wife? If not, explain when and why his feelings changed. Debate whether or not her feelings for him have changed.

Macbeth has been told of the advancing army, and, as if that wasn't bad enough, his men are deserting him like rats from a sinking ship, or, in this case, a doomed castle. But when Macbeth remembers the prophesies of the apparitions, he laughs in the face of danger. Ha! How can Macduff, or anyone else, hurt him if he cannot be defeated by a man of woman born? Ha! Ha! He is invincible until the woods take a walk! Ha! Ha! Ha! **"Hang out our banners on the outward walls; the cry is still, 'They come.' Our castle's strength will laugh a siege to scorn; here let them lie till famine and the ague eat them up**."

While Macbeth is congratulating himself on being Mr. Wonderful, Macduff and his army have arrived and are in Birnam Wood. They have heard that Macbeth's army is thin on the ground, and it appears there won't be too much of a battle, so they decide to make things a bit more interesting. They have marched a long way for this fight, and they want to get as much out of it as they can! They decide to make it more challenging by seeing how close they can get to Dunsinane Castle before being spotted. They camouflage themselves with tree branches and plan to sneak up to the castle disguised as a small wood. Does this ring a bell?

While the enemy is branching out in the woods, Macbeth is strolling around in his castle, feeling very smug. Then, the first piece of bad news arrives. A servant rushes in and announces, **"The queen, my lord, is dead**."

Discuss Macbeth's possible reaction to the news of his wife's death. Give a reason for your prediction.

Macbeth gives a shrug and says, "Oh well, it had to happen sometime!" Is that cold or what? **"She should have died hereafter; there would have been a time for such a word. To-morrow, and to-morrow, and to-morrow**." He has no time for remembering the good old days, even if he wanted to, because in rushes a messenger to break the news that the woods are moving! Macbeth finds this very hard to believe (wouldn't you?), but even after being threatened with hanging, the messenger still sticks to his story, and Macbeth realizes that he had better get his butt in gear. He was told he would be undefeated until Great Birnam Wood comes to Dunsinane, and the woods are almost there! **"I will not be afraid of death and bane till Birnam forest come to Dunsinane**."

Discuss the following: If Macbeth had one wish at this point, what would it be?

Although he was promised he would not be harmed by man of woman born, he slaps on his armor just to be on the safe side. He is beginning to realize that these prophesies are not all he thought they would be.

The woody army has arrived at the castle and Macduff finds Macbeth in no time flat. Macbeth doesn't want to fight Macduff because the little conscience he has left has made him regret killing the very unimportant, and boring, Lady Macduff and the little Duffs. He doesn't want any more Duff blood on his hands: "**Of all men else I have avoided thee: but get thee back, my soul is too much charg'd with blood of thine already**."

Is it surprising that Macbeth still has some honor, after all he has done? Debate: Who is the "real Macbeth"—the noble or the knave?

Macbeth tells Macduff to clear off, but Macduff hasn't marched all this way for nothing. He is here to fight, and fight he will. He says that Macbeth is a lily-livered coward, with a yellow streak a mile wide. This makes Macbeth mad. He tells Macduff that he will fight him but that he is bound to win because he can't be hurt by any man of woman born: "**Let fall thy blade on vulnerable crests; I bear a charmed life, which must not yield to one of woman born**." It is at this point that Macduff drops his bombshell! He wasn't born but taken from his mother by an operation. (Discuss, as tastefully as possible, a Caesarian section. Several of the children may know they were born that way and will enjoy sharing this tidbit!) "**Despair thy charm; and let the angel whom thou still hast serv'd tell thee, Macduff was from his mother's womb untimely ripp'd**." When Macbeth hears this news, he knows his time has come. The witches have been making a fool of him all along.

Discuss the witches. What do you think of their treatment of Macbeth?

Macbeth decides to go out like a man, even though he has been acting like a dirty dog for quite some time. "**Yet I will try the last. Before my body I throw my warlike shield; lay on, Macduff, and damn'd be him that first cries, 'Hold, enough!'**" He puts up a great fight, but in the end Macduff wins. He kills Macbeth and cuts off his head. Then Macduff shows the head to his friends. This is a bit tacky, and very messy, but Macbeth had been a royal pain in his you-know-what!

Debate this statement: "Macbeth only has himself to blame."

The people of Scotland get a new king, Malcolm, the son of King Duncan, and they all live happily ever after. "**Hail, king! for so thou art. Behold, where stands the usurper's cursed head; the time is free. I see thee compass'd with thy kingdom's pearl, that speak my salutation in their minds; whose voices I desire aloud with mine: Hail, King of Scotland!**"

Will's Words—Selections for Recitation

Lady Macbeth (to Macbeth)

Glamis thou art, and Cawdor and shalt be
What thou art promis'd. Yet do I fear thy
nature
It is too full o' the milk of human kindness
To catch the nearest way. Thou would be
great,
Art not without ambition, but without
The illness should attend it;

(Act 1, Scene 5)

Say What??

thou—you
shalt—shall
thy—your
illness—ruthlessness

Kidspeak

Lady Macbeth is saying that her husband is already Thane (Lord) of Glamis and Thane of Cawdor. She believes he is going to be everything that the witches promised, including king of Scotland. She is worried that her husband is too nice to do what has to be done to ascend the throne. She knows that he wants to be great and that he has ambition, but she also knows that he may not be hard-hearted, harsh, and savage enough to do what must be done, namely, get rid of King Duncan.

NAME:____

Lady Macbeth (to herself)

Come, you spirits
That tend on mortal thoughts! unsex me
here,
And fill me from the crown to the toe top-full
Of direst cruelty; make thick my blood,
Stop up the access and passage to remorse,
That no compunctious visitings of nature
Shake my fell purpose,

(Act 1, Scene 5)

Say What??

tend—take care of
direst—worst
remorse—regret, feeling sorry
compunctious—guilty consciences
fell—wicked

Kidspeak

Lady Macbeth is praying that she can be tough enough to do the evil things needed to acquire the throne of Scotland for her husband. She asks the spirits to take away her womanly, tender feelings and fill her up with cruelty. She wants her blood to thicken so that no feelings of guilt, sorrow, or regret can enter her and stop her from doing the wicked things she is planning to do.

NAME:____

Lady Macbeth (to Macbeth)

Drawn by Rachel Weintraub

But screw your courage to the sticking-place,
And we'll not fail. When Duncan is asleep,
Whereto the rather shall his day's hard journey
Soundly invite him, his two chamberlains
Will I with wine and wassail so convince,
That memory, the warder of the brain,
Shall be a fume,

(Act 1, Scene 7)

Say What??

chamberlains—servants
wassail—merrymaking
fume—fog

Kidspeak

Lady Macbeth is feeling very frustrated with her husband. He wants to be king, but he seems to be chickening out now that she is all ready to do the dirty deed. She is giving him a good talking to, trying to boost his spirits. She is like a football coach talking to a player during halftime and telling him to stop acting like a wimp and to get out there and take care of business. Of course, this is murder, not football!

She tells her husband to screw up his courage until it is as tight as can be. The sticking place is the point at which he will not change his mind but stick to his decision to act against King Duncan. If he can be strong, they will not fail in the attempt to sieze the throne of Scotland. She explains that the plan is simple: She will give the king's servants so much wine that they will be in a deep, drunken sleep in the king's bedroom. The servants will not be fit to protect the king when she and Macbeth come to murder him. When the servants wake up, they will not be able to remember anything. This will make it very convenient for putting the blame on them!

NAME:____________________________________

Macbeth (to himself)

Is this a dagger which I see before me,
The handle toward my hand? Come, let
me clutch thee:
I have thee not, and yet I see thee still.
Art thou not, fatal vision, sensible
To feeling as to sight? Or art thou but
A dagger of the mind, a false creation,
Proceeding from the heat-oppressed brain?

(Act 2, Scene 1)

Say What??

clutch—hold
thee—you
thou—you

Kidspeak

Macbeth is a mental mess at this point. He wants to be king, but he really does not want to have to murder the king, who is also his cousin. He had already decided against it, but when he told his wife, she pitched a fit at him, called him a coward, and accused him of breaking his word to her. He finally agreed to kill the king, but he is not at ease about things.

Seeing things that are not really there is always a sure sign that something is wrong! Macbeth sees a dagger with the handle facing his hand as if inviting him to take hold of it, but when he tries to grab it, he finds he cannot. He wonders why the dagger can be seen but not touched. He considers that the dagger could be a figment of a feverish, confused mind, but finally he decides that it has been sent to him as a sign. He decides that the dagger is trying to tell him that he should go ahead and stab the king. The dagger has been sent to encourage him, and lead him to the king's bedroom—and to murder. He lets the imaginary dagger make the decision about the murder of King Duncan.

NAME:______________________________________

First Witch

Round about the cauldron go;
In the poison'd entrails throw.
Toad, that under cold stone
Days and nights hast thirty-one
Swelter'd venom, sleeping got,
Boil thou first i' the charmed pot.

(Act 4, Scene 1)

All Witches

Double, double, toil and trouble;
Fire burn and cauldron bubble.

(Act 4, Scene 1)

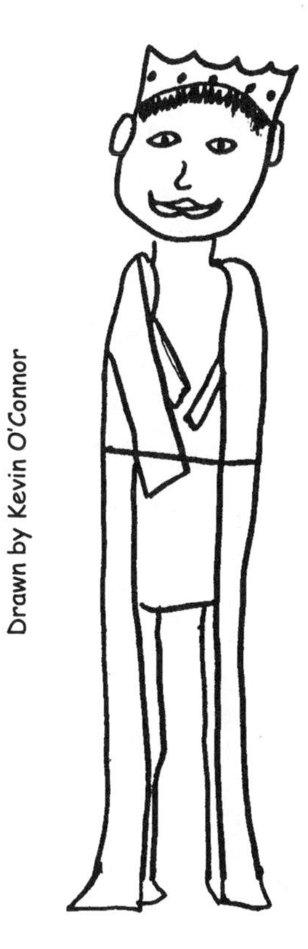
Drawn by Kevin O'Connor

Say What??

cauldron—round, black pot
swelter'd—sweated
venom—poison
thou—you
toil—work

Kidspeak

The witches are conjuring up a powerful spell because they know that Macbeth is coming back. The ingredients they use for their spells are all supposed to be poisonous. Witch number one puts in poisoned intestines and the poisonous sweat from a toad that was caught while it was asleep. They have no pity for Macbeth and wish him double the problems he has had already.

NAME:____

Second Witch

Fillet of a fenny snake,
In the cauldron boil and bake;
Eye of newt, and toe of frog,
Wool of bat, and tongue of dog,
Adder's fork, and blind-worm's sting,
Lizard's leg, and howlet's wing,
For a charm of powerful trouble,
Like a hell-broth boil and bubble.

(Act 4, Scene 1)

All Witches

Double, double, toil and trouble;
Fire burn and cauldron bubble.

(Act 4, Scene 1)

Say What??

fillet—boneless slice
fenny snake—snake from a marshy area
wool—short fur close to a bat's skin
adder's fork—tongue
howlet—baby owl
hell-broth—soup for the devil
toil—work
cauldron—round, black pot

Kidspeak

The witches are conjuring up a powerful spell because they know that Macbeth is coming back. The ingredients they use for their spells are all supposed to be poisonous. Witch number two puts in more poisonous ingredients. They have no pity for Macbeth and wish him double the problems he has had already.

NAME:____

Third Witch

Scale of dragon, tooth of wolf,
Witches' mummy, maw and gulf
Of the ravin'd salt-sea shark,
Root of hemlock digg'd i' the dark.
Liver of blaspheming Jew,
Gall of goat, and slips of yew
Sliver'd in the moon's eclipse,
Nose of Turk, and Tartar's lips,
Finger of birth-strangled babe
Ditch-deliver'd by a drab,
Make the gruel thick and slab;
Add thereto a tiger's chaudron,
For the ingredients of our cauldron.

(Act 4, Scene 1)

All Witches

Double, double, toil and trouble;
Fire burn and cauldron bubble.

(Act 4, Scene 1)

Say What??

maw—stomach
gulf—throat
ravin'd—full of flesh
gall—bile, bitter liquid
slips—small pieces
yew—a tree
sliver'd—sliced off
ditch-deliver'd—born in a ditch
drab—woman
gruel—like oatmeal
slab—sticky
chaudron—intestines
toil—work
cauldron—round, black pot

Kidspeak

The witches are conjuring up a powerful spell because they know that Macbeth is coming back. The ingredients they use for their spells are all supposed to be poisonous. Witch number three puts in more poisonous ingredients. They have no pity for Macbeth and wish him double the problems he has had already.

NAME:____

Lady Macbeth (to herself)

Out, damned spot! out, I say!—One: two: why,
then 'tis time to do't.—Hell is murky!—Fie my
lord, fie! a soldier, and afeared? What need we
fear who knows it, when none can call our power to
account?—Yet who would have thought the old man
to have had so much blood in him?

(Act 5, Scene 1)

Say What??

fie—used to express disgust or shock
afeared—frightened

Kidspeak

Lady Macbeth is not feeling at ease with the situation. She is showing signs of stress by sleepwalking and talking. As she sleepwalks, she rambles on about the murder, about getting caught, about hell, and about how there was so much blood. She washes her hands constantly while awake and mimes the action while asleep. She is overwhelmed by guilt, but her instinct to cover up and not to get caught is strong. She asks, "What have we to fear? No one knows we did it." Then she adds a comment about the amount of blood there was. The image of blood everywhere and on everything has made a great impression on her subconscious and causes the constant "hand washing." She was so strong before the murder. She urged her husband to do the evil deed, but now that he has done it, she has seen signs that her husband is losing his cool, and she is becoming more and more unstable, too.

NAME:________________________________

Doctor (to servant)

Foul whisperings are abroad: unnatural deeds
Do breed unnatural troubles: infected minds
To their deaf pillows will discharge their
secrets:
More needs she the divine than the physician.
God, God forgive us all! Look after her;
Remove from her the means of all annoyance,
And still keep eyes upon her. So, good night:

(Act 5, Scene 1)

Say What??

foul—nasty
whisperings—rumors
divine—priest

Kidspeak

The doctor has been sent for, and he is shocked by Lady Macbeth's appearance. He hints that he has heard rumors about the king's murder and he says that when people do bad things, it causes other bad things to happen. He says that people who have secrets can only talk to their pillows. He thinks Lady Macbeth needs to talk to a priest so that she can confess the deeds that are bothering her conscience. He tells the maid to look after Lady Macbeth and make sure there is nothing around that she could use to kill herself. He then leaves, knowing that there is nothing a doctor can do for her.

NAME:_______________________________________

Macbeth (to servants)

Bring me no more reports; let them fly all:
Till Birnam Wood remove to Dunsinane
I cannot taint with fear. What's the boy Malcolm?
Was he not born of woman? The spirits that know
All mortal consequences have pronounc'd me thus:
"Fear not, Macbeth; no man that's born of woman
Shall e'er have power upon thee."

(Act 5, Scene 3)

Say What??

remove—move
taint—go bad
e'er—ever
thee—you

Kidspeak

Macbeth seems to have recovered from his attack of the jitters. Things can hardly get any worse than they have been, so now he is going to "tough it out." The witches' prophesies have all come true so far, and they have told him that he is safe until the woods move to Dunsinane Castle. Macbeth figures the chances of that happening are very slim! Also, the weird women said that he cannot be harmed by anyone of woman born; that's everyone, right? So, at this point, Macbeth feels like Superman.

NAME:____________________________________

Macbeth (to himself)

She should have died hereafter;
There would have been a time for such a word.
To-morrow, and to-morrow, and to-morrow,
Creeps in this petty pace from day to day,
To the last syllable of recorded time,
All our yesterdays have lighted fools
The way to dusty death. Out, out, brief candle!

(Act 5, Scene 5)

Say What??

Candle—life

Kidspeak

Macbeth appears to be quite depressed and gloomy is this section; of course, his wife has just killed herself and his castle is under attack by former friends who are after his blood, so there is not a whole lot for him to be cheerful about!

In the first two lines of this section, Macbeth is saying that his wife would have died eventually, and that he would have heard this bad news sometime. He sees life as one meaningless day dragging after another to the end of time. Everyone who has ever lived has had to die, so what is the purpose of living? Bummer!

NAME:___________________________________

Macbeth (to Macduff)

I will not yield,
To kiss the ground before young Malcolm's feet,
And to be baited with the rabble's curse.
Though Birnam Wood be come to Dunsinane,
And thou oppos'd, being of no woman born,
Yet I will try the last. Before my body
I throw my warlike shield: Lay on, Macduff,
And damn'd be him that first cries, "Hold, enough!"

(Act 5, Scene 8)

Say What??

yield—give in, surrender
baited—teased
rabble—crowd
thou oppos'd—you fighting against me
hold, enough—I surrender

Kidspeak

In this brief section we can see Macbeth the way he used to be—brave, courageous, daring, and bold. He finally realizes that he has no lucky charms or spells to keep him safe, and that it has all been a cruel trick by the witches. As he faces death he refuses to beg Macduff for mercy and is determined to fight, honorably, to the end.

NAME:____________________________________

Lights, Camera, Action

Movie Making

Please don't skip this section!! Movie making with elementary students will not drive you to an early retirement! Putting on a live performance is guaranteed to drive you up the nearest wall in no time flat, but, through the miracle of technology—in the shape of a camcorder—you will help your students experience the excitement of performing—and you *will* live to tell the tale!

You are about to discover how simple the movie making process can be. All you need is a camcorder, props, simple costumes, a "castle" wall, some actors, and a little self-confidence! The question is how to get everything with a minimum of effort on your part. (You must save your energies for the creative process!)

1. Camcorder. If your school doesn't have one, send home a begging letter liberally sprinkled with veiled references as to how guilty the parents should feel if a camcorder is not forthcoming! Be sure to familiarize yourself with the camcorder before the actual filming. Nothing kills enthusiasm faster than a fumbler who misses an award-winning performance through technical ineptitude!

2. Costumes. A lot can be done with cardboard and silver spray paint in this play. It might be worth approaching the art teacher and humbly throwing yourself on her mercies. Explain your dilemma: You need costumes but you lack the art teacher's talent. You are humbly begging for help. Could she help out by having the students make a few "little things" during art class time, thus relieving you of the burden of organizing it in your room and having to deal with the mess. *Do not say this to the art teacher!* She must believe that you are admiring her talent, not using the scheduled art time as an opportunity to spread the work around! It's not only the students who have to do a little acting to get this show on the road!

   Lady Macbeth's flowing dress should be easy to rustle up. If one is not donated, check the secondhand clothing stores. You will find a variety to choose from, at little cost.

3. Props. We have included a list of props. Dropping a few hints about what is needed usually results in instant props! (Remember: Crowns can be found in abundance at certain local hamburger joints that are named after royal personages!) Have your students make a large sign that says "MACBETH" for the camera to focus on as an introduction to the movie. Your students could also make a mural, or some other visual, for added effect.

4. Sets. The best thing about a camcorder, apart from the ability to edit out the disasters instantly, is its mobility. You can shoot in a variety of locations. The castle scenes require only a painted cardboard wall that can represent both indoors and out. Perhaps, if you haven't pushed your luck too far with the breastplates, swords, daggers, and "sundries," the art teacher might turn his or her talented hand to this, too! Here are some location suggestions for the narrators:

- Hallway
- Cafeteria
- Grassy area (for the blasted heath!)

Your enthusiastic students will be overflowing with ideas for locations with atmosphere. Let them have lots of input so that they feel the responsibility for the performance, as well as ownership. Remember, to have control you must give control. Do you realize how much better Macbeth's life would have been if he had followed that philosophy? Of course, the play would not have been so interesting!

5. Actors. This is the hardest part of all because everyone wants the BIG parts, and it is up to you to choose who does what. Here is an almost painless way:

   - Have the students write down why they want to be a certain character.
   - Have students list several parts they would like to play. This gives you some leeway.
   - If all else fails, flip a coin—remember, auctioning off parts to the highest bidders is not an option!

6. Tips.

   - The narrator's scenes are very informal with lots of kid talk to make it seem real; therefore, it is important that one narrator for each scene has a key phrase that will focus the others on the story line and bring the conversation to the upcoming scene.
   - Slip written dialogue into books, or tape them onto props to aid the memories of nervous actors!
   - Manufacture extra parts by including lots of servants and soldiers. Shakespeare wouldn't mind—the play's the thing!
   - Your movie will take on a very professional look if you have an introduction consisting of a title, visuals, and even mood music!
   - Give the following script outline to actors and let them pad their own scenes with improvisation. The key to successful improvisation is a thorough understanding of the play!
   - Hold lots of practice sessions before to film day—and for the sake of your sanity, don't try to film all the scenes in one day!
   - Show credits at the end of the movie. All the students who played Macbeth are filmed holding a large sign that says "Macbeth"; all the King Duncans hold his name; all Lady Macbeths hold her name, and so on.

Now that you have everything you need, *go make a movie!*

Cast of Characters

*Duncan (king of Scotland)

*Thanes (Lords) of Scotland

*Macbeth (a commander of the Scottish army)

*Banquo (a commander of the Scottish army)

Macduff

Lennox

Ross

Menteith

Angus

Caithness

*Lady Macbeth (wife of Macbeth)

*Three witches

Two soldiers to patrol the walls of Dunsinane Castle

Narrators (the number of narrators can vary from two to as many as the teacher is brave enough to include!)

*These characters are portrayed by different students in each scene. Continuity is maintained through costumes and props, which identify the characters, regardless of the actor. This allows more students to participate, and also eliminates the stress of one student having to learn lots of lines!

Props*

- Duncan: crown, breastplate, sword
- Macbeth: breastplate, sword, dagger
- Banquo: breastplate, sword
- Macduff: breastplate, sword
- Lennox: breastplate, sword
- Ross: breastplate, sword
- Menteith: breastplate, sword
- Angus: breastplate, sword
- Caithness: breastplate, sword
- Lady Macbeth: long, flowing dress; scroll letter
- Three witches: witchy outfits, cauldron
- Narrators: regular clothes
- Scenery: castle wall for background**

*Purchased props may have a more polished look, but to get the students really invested in the performance, encourage them to make their props and costumes whenever possible.
**Much of the action takes place outside, so scout around your building for sites with atmosphere.

Management Notes

The play unfolds through the conversation and interaction of the narrators. The "plot" of this version is that one (two, three, or a small group) student has been to see the play *Macbeth* and is telling the story line to the others. As the story is told by the narrators, the action shifts to the performance of the scene being described, similar to a flashback. The basic formula for the play is a) the narrators discuss a scene; b) actors perform that scene. This a/b rotation continues throughout the play and results in an effective performance that is easy to stage-manage.

The Key Lines are cues for the narrators. When they hear these lines, they know they must focus their discussion on the coming scene and provide a clear "bridge."

As we have stated, the number of narrators is very flexible, and this is the perfect part for your less extroverted students! The narrators portray a group of modern-day kids (this shouldn't tax anyone's acting ability!) in any school setting your students choose.

The play that follows has the narrators in several locations, none of which is set in stone. Please set your narrators in the locations most appealing to your students. Some likely sites would be the front of the school, in a locker hallway, lunchroom, playground, or grassy picnic area. The narrators can change sites as the play progresses, to show the passage of time in the "real" world.

The Quality Quotes appear at relevant points in the text and enable those students who want to recite the "real" lines to do so.

The stage directions are intended to guide the students as they improvise each scene.

Macbeth

Act 1, Scene 1

The narrators are in front of the school. It is first thing in the morning. They greet each other and talk a while.

Narrator 1 (*key line*)**:** Hey guys, did you see that old movie on TV last night? It was pretty weird, but cool. It was called *Mac-something*—yeah, *Macbeth*; it was about . . .

The narrators describe the following: Macbeth and his friend Banquo are going to a meeting with King Duncan. They are crossing a moor when they come across the three witches.

Act 1, Scene 2

Macbeth and Banquo meet the witches and hear their predictions. They meet a messenger from the king, who tells Macbeth he is now Thane of Cawdor.

" Quality Quotes

Banquo (*when he first sees the witches*)**:** What are these,
So wither'd and so wild in their attire,
That look not like the inhabitants of the earth,
And yet are on it?

First witch (*greeting Macbeth*)**:** All hail Macbeth! Hail to thee, Thane of Glamis!

Second witch (*greeting Macbeth*)**:** All hail Macbeth! Hail to thee, Thane of Cawdor!

Third witch (*greeting Macbeth*)**:** All hail Macbeth! That shalt be King hereafter!

Act 2, Scene 1

The narrators are at their lockers, getting ready for class. Talking, etc.

Narrator 2 (*key line*)**:** I saw that movie you were talking about. I thought Macbeth had some nerve to face the king and not say a word about the witches' predictions.

The narrators describe the meeting between King Duncan, Macbeth, and Banquo.

Act 2, Scene 2

Macbeth and Banquo are confused and excited by the news the witches gave them. They meet King Duncan, but they say nothing to him about the strange prediction. King Duncan is pleased to see them and congratulates them on their bravery in battle. Then the king says he would like to come and visit Macbeth and his wife.

" Quality Quotes

Macbeth (*just before he leaves the king*)**:**
Stars, hide your fires!
Let not light see my black and deep desires

Act 3, Scene 3

Still at the lockers. Discussing the meeting between Macbeth and the king.

Narrator (*key line*)**:** Macbeth sure wanted to be king! Do you think he would have done anything without his wife? What about her? What a pushy woman! Didn't she plan the murder?

The narrators describe the interaction between Macbeth and his wife.

Act 3, Scene 3

Lady Macbeth reads a letter from Macbeth, which tells the prophesies. Macbeth arrives home and they discuss the three witches, their predictions, and the coming visit of the king. She tells him that this is their chance to get rid of the king. Macbeth does not want to do it but she talks him into it. They plan to get the king and his guards drunk so that they will not wake up when Macbeth goes in to kill the king. King Duncan arrives.

" Quality Quotes

Lady Macbeth (*after reading Macbeth's letter*)**:**
Glamis thou art, and Cawdor and shalt be
What thou art promis'd. Yet do I fear thy nature
It is too full o' the milk of human kindness
To catch the nearest way.

Act 3, Scene 3

The time has come for Macbeth to commit the murders, and he is chickening out. Lady Macbeth says she will do it; she takes his daggers and leaves. When she comes back, she says that she could not kill the king because he looks like her father. Macbeth takes the knives and leaves. He returns with the bloody daggers.

" Quality Quotes

Lady Macbeth (*encouraging Macbeth to commit the murder*)**:**
We fail?
But screw your courage to the sticking-place,
And we'll not fail.

Macbeth (*after the murder*)**:** Methought I heard a voice cry "Sleep no more!
Macbeth does murder sleep."

Lady Macbeth (*after the murder*)**:**
Give me the daggers. The sleeping and the dead
Are but as pictures; 'tis the eye of childhood
That fears a painted devil. If he do bleed,
I'll gild the faces of the grooms withal;
For it must seem their guilt.

Act 4, Scene 1

Outside a classroom door, the narrators are chatting and waiting for the bell.

Narrator (*key line*): Hey what happened after the murder in that movie? I was watching it but I fell asleep!

The other narrators describe the discovery of the murder, Macbeth's feelings of guilt, and his plan to revisit the witches.

Act 4, Scene 2

Macduff and Lennox arrive and the murder is discovered. The servants get blamed and eventually Macbeth becomes king. He is still not happy, and he decides to go back to see the three witches for another glimpse into the future. The witches give him three more predictions; Macbeth is happy and believes he will not be defeated.

“ Quality Quotes

(*on the heath before Macbeth arrives*)

First witch: Round about the cauldron go;
In the poison'd entrails throw.
Toad, that under cold stone
Days and nights hast thirty-one
Swelter'd venom, sleeping got,
Boil thou first i' the charmed pot.

All witches: Double, double, toil and trouble;
Fire burn and cauldron bubble.

Second witch: Fillet of a fenny snake,
In the cauldron boil and bake;
Eye of newt, and toe of frog,
Wool of bat, and tongue of dog,
Adder's fork, and blind-worm's sting,
Lizard's leg, and howlet's wing,
For a charm of powerful trouble,
Like a hell-broth boil and bubble.

Third witch: Scale of dragon, tooth of wolf,
Witches' mummy, maw and gulf
Of the ravin'd salt-sea shark,
Root of hemlock digg'd i' the dark,
Liver of blaspheming Jew,
Gall of goat, and slips of yew
Sliver'd in the moon's eclipse,
Nose of Turk, and Tartar's lips,
Finger of birth-strangled babe
Ditch-deliverd by a drab,
Make the gruel thick and slab;
Add thereto a tiger's chaudron,
For the ingredients of our cauldron.

Second witch: By the pricking of my thumbs,
Something wicked this way comes.
Open, locks,
Whoever knocks.

(*Macbeth arrives*)

Macbeth (*to the witches*)**:** How now, you secret, black, and midnight hags!
What is it you do?

First apparition: Macbeth! Macbeth! Macbeth! Beware Macduff;
Beware the Thane of Fife. Dismiss me. Enough.

Second apparition: Be bloody, bold and resolute; laugh to scorn
The power of man, for none of woman born
Shall harm Macbeth.

Third apparition: Be lion mettled, proud and take no care
Who chafes, who frets, or where conspirers are:
Macbeth shall never vanquished be until
Great Birnam Wood to high Dunsinane Hill
Shall come against him.

Act 5, Scene 1

Narrators go into the classroom.

Narrator 1 (*key line*)**:** Well, don't keep me in suspense! What happened at the end?

Narrator 2 (*key line*)**:** Don't worry, you'll find out. I did it for my movie review assignment!

Narrator goes to the front of the class and describes the final scene.

Act 5, Scene 2

A servant brings Macbeth the news that the queen is dead. Then he is told the woods are moving, and he knows the end is near. He puts up a fight, and meets his death bravely. Macduff and Malcolm bring closure to the play.

“ Quality Quotes

Servant (*to Macbeth*)**:** The queen, my lord, is dead.

Macbeth: She should have died hereafter;
There would have been a time for such a word.
To-morrow, and to-morrow, and to-morrow,
Creeps in this petty pace from day to day,
To the last syllable of recorded time;
And all our yesterdays have lighted fools
The way to dusty death. Out, out, brief candle!

Messenger (*to Macbeth*)**:** As I did stand my watch upon the hill,
I looked toward Birnam, and anon, methought,
The wood began to move

Macbeth: Liar and slave!

Messenger: Let me endue your wrath if it be not so:
Within this three mile you may see it coming;
I say, a moving grove.

Macbeth (*to Macduff*)**:**
I bear a charmed life which must not yield
To one of woman born.

Macduff: Despair thy charm;
And let the angel whom though hast served
Tell thee, Macduff was from his mother's womb
Untimely ripped.

Macbeth: I will not yield,
To kiss the ground before young Malcolm's feet,
And to be baited with the rabble's curse.
Though Birnam Wood be come to Dunsinane,
And thou oppos'd, being of no woman born,
Yet I will try the last. Before my body
I throw my warlike shield: lay on, Macduff,
And damn'd be him that first cries, "Hold, enough!"

Act 6, Scene 1

The narrator who is presenting the movie review concludes with the following line: "And that was the story of Macbeth!"

This version is missing some very interesting scenes: Banquo the Bloody Ghost scene; the "Is this a dagger I see before me?" scene; and the "Out, dammed spot" sleepwalking scene, which could be inserted very easily using the narrator/actor format. Add more scenes if you wish, or abridge it further, and tailor your production to fit your time frame—and energy level! Whatever you choose to perform, we guarantee your students will amaze you with their enthusiasm, commitment, and ability!

Don't Just Sit There!

Knowledge, the wing wherewith we fly to heaven.
(*Henry VI*, 4.7)

The following activities are intended to bring the play into all curriculum areas and thus enhance students' understanding and interest. The teacher may select several activities to deepen students' understanding of a certain aspect of the play, or only one or two, merely as fun breaks during rehearsals. On a grander scale, the teacher may decide to use *Macbeth* as the core of a thematic study. In brief, the thematic, or project, approach to learning involves an extended study of a topic that crosses all curricula areas. The benefits of this approach lie in the total immersion of the students in the topic, and the learning that occurs from connections students make between their lives and experiences and the topic. For a more detailed look at thematic learning and the aims of this approach, we highly recommend *Engaging Children's Minds: The Project Approach* by Lillian Katz and Sylvia Chard.[1]

We have grouped the activities by curriculum subjects, beginning with language arts, and we strongly encourage teachers to adapt, expand, or condense the activities to meet the needs and interests of their students. We have described the first two activities in detail to provide as complete a picture as possible of the process of classroom application. Following these two activities are lots of "bare bones" that you can discard or fatten up for classroom consumption! Enjoy!

Language Arts

Let the Games Begin!

- Level: second grade and up
- Time: 30 minutes
- Grouping: whole class working in groups of three or four
- Supplies: pencils, lots of two-inch squares of paper (20 times the number of students!), and one sheet of writing paper per child
- Procedure: Ask students to connect any item, person, or place to the character Macbeth (or any major character in the play).
- Objectives: This game will stimulate creative thinking and help reinforce your students' knowledge of the main character in the play.

It is a good idea to divide the class into small groups, with paper and pencils ready, before explaining the task. Explaining the task and then getting supplies and forming groups tend to disrupt the flow, and there will always be someone who will have forgotten what to do by the time he or she is organized to do it!

When the groups are settled with their supplies, explain that they are going to make and play a game. Then explain how to prepare, how to play, and how to win.

- Preparation: Ask each student to brainstorm a list of 20 objects, places, or people and write the names on pieces of paper—two inches square is a good size.

- To play: Ask the students to combine and shuffle all the papers from their individual groups and place them in a pile, facedown, between the players. Explain that player one turns over the first word and lays it faceup on the table; each player writes the word on his or her paper and proceeds to add words that will link the chosen word to *Macbeth.* Speed is not a requirement, as players are allowed to work on linking until you call time. (One minute should be an adequate amount of time, but adjust the time allowed to the skill level of your class.)
- To win: Be the player to connect the selected word to *Macbeth* in the shortest number of links. For example, if the selected word was *pizza,* a connection might look like this: Pizza, Italy, Europe, Scotland, *Macbeth*—three links.

Check your students' understanding of the procedures by asking, "How do we prepare the game?"; "How do we play?"; "How do we win?" Sum up the procedures one more time; then tell your students to get busy. Monitor the time, and when you think the students should have their 20 two-inch squares completed, announce this and encourage everyone to begin the game. When time is running out, give a five-minute warning, then a two-minute warning, rather than abruptly announcing that time is up. This practice makes closure and transitioning so much easier.

Allow time for discussion after the game to hear about the clever and creative connections the students made. There's always time for a pat on the back!

The previous activity is one of the most complicated, taking time to prepare, explain, and play. The following is the type of activity that can be squeezed into any spare minute or, alternatively, elaborated and extended for a more structured presentation.

Lovely Long Lists!

- Level: kindergarten and up
- Time: 5–15 minutes (minimum)
- Grouping: whole class or small groups
- Supplies: whole class approach (short version) needs no supplies; small group approach needs pencils and one sheet of paper per group for writing on

Procedure (*short version*): Ask the students, as a whole class, to help make creative, witty, and humorous lists. The teacher selects a list topic, for example, *qualities a good leader should have,* and asks students to complete the list by calling out ideas. The teacher should record their suggestions on the board, or on butcher paper for a more permanent record. It makes the activity more exciting when the teacher uses a timer and emphasizes that the class only has two (or three, four, five) minutes to complete one (or two, three, four, five) lists.

Procedure (*long version*): The students should work in cooperative groups for this version of the activity. Always divide the class into small groups with paper and pencils ready before explaining the task. Explaining the task and *then* getting supplies and forming groups leads to unnecessary confusion.

When the groups are settled with the supplies they need, explain that a list topic has been selected, for example: *Things Macduff could have done rather than kill Macbeth.* Each group has five minutes to make a list for that topic. The group with the longest list is the winner, but special recognition should be awarded the group that comes up with the most thoughtful response, most witty, most unexpected, etc. Start the timer and watch them go! Spur the enthusiasm by circulating around the room and making such comments as, "Oh, my goodness, this group has 20 items on its list!" Give a two-minute warning when time is running out to spur on extra ideas.

When time is up have each group share its list and encourage the class to appreciate everyone's efforts.

Further extension: When the groups have completed the activity as described above, give the groups two more minutes to select their two favorite items. Use these items to form the "Champion List of All Time." The teacher should record this list on the board, or on butcher paper for a more permanent record.

Objectives: This game will stimulate creative thinking and help reinforce the students' knowledge of the play.

List Topics:

- Questions Macbeth should have asked the witches
- Things you would not want to know if you could see into the future
- Things Macduff could have done rather than kill Macbeth
- Reasons Macbeth should have divorced his wife
- Things you would like to know if you could see into the future
- Qualities a good leader should have

Cross My Palm with Silver

Macbeth's problems arose because of his belief in the witches' power to foretell the future. Fortune-telling is done in many ways, for example, through a crystal ball or with playing cards. What other things do people use to foretell the future? What is your opinion of fortune-telling?

Just Tell Me the Lotto Numbers!

If someone offered to tell you what your future holds, would you want to know? Organize a debate about the pros and cons of knowing what life has in store for you.

A Picture Is Worth a Thousand Words

Select your favorite scene and describe what happened in "Kidspeak" (ordinary language). Imagine that you are explaining the scene to a younger child, and be sure to keep it simple. Practice the retelling of the story until you feel confident enough to do a presentation for another class.

A Thousand Words Is Worth a Picture

Select your favorite lines from the play and illustrate them.

And They All Lived Happily Ever After!

Rewrite the ending of the play so that Macbeth and his wife do not die, and everyone lives happily ever after.

Mix and Match

If you could remove one character from the play, other than the title character, to change the outcome of the story, who would that be? Explain your selection.

or

If you could add one more character to the play to change the outcome of the story, who would that be? Explain your selection.

MacModern!

Rewrite the play *Macbeth,* changing the time from medieval to modern. Dunsinane would no longer be a castle—it might be a hotel and Mr. Macbeth, the tycoon, might live in the penthouse suite!

Rap It Up

Tell the story of *Macbeth* in the form of a poem. Set it to a beat and you have a rap!

Smaller Rap!

If the thought of rapping the whole play seems overwhelming, do only one scene. Perhaps you could get some friends together and do a scene each—*then* you will Rap It Up!

Board to Tears?

Design a board game based on the story of *Macbeth.* The characters could be racing to the throne of Scotland—first one there is crowned and wins the game!

A Scene to Be Seen

Create cooperative groups to give impromptu performances of scenes from the play. To get the groups started, write the scenes on strips of paper; the one picked is the one performed.

Split Personality

If you were an actor, which character would you like to portray in the play? Explain your choice.

If you actually had to live your life as one of the people in the story, who would you choose to be? Explain your choice.

Happy New Year!

Write an appropriate New Year's resolution for each of these characters:

- Macbeth
- Lady Macbeth
- Banquo
- Witch
- King Duncan
- Macduff

Spiderman?

Draw an idea web. Write a character's name in the center and surround the name with adjectives that describe that person.

Lists and More Lists

Compete with a friend to make the longest lists with these titles:

- Things you would find in a castle
- Weapons
- Kings
- World leaders
- Countries that have "land" in their names
- Countries in Europe
- Scottish things
- Qualities a good leader should have

Letter Perfect

Choose a character in the play to write a letter to. Who would it be and why? Would you give the character advice, a warning, or a good "telling off" for his or her behavior? Write the letter and share it with a friend. Did your friend agree with your choice? Would he or she have said the things you said?

Acrostics

Supply an adjective for each letter of the following names:

M	M	D
a	a	u
c	c	n
b	d	c
e	u	a
t	f	n
h	f	

Going Far?

Macbeth was a very ambitious person, which is not necessarily a bad thing—except when ambition drives a person to extreme measures. (Killing the competition could be considered extreme!) What are your ambitions in life? Write a plan showing how you plan to reach your goals.

As Easy as Pie!

Choose one of the main characters and an adjective that describes that character. Then use the adjective to create as many similes as you can. For example: *The witch was as old as dirt; The witch was as old as last year's news; The witch was as old as the carrots in your refrigerator!*

Compete with a friend to come up with the longest list.

Seen but Not Heard

Imagine that you are a servant in Macbeth's castle. You see a lot of the goings-on, but you say nothing. Create a diary that a servant might have written from the day Macbeth came home until the day of his death.

So the Saying Goes

The following are popular colloquial expressions. Investigate their meanings and find a scene in the play that fits each phrase. For example: *To keep up appearances means to put on a show*. Lady Macbeth was keeping up appearances at the banquet where Banquo's ghost appeared.

- To throw dust in the eyes
- To get in hot water
- To chew the fat
- To play with fire
- To skate on thin ice
- To smell a rat
- To let the cat out of the bag
- To mind your Ps and Qs

Oscar Time

Watch a movie version of Macbeth, then draw a Venn diagram and compare and contrast the movie version and the "real" version of the play.

A Man of Many Words

Scholars believe that Shakespeare's vocabulary was a least double that of ordinary people. Often, and to achieve just the right effect, the playwright would make up a word to fit his needs! He accomplished this by combining two words with a hyphen, making what we now call a compound word. That explains why he was never at a loss for words! Search through the text and list all the hyphenated words you find. These are Shakespeare originals—designer words! Can you invent some new words? Try!

Inquiring Minds Want to Knoweth

How do you think Lady Macbeth died? You are the ace crime reporter for the local newspaper. Write an account of Lady Macbeth's final hours based on an exclusive interview you had with one of her ladies-in-waiting.

Can We Talk?

With a few friends, put together a talk-show skit. One person is the host; the panel of guests comprises three or four characters from *Macbeth*, for example, Lady Macbeth, King Duncan, Macbeth, and a witch. The host should compose some probing questions and encourage lively conversations among the guests. Present your talk show to an audience and encourage participation through questions and comments.

Don't Get Cross

Design a crossword puzzle to challenge your friends' knowledge of the play. Include characters' names, places, feelings, and key words from the text.

Triple, Triple Toil and . . .

Macbeth's problems began when he chose to believe the predictions of the three witches. The seeds they planted led to his taking fate into his own hands instead of allowing it to take its course. What would have happened to Macbeth if he had ignored the prophesies of the three witches? Create a story in which Macbeth ignores the witches and tell what you think the outcome would be.

You Can't Judge a Book by Its Cover—or Can You?

King Duncan states that it is easy to tell what a person is really like from his looks: "There's no art to find the mind's construction in the face." Do you agree? Organize a debate with class members regarding King Duncan's words.

Macbeth@scot.com

Suppose the witches and Macbeth had carried on their conversations via E-mail. How might their messages have looked?

A Little of This and a Little of That

The weird sisters had some interesting stuff in their cauldron. You can be just as disgusting—and even more creative. With a couple of friends, brainstorm a list of modern-day yuckies and then act out the "Double, double" scene, substituting your gross items for theirs in their speeches.

Social Studies

Sad, but True

The murder of a political figure is called an *assassination*. The murder of King Duncan was an assassination. Many world leaders have been assassinated. Research three assassinations and write a paragraph about each, explaining what took place, the motives behind it, and the outcome.

Settle It Peacefully

Why were the Scots fighting the English? Research the problem and set up a debate in front of an impartial arbitrator who will make a ruling in the dispute.

Medieval Museum

With a group of friends, collect items for a museum display in a corner of the classroom. Be creative—even if it is a little dishonest! You could have the dagger Macbeth saw before him, Shakespeare's very own quill pen, and Anne Hathaway's favorite cooking pot.

Fun and Games

Life was simple way back when, and so was entertainment: no video games and the like, and reality was real, not virtual! People had to create their entertainment from everyday things. Can you devise a game that can be played outside by four or more players using a shield and a ball? Describe the method of play and list the rules. Give your game a name and arrange a competition between two teams, or more, for the World Championship Title!

The Dark Ages—Ages Ago

The Dark Ages, also known as the Middle Ages, spanned the period from around 476 A.D. to 1000 A.D. *Macbeth* takes place during this period. What was life like then? How does it compare to modern times? When you have researched some basics such as houses, entertainment, food, transportation, and dress, make a picture book for younger children contrasting the way things were then and the way they are now. Draw the medieval on one page and the modern on the page opposite.

It Tickled Your Fancy!

Has the play *Macbeth* sparked your interest in Scotland? Would you like to know more about this ancient country and its inhabitants? With a little detective work, you should be able to track down a Scot to interview. If the "friend of a friend of a friend" approach does not work, look in the phone book for a local chapter of the St. Andrew's Society, a society for people of Scottish descent, and see if they can help you. Prepare your interview questions before meeting with someone, or speaking with someone on the phone, so that you will be time efficient.

Seek 'Em

Research these famous Scots: Mary, Queen of Scots; Bonnie Prince Charlie; Robert the Bruce; Robert Burns; Cindie Lauper.

Don't Judge a Book by Its Cover

The three witches in *Macbeth* are among the most famous characters in the play. They are always referred to as "witches," and yet in the play that name appears only once. This is a case of stereotyping. What can you discover about the history of the persecution of old women for witchcraft? What methods were used to prove innocence or guilt? Did they get a fair trial? What is your opinion of this issue?

Everything in Its Place

Draw a map of Scotland; then put the following places on it: Glamis, Cawdor, Ross, Lennox, Menteith, Angus, Caithness, Fife, Dunsinane, Great Birnam Wood, Edinburgh, and Loch Ness.

MacMovie

The Academy Award–winning movie *Braveheart* gives a gripping depiction of life and death in medieval Scotland. With your parents' permission, watch the movie and then write a review giving your opinions.

Bonnie Scotland

Scotland is often overshadowed by its southern neighbor, England. Do your part to boost Scotland's tourist trade by designing a brochure that will show some of the wonderful things that can be seen, and done, there.

The Coronation of Macbeth

Macbeth's coronation is not described in the play. Do some coronation research to discover all you can about the coronation ceremony; then write an account of the coronation of Macbeth as it would probably have taken place. Your writing could take the form of a newspaper article or even an additional scene for the play.

Art

If Music Be the Food of Love . . .

The skirl of bagpipes is a stirring sound, and the grace and energy of Scottish dancers is amazing. See if you can find some Scottish music and/or a video of Scottish dancers and enjoy a little of the culture of Scotland. Bagpipes have a fascinating history. They were not solely intended for entertainment. What information can you find out about these very interesting instruments? Prepare a presentation on your research results.

Mood Music

With a group of friends, decide which scene you will ad lib and then create sound effects and/or music to accompany the scene.

It Pays to Advertise

Get a large sheet of paper and design an eye-catching poster for the play. Ask the principal if you, and other students, could display the posters throughout the school for a week or so.

Let's Give Them a Hand

Create a puppet of your favorite character and then get together with friends to put on a MacPuppet show!

Marvel-ous!

Draw your favorite scene in the form of a comic strip. Work with friends to create a MacComic book version of the play.

The Mask

Create a Renaissance half-mask. Decorate it with ribbon, fabric, sequins, glitter—and just about anything else you can get your hands on!

Knit-Wit!

The Scottish highlands are famous for their heavy woolen sweaters. Research what Arran- and Shetland-patterned sweaters look like. These designs may be too difficult for you right now, but see if you can knit a 12-inch square. Once you have accomplished this, you might be ready for an Arran!

Show Your True Colors

Tartan is a plaid textile design of Scottish origin. Each clan has a unique tartan of its own. The traditional Scottish kilts are made from a tartan fabric that represents the clans' colors. In a battle, clan tartans were just like uniforms indicating whose side one was on. There is a tartan for every clan. Can you find the tartan for the clan Macbeth? Become an honorary Scot for a day by adding "Mac" to your last name and design your own clan tartan.

Crafty Craftsmen

The recently completed Globe Theatre in London is as exact a replica of the old Globe as was possible. No nails were used in the building of the theater and all the beams were fitted together through a variety of special joints. Construct a building, without using tape or any other "joining material." Pieces should be wedged and/or supported by other parts of the building. It isn't easy, but it is possible!

Shield

A shield is a piece of armor that was carried on the arm to protect a warrior in battle. Some were plain and strictly functional; others were ornate and, through colors, pictures, and symbols, told about the owner. Research the meaning of shield decorations. Then design a shield that signifies you and the things you value.

Math

Venn? Now!

Use a Venn diagram to show similarities and differences between the following:

- Macbeth and King Duncan
- Macbeth and Lady Macbeth
- Life in medieval times and life in modern times

A Rose by Any Other Name

Write 10 different titles for the play. Then survey your classmates to find out which one they prefer.

Glad You Asked!

- Design a survey to discover which character in the play people enjoy the most.
- Design a survey to discover which character in the play people think is the meanest.
- Design a survey to discover which character in the play people think would make the best friend.
- Design a survey to discover which character in the play people think could have been left out.

Graph the results of each survey.

Venn? Anytime!

Create a Venn diagram that compares Macbeth with any world leader. Find as many ways as you can in which they are alike and ways in which they are different.

Science

Double, Double—Don't Get in Trouble!

You may not have access to fenny snakes, newt's eyes, or blind-worm's sting (thank goodness!), but with a little creativity you can cook up a powerful potion! Create a potion, either as a written recipe or an actual yucky liquid. Make a list of the amazing effects this potion has—*but* make sure that *no one drinks it.* This is an exercise in creativity, not homicide!

Who Would Have Thought the Old Man Had So Much Blood in Him?

How many facts can you find out about blood? Challenge a friend to a fact-finding frenzy! Who can make the longest fact list?

Betty McCrocker

Create a witch's recipe book. Include breakfast, lunch, and dinner recipes, and a special section for potions of all kinds. Be sure to be as disgusting as possible.

Creative Thinking

Swords into Ploughshares?

List at least 10 uses for a sword, other than fighting, killing, and maiming!

Separated at Birth

In what ways is . . .

- Macbeth like your teacher?
- Lady Macbeth like your mom?
- King Duncan like you?
- A witch like a newsreader you watch on television?
- Shakespeare like Stephen King?

Hot Stuff

Notes

1. Lillian Katz and Sylvia Chard, *Engaging Children's Minds: The Project Approach* (Norwood, NJ: Ablex, 1989).

Annotated Bibliography and Resources

Following is a list of great books that have been referenced and/or recommended, as well as other resources that provide inspiration, information—and fuel for the fire!

One final suggestion: Having maps—ancient and modern—of Scotland and its neighbors will give this play a new dimension. Comparing old and new maps reveals changes in a country's borders and provides stimulus for further social studies investigations.

Burdett, Lois. *Macbeth for Kids*. Ontario, Canada: Black Moss Press, 1996.

This is an outstanding rhyming version of the story. Young children will enjoy hearing it read aloud, and older students may even memorize it!

Chorzempa, Rosemary. *Design Your Own Coat of Arms*. New York: Dover Publications, 1987.

Children and adults find it very exciting to design their own coats of arms, and this is the book to provide lots of clear help. Components within the coats of arms are explained, with clear illustrations and instructions regarding what should and should not be included in your design.

Garfield, Leon. *Shakespeare Stories*. Boston: Houghton Mifflin, 1985.

There are 12 stories in this volume, including *Macbeth*, *Hamlet*, *A Midsummer Night's Dream*, and *Romeo and Juliet*. They are well written and are a great way to get a handle on the story lines before tackling the plays.

———. *Shakespeare Stories II*. Boston: Houghton Mifflin, 1994.

Among the nine stories in this volume are *Julius Caesar*, *Much Ado About Nothing*, and *The Winter's Tale*. As with the first book, the stories are well written and a great introduction to the plays.

Karbiener, Karen. Study guide book essay to *Macbeth* by Shakespeare, ed. Karen Karbiener. Classics Illustrated edition. New York: Acclaim Books, 1997.

McCaughrean, Geraldine. *Stories from Shakespeare*. New York: Margaret K. McElderry Books, 1995.

When trying to figure out who's who and what's what in Shakespeare's plays, good retellings are very useful. This book should be on your "Must Read" list.

Shakespeare. *Macbeth*. Cambridge School Shakespeare Series, ed. Rex Gibson. Cambridge, England: Cambridge University Press, 1993.
This is the full text and is a useful reference for the teacher, as well as for those students who get so fired up they want more, more, more! The pages on the right contain text and the facing pages are full of ideas and suggestions for enhancing students' understanding of what is happening at that particular point in the play.

Shakespeare. *Macbeth*. Retold by Bruce Coville. New York: Dial Books, 1997.
Wonderful illustrations. Your students, and you, will fall for this one! A succinct retelling.

Shakespeare. *Macbeth*. Shakespeare for Everyone Series, ed. Jennifer Mulherin. Morristown, NJ: Silver Burdett Press, 1988.
A must for those enthusiastic students!

Shakespeare. *Macbeth*. Shakespeare Library, ed. Wendy Greenhill. Oxford, England: Heinemann, 1996.
This is another great book for the "Big Mac" lover! It is user-friendly for children and adults.

Shakespeare. *Macbeth for Young People*. Shakespeare for Young People Series, ed. Diane Davidson, bk. 4. Fair Oaks, CA: Swan Books, 1986.
This series is an excellent resource for teachers and is user-friendly for students.

Shakespeare. *Shakespeare, the Animated Tales: Macbeth*. Produced and directed by Dave Edwards. 30 min. Random House. Videocassette.
The video gives an abridged version of the play but keeps the main story lines intact. Quotes and "Kidspeak" are interspersed for ease of understanding. The animation is very well done.

A Midsummer
Night's Dream

What You Should Know About *A Midsummer Night's Dream*

Who's Who

When presenting Shakespeare to young children, we believe it is necessary to simplify the plays by removing nonessential (in our opinion!) characters whose presence would contribute little to the students' understanding of the fundamental story line—but would contribute much to their confusion! If your particular favorite minor character has been axed, please keep in mind that it was for a good cause.

> *"Let us from point to point this story know, To make the even truth in pleasure flow"*
> *(All's Well That Ends Well, 5.3).*

The Major Characters

Hermia (HER-me-uh)

> O me! you juggler! you canker-blossom!
> You thief of love!
> **(3.2)**

A petite brunette, Hermia makes up for her lack of physical size with an oversized assertive attitude. Like all "normal" teenagers, Hermia is going through a rebellious stage. She wants things "her way" and won't put up with anyone getting in "her way," not her best friend, not her father, and not even the duke. In essence, Hermia is a pint-sized, quick-tempered teen who will get what she wants at any cost. And what she wants is to choose her own husband. Is that so bad?

Lysander (lie-SAND-er)

The course of true love never did run smooth.
(1.1)

The object of rebellious Hermia's desire. He is the dashing "Romeo" who brushes aside the law, Hermia's father's wishes, and good taste to follow his heart. In the name of love, Lysander intends to elope, thus avoiding the entire problem of Hermia's previously arranged marriage to Demetrius, but in doing so he creates a much larger problem that ends up seeming more like a midsummer nightmare than a dream.

Demetrius (de-MEE-tree-us)

I love thee not; therefore pursue me not.
Where is Lysander and fair Hermia?
The one I'll slay, the other slayeth me.
(2.1)

He's got Hermia's dad and the duke on his side. Demetrius is the creep that Hermia is supposed to marry. He is a lot like Hermia, and perhaps they deserve each other. Like her, Demetrius wants his own way no matter what. What he wants is Hermia, even though she definitely does not want him. But as the saying goes, there is someone for everyone. That someone for Demetrius is Helena, or at least she would like to be. Demetrius had the hots for Helena earlier, but he is not the slightest bit interested in her now.

Helena (HEL-e-nuh)

The more I love, the more he hateth me.
(1.1)

The overly sensitive, super-model of the story, Helena is a timid blond who has trouble letting go. Having been previously seduced by Demetrius, Helena is passionately in love with him, but as they would say in Nashville, she is traveling down a one-way street to heartache. Demetrius is no longer interested in her. Even in the face of his cold shoulder, deaf ear, and degrading insults, Helena proclaims her undying love for him. Pride, self respect, and playing hard-to-get are beyond her comprehension. There seems to be nothing this girl won't do to get her man, including divulging her best friend Hermia's secret. All's fair in love and war.

Oberon (OH-ber-on)

> What thou seest when thou dost wake,
> Do it for thy true-love take . . .
> Wake when some vile thing is near.
> **(2.2)**

When night falls on the wood, the fairy kingdom reigns. The domineering king of the fairies, Oberon, wields great power. He has the ability to become invisible, and he uses this ability to spy on the four lovers. He also demonstrates his superior magical talents by acquiring the enchanted "love potion" that he uses to make an ass of his queen and confuse the four lovers. Oberon demonstrates his dominance over the "mortals" by manipulating them like puppets in a play.

Titania (ti-TAH-nee-uh)

> What jealous Oberon? Fairy, skip hence.
> I have forsworn his bed and company.
> **(2.1)**

Titania, the elegant queen of the fairies and Oberon's wife, is accompanied by a throng of singing and dancing attendants. She seems to be nobler than her husband, and she displays many fine qualities that Oberon appears not to possess. She demonstrates her loyalty by caring for a small boy after his mother had died. Rather than lose the child to Oberon to be his servant, Titania puts up a spirited fight to keep him. However, her resistance leads to the nasty trick that results in her falling in love with a donkey (ass) and losing the child to Oberon anyway.

Puck

> Lord, what fools these mortals be!
> **(3.2)**

Puck, a.k.a. Robin Goodfellow, is the fairy fool and trickster in the story. He is Oberon's right-hand hobgoblin. He is a sneaky sprite who lurks around the wood looking for mischief. It is Puck who mistakes Demetrius for Lysander and eventually causes both of them to fall in love with Helena. It is Puck who turns an actor into an ass and leads him to Titania's flowery bed. It is Puck who causes confusion and much amusement in the wood. However, it is also Puck who makes everything right again only after a direct order from his boss, Oberon, of course.

Bottom

> I see their knavery.
> This is to make an ass of me,
> to fright me if they could.
>
> **(3.1)**

Named for his occupation as a weaver (a "bottom" is a reel on which thread is wound) rather than his backside, Nick Bottom is also an amateur actor. In his opinion, he is talented enough to play all the parts and carry the entire play alone. Unfortunately, his opinion is not shared by the other characters, especially Puck, who happens upon him practicing in the wood. Bottom is arrogant and loudmouthed even before Puck turns his head into an ass's. Bottom never realizes that he has been transformed, which points to his ignorance and provides most of the humor in the play.

The Minor Characters

Theseus (THEE-see-us)

> Either to die the death, or to abjure
> Forever the society of men.
> Therefore fair Hermia question your desires.
>
> **(1.1)**

Theseus, Duke of Athens, is a heroic leader whose job it is to enforce to laws. He is a powerful warrior who has just returned from battle with the Amazons, whose queen, Hippolyta, is to become his wife. As a judge, he makes decisions swiftly and some might say fairly (offering Hermia a nunnery over death). It is possible that, not wanting an execution on his wedding day, Theseus was looking for a loophole in the law in order to spare Hermia's life. What a nice guy!

Egeus (e-JEE-us)

> Full of vexation come I, with complaint
> Against my child, my daughter Hermia.
>
> **(1.1)**

Parenting skills were lacking in Athens: Hermia's father, Egeus, dragged her before the duke to force her to obey him. Egeus did have the law on his side, and the law superseded all reasoning. Where were his loving feelings toward his daughter? Where was his concern for her happiness? Apparently nowhere! He gave no reason for his choice of Demetrius over Lysander in his daughter's arranged marriage. Thanks, Dad!

The Actors

> O monstrous! O strange! We are haunted. Pray,
> masters! Fly, masters!
> Help!
>
> **(3.1)**

Also called "the mechanicals," or workers, Quince, Flute, Snug, Snout, Starveling, and Bottom are each named for his occupation. They are attempting to practice a play for the wedding of Theseus and Hippolyta. Their acting abilities are virtually nonexistent, but what they lack in talent they make up for in enthusiasm. They provide much amusement for their audience. These "actors" are the clowns of the story (even though they are performing a tragedy).

What's What

Background Information

A Midsummer Night's Dream has been called Shakespeare's "first mature play." Written between 1594 and 1596, it is believed to have been initially intended as entertainment for a wedding rather than a work for the theater. That must have been some wedding! The play was written at about the same time *Romeo and Juliet* was being performed. In a way these two plays are two sides of the same coin with *A Midsummer Night's Dream* being the comic counterpart. Both share the themes of forbidden love, angry parents, and rebellion. Curiously enough, the play that Bottom and his friends are practicing in the wood, called *Pyramus and Thisbe*, shares almost the same plot as *Romeo and Juliet*. It is thought that this play within a play intentionally pokes fun at the ludicrous lengths to which Romeo and Juliet go to "be together," although both plays are technically tragedies.

At times it seems that Shakespeare was more interested in telling a good story rather than telling an accurate story. In *A Midsummer Night's Dream*, the story does not even take place in midsummer. In fact, the people of Athens are celebrating May Day with the wedding of Theseus and Hippolyta. At the end of the play, upon seeing the sleeping lovers in the wood, Theseus states, "No doubt they rose up early to observe the rite of May" (4.1). Some think that the title may actually refer to the time of year the play was first performed rather than to any reference to the story. To add to the confusion, Hippolyta tells Theseus as the play opens, "Four days will quickly steep themselves in night, four nights will quickly dream away the time" (1.1). She is referring to the amount of time left until their wedding; however, she may not have realized just how true her statement really was. You see, between the time this statement was made and the time the wedding actually took place, only one night had passed. Did Shakespeare lose his calendar or was time really "dreamt" away? Should this play really have been called *A May Day Four Night's Dream*?

Whatever else this play might have been called, it was a clear reflection of both the beliefs and the audiences of the time. Being set in mythical Athens, Greece, there must have been a strong temptation to write about Mount Olympus, gods, and goddesses. Instead, he played on the real superstitions of English society at the time—hence the fairies. Like the leprechauns of Ireland, fairies were blamed when things were lost or when something went wrong in people's lives.

Since his audiences ranged from the common folk of the open-air Globe Theatre to the nobility of the enclosed Blackfriars Theatre, Shakespeare included all elements of society in his play. The amateur actors who rehearsed in the wood in *A Midsummer Night's Dream* reflected the custom of the time. Tradesman-actors would put on grand productions and compete at festivals. Even the costumes used were sixteenth-century English rather than traditional Greek togas. Shakespeare knew his audience, and because his audiences were also his customers, he gave his customers what they wanted. He would have been highly successful as a movie producer in Hollywood, don't you think?

A Midsummer Night's Dream is set apart from Shakespeare's other plays by his character development, or the lack thereof. In almost all of the Bard's plays, the characters come to life in vivid and memorable ways; however, only the fantasy characters appear real (your students will not soon forget them), whereas the real characters lack substance. If we had a dollar for every time we confused the names of the four lovers, we would be sunning ourselves on an exotic beach instead of writing this book. The four lovers are almost interchangeable. It is obvious that the names Helena and Hermia were chosen to cause confusion, and the Helena loves Demetrius loves Hermia loves Lysander "love chain" that winds its way through the play just adds to the confusion and comedy.

It is not certain that Shakespeare intended a play on words when he chose to have Bottom's head turned into an ass's instead of a mule's or a donkey's. In England, that particular posterior part of the anatomy is spelled *arse* (pronounced ar-ss), and consequently does not lend itself to the pun. However, no matter what the Bard intended, for American students, *ass* is too obvious a joke to overlook—so be prepared! Depending on the age of your students and the complexity of their wit, it is perfectly acceptable to avoid this joke altogether by substituting *donkey* for *ass*.

After you have tried to untangle the story line and keep the characters straight, you will be comforted by thinking of this entire play as a dream; indeed, you may feel as though you need to lie down before it is over. This may explain why the play ends with this from Puck:

> If we shadows have offended,
> Think but this, and all is mended—
> That you have but slumb'red here
> While these visions did appear.
> And this weak and idle theme,
> No more yielding but a dream,
> Gentles, do not reprehend.
> If you pardon, we will mend.
> And, as I am an honest Puck,

If we have unearned luck
Now to scape the serpent's tongue,
We will make amends ere long;
Else the Puck a liar call.
So, good night unto you all.
Give me your hands, if we be friends,
And Robin shall restore amends.

(5.1)

What's Happening

The Story

As described in the introductory section, introducing Shakespeare to children follows the hook, line, and sinker approach to teaching!

Activities and games for presenting the hook (a tantalizing mention of a great story waiting to be told), and the line (the introduction of the characters), can be found in the introduction and should be presented to the students before continuing the story.

After studying many different ways of retelling this play, and after introducing the story to many different students, we would like to share with you our version of *A Midsummer Night's Dream*. Through experience, we have found it much more effective to "tell" the story rather than to "read" the story. We have separated the story into sections that represent natural pauses; one section per sitting is "just right." Included within each section are discussion and debate ideas (Let's Talk).

We have sprinkled popular lines from the actual play throughout the story. These verses correspond with the reproducible verses in the section of this book called Will's Words. You may wish to offer the verses for memorizing and reciting to your class as you tell the story. Even better, you may want to have your students perform short scenes from the story as you tell it. We find that, by placing Shakespeare's words and actions into the mouths and bodies of the children, they understand and appreciate the play more completely.

Let's Talk

We have found great success in increasing our students' connection to the play by providing frequent opportunities to discuss, debate, and just plain talk about it. Let's Talk can be done in a variety of ways:

1. Student-led discussion. Intriguing questions can be posed to the whole class; however, instead of you (the teacher) selecting the speaker, let the student who is speaking choose the next speaker.

2. Let's not talk. After asking a question of the whole class, give individual students "sticky notes" to write their responses on. After writing, students will place their responses on the chalkboard. As a whole class, group the "sticky notes" in categories and summarize the results.

3. Small group discussion. Following your question, place students in groups of two to four. Within their groups, select a leader and a recorder. The leader will choose who speaks, and the recorder will write down what is said. At the end of the discussion, the recorder will report what was said to the rest of the class.

4. Debate. You will need a podium (music stand) and a controversial dilemma. After posing the dilemma to your students, allow them to choose sides and move to either side of the podium. Once in place, students will take turns explaining why their point of view is "right." After each side has had a turn to state its position, students may choose to change sides. This will continue until a strong majority prevails or you run out of time. Wait until the end of the debate to share your opinion, or you run the risk of polluting the process as your students might choose to agree with you rather than think for themselves.

Look for the Let's Talk symbols for discussion and debate topics. They are located at relevant points in the story and may be used in two ways:

1. in natural breaks during your telling of the story;

2. after the entire story has been told, as a way of reviewing and solidifying the story in your students' minds.

The Sinker

The enthusiastic telling of the story.

Our Version

For information on some of the many excellent read-aloud versions of *A Midsummer Night's Dream,* see the Annotated Bibliography; it is worth shopping around to find the version that suits your style. The following is the version that suits *our* style—our version!

Read it (or, preferably, loosely recite from memory) with gusto and enthusiasm—without inhibition!

Kidspeak and Shakespeak

The following story of *A Midsummer Night's Dream* is written in simple English, Kidspeak, and at certain points in the story actual text from the play is included, Shakespeak! Don't be afraid to introduce young students to Shakespeak. The strangeness of the language is often appealing to children; when they are familiar with the story, they can relate more easily to the difficult language.

The following is only one way to retell the story of *A Midsummer Night's Dream*. You should infuse it with your personality and enthusiasm: "Here we go! Get ready to study Shakespeare!! Even though you are such itty-bitty kindies (first, second, and third graders)! Get your brains in gear 'cause here it comes! This is a really cool story all about . . ."

A Midsummer Night's Dream

Section I

Have you ever had a friend that your parents didn't approve of? What did they do about it? Pause here for discussion. What did you do about it? Pause here for discussion.

Kids have been faced with problems like this forever. A long time ago in a place called Athens, Greece, there was a girl named Hermia who was confronted with this very same problem. Unlike today, when probably the worst thing that could happen to you for not obeying your parents is that you would get grounded, back in Athens you could lose your head. You see, there was a law in Athens that stated a father had the right to choose his daughter's husband. It was called an *arranged marriage*. If the daughter did not obey her father's wishes, she could be put to death. Now, how many girls do you think chose to disobey their fathers in Athens?

Debate the role of punishment in discipline.

Hermia loved Lysander, but her father, Egeus, did not. Hermia wanted to marry Lysander, but her father had other plans for her. Hermia's father had chosen a man named Demetrius to marry his daughter whether she liked it or not! You can imagine the fights they must have had over who would marry whom. Their house was not a very pleasant place to be, I'm sure. Having reached the end of his rope, Egeus dragged his daughter and the two men they were fighting about to the grand palace of Duke Theseus to settle this problem once and for all.

Discuss various types of governments and their advantages and disadvantages. If we were to choose one form of government for the entire world, debate which form would be the best.

Duke Theseus had just returned as the hero from a battle with the Amazons, and he had taken the queen of the Amazons, Hippolyta, to be his new wife. They were getting married in four days. Theseus was definitely in a good mood. With his bride-to-be seated next to him and marriage on his mind, I can't imagine that he was thrilled to see Egeus with his daughter in tow proclaiming, "**Full of vexation come I, with complaint against my child, my daughter Hermia.**" Because nobody wants an execution on his or her wedding day, Theseus pleaded with Hermia to do what her father wished. He even reduced the sentence from death to life in a nunnery. In other words, do what your dad says or you can't marry anyone. Hermia stuck to her guns and to her man. She wanted Lysander and no one else. She would rather never get married than to marry dad's dude, Demetrius. Theseus told her to "**Take time to pause; and by the next new moon either prepare to die for disobedience to your father's will, or else to wed Demetrius**." In other words, sleep on it.

As you can imagine, Hermia had no intentions of changing her mind or her man. Fortunately, Lysander, with a love that was equally strong for Hermia, had a plan. When they were alone, he suggested that they run off and get married anyway. Lysander and Hermia planned to meet in the woods outside Athens after sunset. During this time, Lysander made the understatement of the day when he proclaimed, "**The course of true love never did run smooth**." No, it ran off, instead.

Discuss the word "love" and what it means or looks like. Debate the existence of "love at first sight."

In the midst of crafting this rebellious plan, the two lovers were joined by Hermia's best friend, Helena. She was hopelessly and obsessively in love with Demetrius. However, everything she said and did to demonstrate her love was met with insult and rejection from him. Hermia revealed her and Lysander's secret plan to Helena: "**Take comfort. He no more shall see my face; Lysander and myself will fly this place. Farewell, sweet playfellow. Pray thou for us; and good luck grant thee thy Demetrius**." Thinking that ratting on her best friend would gain points with Demetrius, Helena ran off to inform him of the secret plan.

As the sun set on Athens that night, four shadowy figures made their way into the woods with love on their minds. Lysander was pursued by his love, Hermia. Hermia was pursued by her love, Demetrius. Demetrius was pursued by his love, Helena. Indeed, Lysander was right: "**The course of true love never did run smooth**."

While all this was going on, a group of hardworking men in Athens were preparing to perform a play to celebrate the upcoming wedding of Theseus and Hippolyta. These men were not actors by trade; they were tinkers, tailors, and cabinet makers who *thought* they were actors. The most arrogant "actor" in the group was a weaver named Nick Bottom. While the parts were given out, Bottom kept interrupting. He seemed to think that he could play all the parts, including the part of the lion, and he proceeded to show them by stomping around the room and roaring at the top of his lungs. After much "showing off," and annoyance, the "actors" divided up the parts and decided to meet in the woods at sunset to rehearse by moonlight.

Section II

As the lovers and actors made their way into the darkening woods, they were not alone. The caretakers of the night and the residents of the forest were the fairies. All was not well in fairyland, however; the king and queen of the fairies were fighting. You see, the queen of the fairies, named Titania, was taking care of a small boy whose mother had died. Wasn't she nice? The king of the fairies, named Oberon, wanted to take the boy away to be his servant. Wasn't he mean?

Discuss superstitions. Choose a popular superstition that your students hold (crossing fingers, rabbits' feet) and debate its existence.

Titania explained to Oberon that their arguing had caused seasons to change, crops to die, and animals to get sick. She pleaded with him to leave the boy with her, but Oberon explained that she could end the argument and return everything to normal if she would just give him the boy. Well, seeing that this was going nowhere, Titania took the boy and stormed off saying, "**Not for thy fairy kingdom. Fairies, away!**" Oberon, angered even more by Titania's exit, vowed revenge when he said, "**Well, go thy way. Thou shalt not from this grove till I torment thee for this injury**."

Oberon's revenge was creative indeed. In order to carry out his cruel and unusual punishment, he called upon his faithful and mischievous fairy-servant, Robin Goodfellow, otherwise known as Puck. Being one to stir things up anytime he had a chance, Puck jumped at the opportunity to serve his king and trick his queen. Oberon told Puck of a magical flower whose juices caused "love at first sight." The flower was called *love-in-idleness*, but love would not be idle for long.

After sending Puck in search of the magical flower, Oberon revealed his plan. "**Having once this juice, I'll watch Titania when she is asleep and drop the liquor of it in her eyes. The next thing then she, waking, looks upon (be it on lion, bear, or wolf, or bull, on meddling monkey, or on busy ape) she shall pursue it with the soul of love**." Oberon wished to humiliate Titania by making her fall in love with an animal; he also saw this as an opportunity to take the child from her to be his servant, therefore getting what he wanted and having a good laugh at the same time.

Discuss manipulation. Share examples of ways adults manipulate children (candy, stickers, etc.). Debate whether manipulation is right or wrong.

While Oberon was hatching his devious plan, and Puck was searching the earth for the magical love juice, who should happen into the woods but Demetrius. Remember him? He was searching for his bride-to-be, Hermia. Following Demetrius like a little lost puppy was Helena. Remember her? She was obsessed with Demetrius, and she would do anything to make him love her. Unfortunately, Demetrius had no use for Helena, and he took every opportunity to tell her so.

After making himself invisible, Oberon overheard Helena's passionate pleas for love, and Demetrius's outright rejection of her:

Demetrius: I love thee not; therefore pursue me not.

Helena: You draw me . . .

Demetrius: Do I not in plainest truth tell you I do not nor cannot love you?

Helena: And even for that do I love you the more.

Demetrius: For I am sick when I do look on thee.

Helena: And I am sick when I look not on you.

Demetrius: I'll run from thee and hide me in the (thickets) and leave thee to the mercy of wild beasts.

Helena: The wildest hath not such a heart as you.

Demetrius: I will not stay thy questions. Let me go!

Helena: I'll follow thee.

Helena just didn't get it. Demetrius did not love her. He wanted to be as far away from her as possible. Witnessing this unrequited love, Oberon vowed to help Helena and Demetrius fall in love. Was it any of his business? No, but I guess being king of the fairies comes with some special privileges!

Discuss what your students would do to make enemies become friends. Debate whether it is right or not to involve yourself in other people's problems.

After Puck returned with the magical flower, Oberon instructed him to find the sleeping Demetrius and place a drop of the love juice in his eye so that he would look upon and fall madly in love with Helena when he woke up. Oberon instructed Puck that **"A sweet Athenian lady is in love with a disdainful youth. Anoint his eyes; but do it when the next thing he espies may be the lady. Thou shalt know the man by the Athenian garments he hath on."** Little did Puck or Oberon know that Demetrius was not the only Athenian man in the woods that night.

Who else was there, and what problems might that have caused? Pause for predictions.

With Puck out on his quest to find the two lovers, Oberon took his portion of the flower and went to find Titania. She was lying down to sleep on a bed of flowers, attended by her fairy servants. When Oberon finally found Titania, he dropped the love juice in her sleeping eyes while he whispered his sweet revenge into her sleeping ears: **"What thou seest when thou dost wake, do it for thy true-love take; love and languish for his sake. Be it (lynx) or cat or bear, (leopard), or boar with bristled hair in thy eye that shall appear when thou wak'st, it is thy dear. Wake when some vile thing is near.**" Oberon could not wait for her to wake up—can you?

Discuss reasons for taking revenge on someone. Debate whether revenge is right or not.

Meanwhile, the other Athenian man, Lysander, followed by his true love, Hermia, were lost in the woods and decided to lay down and rest for the night. As the two lovers fell into a deep sleep, Puck came wandering by. When he saw the man in Athenian clothes, he knew his search was over. Little did Puck know that he was about to put the love juice in the wrong man's eyes! Had he have known, I'm sure he would have done it anyway!

With the love juice in Lysander's eyes just waiting for the "first sight," Helena came by searching for Demetrius. Seeing Lysander lying on the ground and thinking that he might be dead, Helena shook him awake. As he woke up, his eyes met Helena's, and he fell madly in love with her. He declared his love for her by saying, "**Not Hermia, but Helena I love. Who will not change a raven for a dove?**" Helena thought that Lysander was playing a cruel joke on her and she ran off. Lysander, with his newfound love in his sights, chased after her. Hermia, who woke up after everyone had gone, was scared, alone, lost, and confused in the dark woods.

Debate the truth of the phrase, "once best friends, always best friends." Discuss what it takes to break up best friends.

Section III

Not far from where Hermia was left standing, who else should enter the woods? None other than Nick Bottom and his group of "wanna-be" actors. Before they could begin rehearsing their play called *Pyramus and Thisbe*, they spent a considerable amount of time debating over how not to frighten or offend anyone in the audience. Should all the killing be taken out of the play? "**Will not the ladies be afeard of the lion?**" When everything was settled, one of the actors dressed like a wall and another carried a lantern to portray the moon. Only half the lion mask remained so that no one would think the lion was real, and a special prologue explained that none of the killing on the stage was real, either. If these things seem silly to you, you are getting the right idea. These "actors" *were* silly, and everyone except themselves thought so. Everyone, including Puck, who was hiding in the trees giggling at the rehearsal.

Choose a popular television show or movie that many of your students have seen. Discuss the appropriateness of it for children. Debate whether or not there is too much violence on television or in movies for kids.

Not being one to pass up an opportunity to cause mischief, Puck turned Nick Bottom's head into an ass's (donkey's). Not knowing what change had taken place, Bottom kept on rehearsing. As his fellow actors ran from him in terror, he declared, "**I see their knavery. This is to make an ass of me, to fright me, if they could. But I will not stir from this place, do what they can. I will walk up and down here, and I will sing, that they shall hear I am not afraid.**" It was here that Bottom's arrogance combined with his ignorance, and the real comedy began.

Bottom's singing wound its way through the night air and entered the ears of the sleeping Titania. Upon waking, the first thing she saw was an ass-headed man standing above her singing out of key. Titania then asked, "**What angel wakes me from my flowery bed?**" The love potion was obviously working because Bottom was no angel, that's for sure. She asked him to continue singing while her fairies attended to him. Titania must have really gotten bit by the lovebug bad! Bottom, realizing that "**reason and love keep little company nowadays,**" gave in and allowed Titania to feed him hay and shower him with love. Puck, once again spying from a distance, was delighted by the turn of events and could not wait to tell Oberon.

"**Titania waked, and straightway loved an ass.**" Puck laughed as he met up with the fairy king. Oberon could not have been more pleased. This was exactly what he had hoped for. But, before he could ask Puck about their other scheme involving the young Athenians, they were interrupted by Demetrius and Hermia walking through the woods. Remember, Demetrius had been searching the woods for his bride-to-be, Hermia, and she would rather never marry than wed Demetrius. "**Stand close. This is the same Athenian,**" interrupted Oberon. "**This is the woman, but not this the man,**" answered Puck. Oops, someone has made a magical mistake, and that someone was . . .

Discuss the difference between mistakes that are "on purpose" and mistakes that are "by accident." Debate whether Puck's mistake was on purpose or by accident.

You guessed it right. It was Puck who put the love potion in the wrong man's eyes. Oberon was furious. "**What hast thou done? Thou hast mistaken quite and laid the love-juice on some true-love's sight.**" In other words, "Puck, you really messed things up!" So Oberon took it upon himself to set the lovers straight, or so he thought. When Demetrius had lain down to rest, Oberon dropped the love juice into his eyes. Who should come along next, but Lysander and Helena, and who should Demetrius see first, but Helena. Am I the only one who sees a problem here? No, Puck saw it, too, and I'm sure he had a huge grin on his face when he said, "**Lord, what fools these mortals be!**"

No matter how much fun Puck was having watching the "fools," the lovers were having anything but fun. You see, because of Puck's magical mistake, Lysander and Demetrius, both of whom used to love Hermia, now both loved Helena, who before was loved by nobody. Confusing? I should say so, but wouldn't it have been fun to watch?!

Not if you were Oberon. He wanted only to help the lovers fall in love, and now he was witnessing anything but love. Demetrius wanted to fight Lysander for Helena. Hermia was yelling and screaming at her once best friend, "**Oh me! you juggler! you canker-blossom! you thief of love! What have you come by night and stolen my love's heart from him?**" Helena, who couldn't believe what was happening, thought everyone was making fun of her. Oberon's plan had fallen completely apart.

To make things right, Oberon demanded that Puck fix this mess. So, Puck caused a fog to fill the forest; by disguising his voice, he led the four lovers together and caused them all to fall asleep. Puck then put the love juice into Lysander's eyes again so he would, Puck hoped, see Hermia first this time. "**When thou wakest, thou takest true delight in the sight of thy former lady's eye.**" Puck and Oberon waited with their fingers crossed for the lovers to wake up. But these four were not the only lovers in the wood on Oberon's mind.

Section IV

Titania and Bottom were snuggling in the flowers not far from where the lovers slept. Titania's fairy-servants tended to Bottom's needs. They scratched his long hairy ears and brought him hay to eat until he grew tired. Wrapped in each other's arms, the queen of the fairies and the ass-headed actor fell sound asleep.

When Oberon and Puck happened upon them, Oberon took pity on Titania, and released her from the spell, but not before stealing away the child they had been fighting over. He then instructed Puck to "**take this transformed scalp from off the head of this Athenian swain and think no more of this night's accidents but as the fierce vexation of a dream.**" So Puck removed the ass's head from Bottom and left him to wake the next morning lost, confused, alone, and planning to write a song to add to the play about the "most rare vision" he had had the night before. Once a Bottom always a Bottom!

At the sound of a hunter's wind horn, the four lovers also woke to find themselves lost and confused, but not alone. Theseus, Duke of Athens, was out for an early-morning hunt. He was with a hunting party that included Hermia's father, Egeus, and Theseus's bride-to-be, Hippolyta. Lysander tried to explain the situation, but Egeus was furious and did not want to listen. He demanded punishment for Lysander and Hermia's rebellion. At this point, Demetrius announced that he no longer wished to marry Hermia. He was now in love with Helena. Seeing an opportunity to avoid any unpleasantness on his wedding day, and to impress Hippolyta, I'm sure, Theseus announced the triple wedding of Demetrius and Helena, Lysander and Hermia, and Hippolyta and himself.

Discuss the experience of déjà vu. Debate whether or not dreams really can come true.

Back in Athens, the actors were joined once again by Bottom, and they prepared for their grand performance. Even though they had rewritten parts, added new lines, and never practiced together, they thought they were ready. As ready as they would ever be, anyway. The resulting play caused more laughter than sorrow, being more of a comedy than the tragedy it was intended to be. The audience ridiculed the play and the actors, but a good time was had by all!

"**Lovers, to bed; 'tis almost fairy time**," Theseus announced as the actors took their final bows. After everyone was asleep, Oberon, Titania, and the fairy court (including Puck) entered the palace to bless the marriages of the three couples. And, as if to apologize to us for all the mischief and confusion that he had caused, Puck ended the story by saying,

If we shadows have offended,
Think but this, and all is mended—
That you have but slumb'red here
While these visions did appear.
And this weak and idle theme,
No more yielding but a dream . . .
Else the Puck a liar call.
So, good night unto you all.
Give me your hands, if we be friends,
And Robin shall restore amends.

So, all's well that ends well—which may have provided the Bard with inspiration for another play!

Will's Words—Selections for Recitation

Theseus (to Hippolyta)

the flower that
Oberon puts in
Demtrisus's eyes
Lysander's eyes
and so on.
Drawn by Jena Bergan

Hippolyta, I wooed thee with my sword,
And won thy love doing thee injuries;
But I will wed thee in another key,
With pomp, with triumph, and with
reveling.

(Act 1, Scene 1)

Say What??

Theseus—pronounced THEE-see-us
Hippolyta—pronounced hip-ALL-it-ah
wooed thee with my sword—Hippolyta was captured by Theseus when he conquered the Amazons
pomp—triumph
reveling—fancy ceremony

Kidspeak

Hippolyta was the queen of the Amazons and Theseus had just conquered them. He took Hippolyta back to Athens with him to get married, but she was not very happy about it. By saying that he will "wed thee in another key," he is trying to make her happy about their upcoming wedding.

NAME:____________________________________

Egeus (to Theseus)

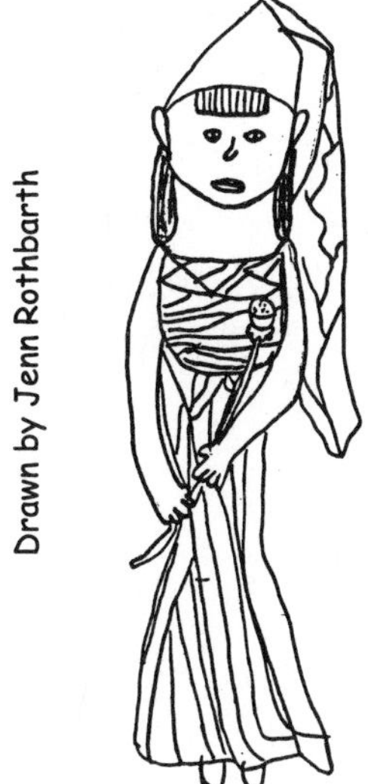

Full of vexation come I, with complaint
Against my child, my daughter Hermia.
Stand forth, Demetrius. My noble lord,
This man hath my consent to marry her.
Stand forth, Lysander. And, my gracious
  Duke,
This man hath bewitched the bosom of my
  child.

(Act 1, Scene 1)

Say What??

Egeus—pronounced e-JEE-us
vexation—feeling annoyed or irritated
consent—permission
my noble lord/my gracious Duke—Egeus is talking to Theseus
bewitched—taken control of
bosom—heart

Kidspeak

Hermia's dad, Egeus, is really mad because she refuses to marry Demetrius, the man he chose for her. Egeus has come before Theseus, Duke of Athens, to complain about Hermia's choosing Lysander instead of Demetrius.

NAME:____

Egeus (to Theseus)

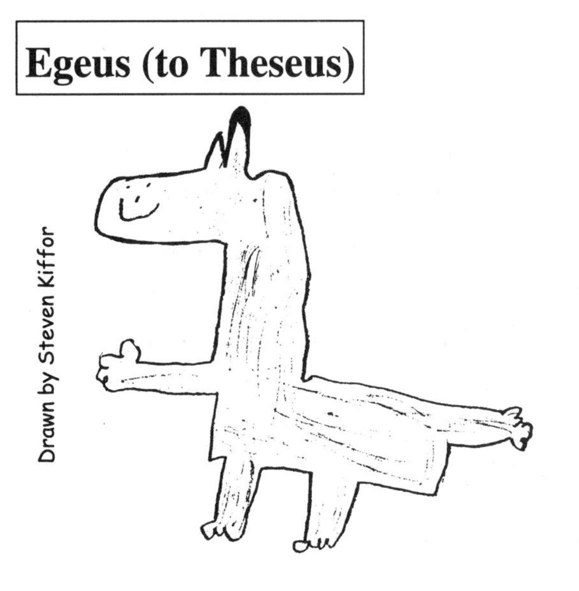

I beg the ancient privilege of Athens:
As she is mine, I may dispose of her,
Which shall be either to this gentleman
Or to her death, according to our law
Immediately provided in that case.

(Act 1, Scene 1)

Say What??

Egeus—pronounced e-JEE-us
ancient privilege of Athens—an old law
dispose—get rid of
this gentleman or to her death—marry Demetrius or die immediately
provided in that case—Egeus wants the law enacted quickly

Kidspeak

An old law in Athens says a daughter who doesn't obey her father's wishes can be put to death, and that is what Egeus wants. Hermia must marry Demetrius or die. He wants this law enacted quickly, too.

NAME:____

Bottom (to the rest of the actors)

Let me play the lion too. I will roar that I will do
any man's heart good to hear me. I will roar that I will
make the Duke say, "Let him roar again; let him roar again."

(Act 1, Scene 2)

Say What??

lion—one of the parts in the play
the Duke—Theseus, who will be in the audience

Kidspeak

Nick Bottom, who has already gotten a part in the play is showing off. He says he can play all the roles including the lion, because he can roar so well.

NAME:____

Oberon (to himself)

Drawn by Rachel Weintraub

Having once this juice,
I'll watch Titania when she is asleep
And drop the liquor of it in her eyes.
The next thing then she, waking, looks upon
(Be it on lion, bear, or wolf, or bull,
On meddling monkey, or on busy ape)
She shall pursue it with the soul of love.

(Act 2, Scene 1)

Say What??

Oberon—pronounced OH-ber-on
juice—the liquid from the magical flower
liquor—the magical part of the juice
meddling—interfere
busy—meddling
pursue it with the soul of love—fall in love at first sight

Kidspeak

As soon as Puck returns with the magical flower, Oberon will find Titania where she is sleeping and drop some of the magic juice in her eyes. When she wakes up, she will fall in love with the first creature she sees.

NAME:____

Demetrius and Helena

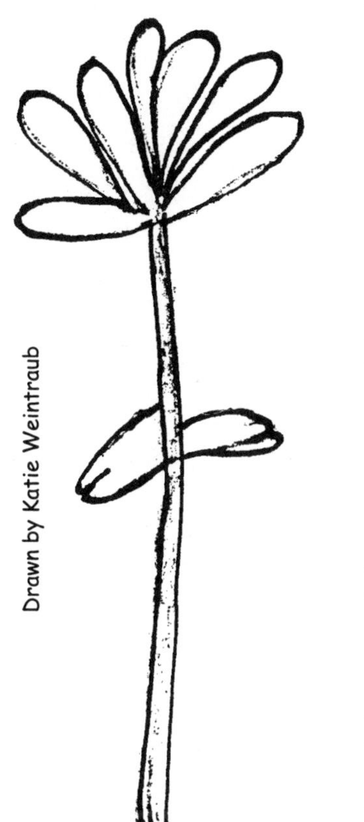

Demetrius: I love thee not; therefore
pursue me not.
Where is Lysander and fair Hermia?
The one I'll slay, the other slayeth me.
Thou told'st me they were stol'n unto this wood;
And here am I, and wood within this wood
Because I cannot meet my Hermia.
Hence, get thee gone, and follow me no more!

Helena: You draw me, you hard-hearted adamant!
But yet you draw not iron, for my heart
Is true as steel. Leave you your power to draw,
And I shall have no power to follow you.

Demetrius: Tempt not too much the
hatred of my spirit,
For I am sick when I do look on thee.

Helena: And I am sick when I look not on you.

(Act 2, Scene 1)

Say What??

Helena—pronounced HEL-e-nuh
Demetrius—pronounced de-MEE-tree-us
pursue—chase
fair—lovely
slay—kill
slayeth—loves
stol'n unto this wood—ran into the forest
wood within this wood—crazy in this forest
adamant—magnet

Kidspeak

Helena is chasing Demetrius into the forest proclaiming her love for him. He is telling her how much he hates her. She says he is like a magnet and she is like steel. He says she makes him sick.

NAME:____

Oberon (to himself)

I know a bank where the wild thyme blows,
Where oxlips and the nodding violet grows,
Quite over-canopied with luscious woodbine,
With sweet musk-roses, and with eglantine.
There sleeps Titania sometime of the night,
Lulled in these flowers with dances and delight;
And there the snake throws her enameled skin,
Weed wide enough to wrap a fairy in.
And with the juice of this I'll streak her eyes
And make her full of hateful fantasies.

(Act 2, Scene 1)

Say What??

Oberon—pronounced OH-ber-on
bank—a small hill
wild thyme—purple flowering bush
oxlips/nodding violet/luscious woodbine/sweet musk-roses/eglantine—different flowers
over-canopied—hanging overhead
lulled—asleep
snake throws her enameled skin—snake sheds its skin
weed—snakeskin
juice—magic flower
hateful fantasies—bad dreams

Kidspeak

Oberon is on his way to put the magic juice into Titania's eyes, and he is talking about where he will find her. She is asleep in a bed of flowers. He also shows his anger with her when he compares her to a snake and hopes that she has bad dreams.

NAME:____

Oberon (to the sleeping Titania)

What thou seest when thou dost wake,
Do it for thy true-love take;
Love and languish for his sake.
Be it ounce or cat or bear,
Pard, or boar with bristled hair
In thy eye that shall appear
When thou wak'st, it is thy dear.
Wake when some vile thing is near.

(Act 2, Scene 2)

Say What??

Oberon—pronounced OH-ber-on
languish—to become weak
ounce—lynx
pard—leopard
vile—disgusting

Kidspeak

As Oberon places the magic flower juice in Titania's eyes, he hopes that when she wakes up, she will fall in love with some disgusting animal.

NAME:____

Lysander (to Helena)

Content with Hermia? No; I do repent
The tedious minutes I with her have spent.
Not Hermia, but Helena I love.
Who will not change a raven for a dove?
The will of man is by his reason sway'd,
And reason says you are the worthier maid.

(Act 2, Scene 2)

Say What??

Lysander—pronounced lie-SAND-er
content—happy
repent—take it back
tedious—boring
raven—large, ugly, black bird
will—choice
swayed—changed
worthier maid—better girlfriend

Kidspeak

Puck has just mistakenly put the love juice in Lysander's eyes, and he has seen and fallen in love with Helena. Lysander is telling her that he no longer loves Hermia, and he now loves Helena.

NAME:____

Titania (to Bottom)

Drawn by Jenny Oster

What angel wakes me from my flow'ry
bed?
I pray thee, gentle mortal, sing again.
Mine ear is much enamored of thy note;
So is mine eye enthralled to thy shape;
And thy fair virtue's force doth move me,
On the first view, to say, to swear, I love
thee.

(Act 3, Scene 1)

Say What??

Titania—pronounced ti-TAH-nee-uh
pray—beg
mortal—human being
enamored—overtaken
enthralled—overtaken
fair virtue's force—power of love

Kidspeak

Titania wakes up to see the donkey-headed Bottom and hear him singing. She tells him how much she loves what she sees and hears and how powerful his love is to her.

NAME:____

Helena and Hermia

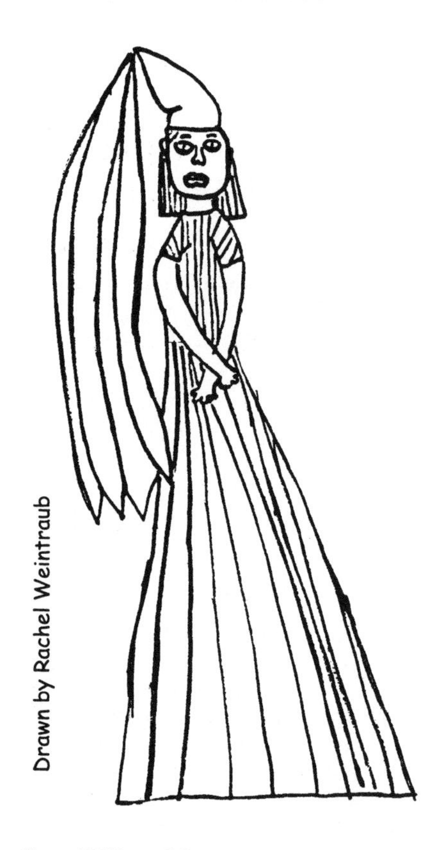

Hermia: O me! you juggler! you canker-blossom!
You thief of love! what, have you come by night
And stolen my love's heart from him?

Helena: Have you no modesty, no maiden shame,
No touch of bashfulness? What, will you tear
Impatient answer from my gentle tongue?
Fie, fie! you counterfeit, you puppet you!

Hermia: Puppet? Why so! Ay, that way goes the game. Now I perceive that she hath made compare between our statures; she hath urged her height; And with her personage, her tall personage, her height, (forsooth), she hath prevail'd with him. And are you grown so high in his esteem; Because I am so dwarfish and so low? How low am I, thou painted maypole? speak! How low am I? I am not yet so low but that my nails can reach unto thine eyes.

(Act 3, Scene 2)

Say What??

Helena—pronounced HEL-e-nuh
Hermia—pronounced HER-me-uh
juggler—trickster
canker-blossom—diseased flower
modesty/maiden shame/bashfulness—ashamed and embarrassed
counterfeit—fake
puppet—short person
game—fight
statures—sizes
forsooth—in truth
prevailed—won
esteem—opinion of you
dwarfish—short
painted maypole—tall person
nails—fingernails

Kidspeak

After discovering that Lysander now loves her tall best friend Helena, the short Hermia starts a fight. She accuses Helena of stealing Lysander, and they insult each other's height. This is a real shouting match.

NAME:____

Puck (to audience)

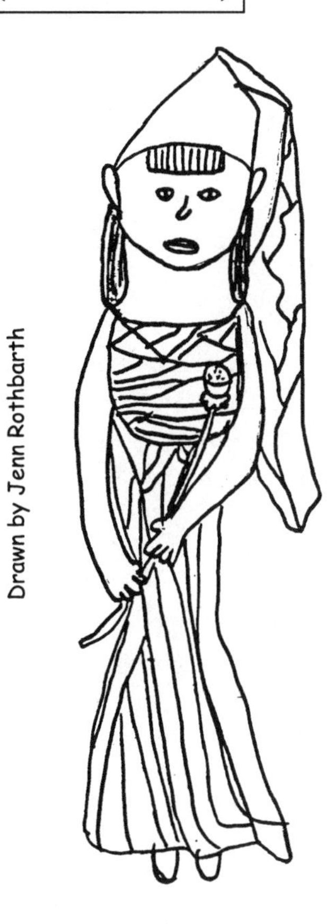

If we shadows have offended,
Think but this, and all is mended—
That you have but slumb'red here
While these visions did appear.
And this weak and idle theme,
No more yielding but a dream,
Gentles, do not reprehend.
If you will pardon, we will mend.
And, as I am an honest Puck,
If we have unearned luck
Now to scape the serpent's tongue,
We will make amends ere long;
Else the Puck a liar call.
So, good night unto you all.
Give me your hands, if we be friends,
And Robin shall restore amends.

(Act 5, Scene 1)

Say What??

offended—hurt you
mended—fixed
slumb'red—slept
idle—foolish
no more yielding—just
reprehend—criticize
scape the serpent's tongue—avoid the "boo's" of the audience
make amends ere long—make things right
give me your hands—clap for us

Kidspeak

This is the very end of the play, and Puck is speaking to the audience. He tells them that everything was just a dream, and he asks them to please clap for the actors (instead of "booing").

NAME:____

Lights, Camera, Action

Movie Making

Please don't skip this section!! Movie making with elementary students will not drive you to an early retirement! Putting on a live performance is guaranteed to drive you up the nearest wall in no time flat, but, through the miracle of technology—in the shape of a camcorder—you will help your students experience the excitement of performing—and you *will* live to tell the tale!

With the complexity of Shakespeare's story lines, we have found that making a "movie" using a camcorder is much easier than preparing for a live performance "onstage." Not only can you practice a scene immediately before you record it, but you can edit out mistakes, shoot "on location," and create special effects. Your grand performance will then become a movie premier, and copies of the video can be sent home for private viewing, or it can become part of a multimedia computer presentation. You may even decide to hold your own Oscar awards!

You are about to discover how simple the movie making process can be. All you need is a camcorder, props, simple costumes, a "castle" wall, some actors, and a little self-confidence! The question is how to get everything with a minimum of effort on your part. (You must save your energies for the creative process!)

1. Camcorder. If your school doesn't have one, send home a begging letter liberally sprinkled with veiled references as to how guilty the parents should feel if a camcorder is not forthcoming! Be sure to familiarize yourself with the camcorder before the actual filming. Nothing kills enthusiasm faster than a fumbler who misses an award-winning performance through technical ineptitude!

2. Costumes. Ask for donations and check the secondhand clothing stores. You will find a variety to choose from, at little cost.

3. Props. We have included a list of props. Dropping a few hints about what is needed usually results in instant props! Have your students make a large sign that says "A MIDSUMMER NIGHT'S DREAM" for the camera to focus on as an introduction to the movie. Your students could also make a mural, or some other visual, for added effect.

4. Sets. The best thing about a camcorder, apart from the ability to edit out the disasters instantly, is its mobility. You can shoot in a variety of locations. Castle scenes require only a painted cardboard wall that can represent both indoors and out. Perhaps, the art teacher might turn his or her talented hand to this, too! Here are some location suggestions for the narrators:

   - Hallway
   - Cafeteria
   - Grassy area

Your enthusiastic students will be overflowing with ideas for locations with atmosphere. Let them have lots of input so that they feel the responsibility for the performance, as well as ownership. Remember, to have control you must give control.

5. Actors. This is the hardest part of all because everyone wants the *big* parts, and it is up to you to choose who does what. Here is an almost painless way:

   - Have students list several parts they would like to play. This gives you some leeway.
   - Have the students write down why they want to be a certain character.
   - If all else fails, flip a coin. Remember, auctioning off parts to the highest bidders is not an option!

6. Tips.

   - Slip written dialogue into books, or tape them onto props to aid the memories of nervous actors!
   - Manufacture extra parts by including lots of servants and fairies. Shakespeare wouldn't mind—the play's the thing!
   - Your movie will take on a very professional look if you have an introduction consisting of a title, visuals, and even mood music!
   - Give the following script outline to actors and let them pad their own scenes with improvisation.
   - The key to successful improvisation is a thorough understanding of the play!
   - Hold lots of practice sessions before the film day; and for the sake of your sanity, don't try to film all the scenes in one day!
   - Show credits at the end of the movie.

Now that you have everything you need, *go make a movie!*

Cast of Characters

*Narrator

*Theseus, Duke of Athens

*Hippolyta (the queen of the Amazons)

*Egeus (Hermia's father)

Hermia

Lysander

Helena

Demetrius

*Oberon (king of the fairies)

*Titania (queen of the fairies)

*Puck (or Robin Goodfellow)

*Fairies (Cobweb, *Mustardseed, Peaseblossom) can use kindergartners

*Nick Bottom (also plays Pyramus)

*The Actors (also play Thisbe [a boy playing a girl's part], the lion, and the wall)

*Indicates that a character will be portrayed by only one student. Please note that the four lovers are changed between Acts 2 and 3, and again between Acts 4 and 5. This allows more students to participate in the *big* roles.

Props

- costumes or distinguishable symbols for each main character (need to be interchangeable) for the four lovers
- sets for the palace and the woods
- magical flower
- signs: *Welcome to Athens, This Way to the Woods,* and *Presenting: Pyramus and Thisbe: A Tragedy*
- flowers for Titania's flowery bed
- play phone, horn, and baby doll

Management Notes

The stage directions 🎬 are intended to guide the students as they improvise each scene.

There are six acts and 13 scenes. A different group of students portrays the four lovers in every other act, using the same costumes for consistency.

Where appropriate, students may memorize actual dialogue from the play. A * indicates a place where actual dialogue can be used during the performance. The Quality Quotes appear at relevant points in the text and enable students who want to recite the "real" lines to do so.

A Midsummer Night's Dream

Introduction

Narrator: Hi, I'm ______________, and I'd like to tell you an amazing story. You are about to see one of the funniest and most confusing comedies ever written. Did you hear that? I called it a comedy. That not only means that the whole thing is supposed to be funny and that you're about to get a good laugh, but that every one will live happily ever after in the end. It is a comedy called *A Midsummer Night's Dream,* and when it is over you will be glad that it was just a dream. In this fantasy world created by William Shakespeare almost 400 years ago, nothing is as it seems. In a forest ruled by fairies, magic is the king when the sun goes down, and if you happen to be in that forest at night, then you had better *watch out!*

However, this is not only a story about magic. It is also about friends and how they do and don't get along. If you have ever really liked someone, but your parents didn't, and they wanted to choose your friends for you, then you will understand. (*Camera films map of Europe, focusing on Greece.*)

Our story begins on the continent of Europe, in the country of Greece, in the ancient city of Athens. It is a time when gods and goddesses ruled the earth from high on Mount Olympus. The Duke of Athens, named Theseus, has just returned from a victorious war with the Amazons, and he has brought back the queen of the Amazons, named Hippolyta, to be his wife. They are to be married in four days.

Act 1, Scene 1

Theseus and Hippolyta are sitting in the palace planning their upcoming wedding.

" Quality Quotes

Theseus (*telling Hippolyta how strong his love is*):
Hippolyta, I wooed thee with my sword,
And won thy love doing thee injuries;
But I will wed thee in another key,
With pomp, with triumph, and with reveling.

Egeus enters the palace with Hermia, Lysander, and Demetrius in tow.

" Quality Quotes

Egeus (*pleading his case before Theseus*):
Full of vexation come I, with complaint
Against my child, my daughter Hermia.
Stand forth, Demetrius. My noble lord,
This man hath my consent to marry her. Stand forth, Lysander. And, my gracious Duke,
This man hath bewitched the bosom of my child . . . I beg the ancient privilege of Athens:
As she is mine, I may dispose of her,
Which shall be either to this gentleman
Or to her death, according to our law
Immediately provided in that case.

Theseus and Hermia discuss her options. Both Lysander and Demetrius are compared. Hermia is given until Theseus's wedding to decide.

Act 1, Scene 2

Narrator: So now you see the problem. Hermia wants to marry Lysander, but her father, Egeus, wants her to marry Demetrius. What's a poor girl to do? Obey her father or obey her heart? What would you do? Remember, if Hermia doesn't do what her father wishes, then she can never get married again. Not to worry, Lysander has a plan.

Lysander and Hermia meet at the palace in secret. Hermia is worried, but Lysander shares his plan to elope.

“ Quality Quotes

Lysander (*after Hermia expresses worry*):
The course of true love never did run smooth.

Helena comes along and Hermia tells her the plan. After Hermia and Lysander leave, Helena calls Demetrius to reveal the plan (have her use a cell phone as a joke). All four lovers run off to the woods.

Act 1, Scene 3

Narrator: In another part of Athens a group of actors are gathering to practice a play called *Pyramus and Thisbe* for the wedding of Theseus and Hippolyta. But these are no ordinary actors; in fact, they aren't actors at all. They are weavers, tailors, and cabinet makers. As the parts of the play are being assigned, one actor (a weaver, actually) named Nick Bottom just can't keep his mouth shut. He wants to play all the parts by himself and he proceeds to show us that he can.

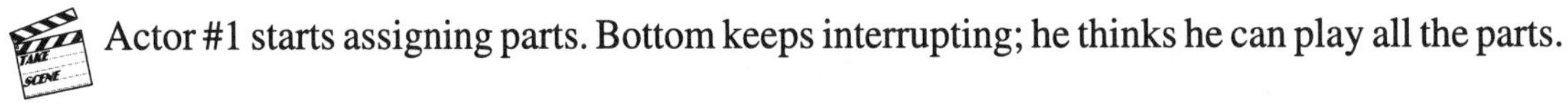

Actor #1 starts assigning parts. Bottom keeps interrupting; he thinks he can play all the parts.

“ Quality Quotes

Bottom: Ready, name what part I am for, and proceed.
(*He is given the part of Pyramus.*)
What is Pyramus? A lover or a tyrant?
(*He is told that Pyramus is a lover.*)
And I may hide my face, let me play Thisbe, too. I'll speak in a monstrous little voice. Let me play the lion, too. I will roar that I will do any man's heart good to hear me. I will roar and let the Duke say "Let him roar again; let him roar again."

The actors decide to meet in the woods at night to practice.

Act 2, Scene 1

Narrator: So as the sun begins to set, the four lovers and the actors make their way into the woods outside of Athens, but they are not alone. After the sun goes down, the fairies come out. Their job is to care for the earth at night, but they have been known to cause a bit of mischief. The fairy who causes the most mischief is named Puck. On this particular night, the king and queen of the fairies, Oberon and Titania, are arguing over a child. Both want him as their servant, and neither will give in.

Oberon and Titania are fighting over a child (use baby doll as prop). Titania storms off and Oberon calls Puck over to plan revenge, and sends him in search of the magical flower.

“ Quality Quotes

***Oberon** (*telling about the plan*)**:** Having once this juice,
I'll watch Titania when she is asleep
And drop the liquor of it in her eyes.
The next thing then she, waking, looks upon
(Be it on lion, bear, or wolf, or bull,
On meddling monkey, or on busy ape)
She shall pursue it with the soul of love.
And ere I take this charm from off her sight
(As I can with another herb)
I'll make her render up (the child) to me.
But who comes here? I am invisible,
And I will overhear their conference.

Helena and Demetrius enter the woods, arguing.

“ Quality Quotes

***Demetrius:** I love thee not; therefore pursue me not.
Where is Lysander and fair Hermia?
The one I'll slay, the other slayeth me . . .
Hence, get thee gone, and follow me no more!
***Helena:** You draw me, you hard-hearted adamant! . . .
Leave you your power to draw,
And I shall have no power to follow you.
***Demetrius:** Tempt not too much the hatred of my spirit,
For I am sick when I do look on thee.
***Helena:** And I am sick when I look not on you.

This dialogue makes Oberon want to help Demetrius and Helena fall in love. Helena and Demetrius walk off into the woods still arguing; Puck returns with the magic flower; Oberon tells Puck to find Demetrius and use the flower to help him fall in love with Helena while he goes to find Titania.

“ Quality Quotes

***Oberon** (*talking about where he will find Titania and what he will do*):
I know a bank where the wild thyme blows,
Where oxlips and the nodding violet grows,
Quite over-canopied with luscious woodbine,
With sweet musk-roses, and with eglantine.
There sleeps Titania sometime of the night,

Lulled in these flowers with dances and delight;
And there the snake throws her enameled skin,
Weed wide enough to wrap a fairy in.
And with the juice of this I'll streak her eyes
And make her full of hateful fantasies.

***Oberon** (*talking to Puck about Demetrius*):
Take thou some of it and seek through this grove.
A sweet Athenian lady is in love
With a disdainful youth. Anoint his eyes;
But do it when the next thing he espies
May be the lady. Thou shalt know the man
By the Athenian garments he hath on.

Act 2, Scene 2

Narrator (*off camera*): Oberon finds Titania asleep on her bed of flowers and he squeezes the juice of the magical flower into her eyes. He is hoping that when she wakes up she will fall in love with something awful.

Titania lays down to sleep and is tended to by fairies; Oberon finds her and puts the love juice in her eyes.

“ Quality Quotes

***Oberon** (*while putting drops in her eyes*):
What thou seest when thou dost wake,
Do it for thy true-love take;
Love and languish for his sake.
Be it ounce or cat or bear, Pard [leopard], or boar with bristled hair
In thy eye that shall appear
When thou wak'st, it is thy dear.
Wake when some vile thing is near.

Act 2, Scene 3

Narrator: While Oberon waits for Titania to see some “vile thing,” Puck has found a man sleeping in the woods wearing Athenian clothes. Thinking that this must be the man that Oberon told him about, Puck squeezes the love juice into his eyes. Unfortunately, the man Puck finds is Lysander, not Demetrius, and the woman that Demetrius sees first is not his true love, Hermia, but her best friend, Helena. Puck has just made a *big* mistake!

Lysander and Hermia stop in the woods to rest. Puck sees the sleeping Lysander, places the love juice in his eyes, and goes away. Helena comes along and wakes up Lysander. Lysander falls in love with Helena and chases her off; Hermia wakes up all alone.

“ Quality Quotes

***Lysander** (*after Helena asks, “What about your love, Hermia?”*):
Content with Hermia? No; I do repent
The tedious minutes I with her have spent.

Not Hermia, but Helena I love.
Who will not change a raven for a dove?
The will of man is by his reason sway'd,
And reason says you are the worthier maid.

Act 3, Scene 1

Narrator: While Lysander is busy falling in love with the wrong girl, Bottom and his merry band of actors are making their way into the woods to rehearse their play. Little do they know that they have an audience. Puck is watching their silliness from behind a tree. Wanting to get in on the act, Puck causes a bit of silliness of his own.

Bottom and the actors enter the woods, watched by Puck. Puck turns Bottom's head into an ass's (donkey's). The ass-headed Bottom scares the other actors away.

" Quality Quotes

***Actor #1:** O Bottom, thou art changed. What do I see on thee?

***Actor #2** (*upon seeing the ass's head*)**:** Bless thee, Bottom, bless thee! Thou art translated.

Bottom starts to sing to show that he is not afraid; Bottom's singing wakes up Titania who falls in love with him.

" Quality Quotes

***Titania** (*after he wakes her up with singing*)**:**
What angel wakes me from my flow'ry bed?
I pray thee, gentle mortal, sing again.
Mine ear is much enamored of thy note;
So is mine eye enthralled to thy shape;
And thy fair virtue's force doth move me,
On the first view, to say, to swear, I love thee.

***Bottom** (*in response to Titania's expression of love*)**:**
Methinks, mistress, you should have little reason for that. And yet, to say the truth, reason and love keep little company together nowadays.

Bottom gives in and the fairies attend to him.

Act 3, Scene 2

Narrator: As you can imagine, Puck cannot wait to find Oberon and tell him the good news of Titania and Bottom's newfound love. And as you can imagine, Oberon is thrilled to hear that his plan has worked. However, the thrill is gone when he realizes that his other plan, the one to make Helena and Demetrius fall in love, is really messed up. Remember, Puck put the love juice in Lysander's eyes—not Demetrius's. If you want something done right, then you have to do it yourself. Oberon does just that. However, he makes things worse!

Puck and Oberon celebrate the success of Titania's plan. Demetrius and Hermia interrupt their celebration, and Hermia wants to know where Lysander is. Puck realizes that he made a mistake.

“ Quality Quotes

***Oberon** (*after Puck realizes his mistake*)**:**
What hast thou done? Thou hast mistaken quite
And laid the love-juice on some true-love's sight.

Oberon decides to fix the mistake by placing the love juice in Demetrius's eyes when he is asleep. When Helena and Lysander enter, Demetrius wakes up and he also falls in love with Helena. Helena thinks it is all a cruel joke.

“ Quality Quotes

***Helena** (*after Demetrius declares his love for her*)**:**
I see you all are bent
To set against me for your merriment.
If you were civil and knew courtesy,
You would not do me thus much injury.
Can you not hate me, as I know you do,
But you must join in souls to mock me too?

Demetrius and Lysander are fighting over Helena, and Hermia fights with Helena.

“ Quality Quotes

***Hermia:** O me! you juggler! you canker-blossom!
You thief of love! what, have you come by night
And stolen my love's heart from him?

***Helena** (*thinking this is all a cruel joke*)**:**
Fie! you counterfeit, you puppet you!

***Hermia** (*thinking that Helena is making fun of her because she is short*)**:**
Puppet? Why so! Ay, that way goes the game . . .
Because I am so dwarfish and so low?
How low am I, thou painted maypole? speak!
How low am I? I am not yet so low
But that my nails can reach unto thine eyes.

Oberon orders Puck to fix the mistakes that have been made so that all the chaos will seem like a dream.

Act 4, Scene 1

Narrator: This is a fine mess, and now it's Puck's job to fix it. Demetrius and Lysander, who both once loved Hermia, now both love Helena. Everybody is fighting with everybody else, and this comedy is looking more and more like a tragedy by the minute. Can Puck really make everything right? Let's hope so.

Puck causes a fog to fall over the forest—this can be accomplished by covering the camera lens with wax paper, or something else translucent. The lovers become separated and lie down to sleep. Puck places love juice in Lysander's eyes and hopes that he will see Hermia first.

“ Quality Quotes

***Puck** (*as he drops the juice in Lysander's eyes*):
When thou wakest,
Thou takest
True delight
In the sight
Of thy former lady's eye:
And the country proverb known,
That every man should take his own,
In your waking shall be shown:
Jack shall have Jill;
Nought shall go ill;
The man shall have his mare again, and all shall be well.

Act 4, Scene 2

Narrator: While Puck waits with his fingers crossed, hoping that Lysander will wake to see his true love Hermia, Oberon finds Titania lying asleep in the arms of Bottom (who still has the head of an ass). Although he finds it funny, Oberon takes pity on Titania and Bottom and so he releases them from their magical spells However, only after he takes the child for his servant. When they wake up, they will think that everything was just a dream. I guess Oberon got what he wanted, after all.

Oberon finds Titania and Bottom asleep. He takes the child and releases Titania and Bottom from their spells.

“ Quality Quotes

***Titania** (*after being released*): My Oberon! what visions have I seen!
Methought I was enamor'd of an ass.

Oberon and Titania leave while Bottom is still sleeping.

Act 5, Scene 1

Narrator: As the sun rises the next morning, a hunter's horn awakens the four lost lovers. Theseus, Hippolyta, and Egeus are out for an early morning hunt, but instead they find Hermia, Lysander, Helena, and Demetrius lying under a tree. Before Egeus can explode with anger, Demetrius proclaims his love for Helena, and Lysander does the same for Hermia. Seeing a happy ending in the works, the duke and Hippolyta announce a triple wedding.

A horn blows. Theseus and the hunting party wake up the four lovers. Egeus is furious and Lysander and Demetrius proclaim their love. Theseus and Hippolyta announce a triple wedding and everyone heads for Athens.

“ Quality Quotes

***Demetrius** (*while leaving for Athens*): Are you sure
That we are awake? It seems to me
That yet we sleep, we dream.

Act 5, Scene 2

Narrator (*off camera*)**:** Wait a minute, we're not out of the woods yet. We can't forget about Bottom. Having been restored to his former know-it-all self, he runs out of the woods to find his friends. Of course, he still wants every part in their play. Some things will never change.

Bottom wakes up, looks confused, feels his head and ears, and runs out of the forest.

Act 6, Scene 1

Narrator: Back in Athens, love is in the air, and three times as much as before. Theseus marries Hippolyta, Demetrius marries Helena, and Lysander marries Hermia. At the reception for the triple wedding, everyone is entertained by the untalented actors. Even though they add parts at the last minute and have never really practiced together, Bottom and the actors are a hit (in their own minds anyway).

All the couples and Egeus are watching the actors perform their play. You may ad lib as much or as little of the play as you like; remember to include Pyramus (leading man), Thisbe (leading lady), a lion, and a wall. Encourage silliness. At the end of the play, Theseus sends everyone to bed.

“ Quality Quotes

***Theseus:** The iron tongue of midnight hath told twelve.
Lovers, to bed; 'tis almost fairy time.

The lights go out and everyone sleeps.

Narrator: Just when you think this has all been just a dream, the fairies return to bless the marriages and the palace. Of course, Puck gets the last word.

Puck, Oberon, Titania, and all the fairies enter. (Use special lighting to make it magical.)

“ Quality Quotes

***Puck:** If we shadows have offended,
Think but this, and all is mended—
That you have but slumb'red here
While these visions did appear.
And this weak and idle theme,
No more yielding but a dream.
Else the Puck a liar call.
So, good night unto you all.
Give me your hands, if we be friends,
And Robin shall restore amends.

Don't Just Sit There!

Knowledge, the wing wherewith we fly to heaven.
(*Henry VI*, 4.7)

The following activities are intended to bring the play into all curriculum areas and thus enhance students' understanding and interest. The teacher may select several activities to deepen students' understanding of a certain aspect of the play, or only one or two, merely as fun breaks during rehearsals. On a grander scale, the teacher may decide to use *A Midsummer Night's Dream* as the core of a thematic study. In brief, the thematic, or project, approach to learning involves an extended study of a topic that crosses all curricula areas. The benefits of this approach lie in the total immersion of students in the topic and the learning that occurs from connections students make between their lives and experiences and the topic. For a more detailed look at thematic learning and the aims of this approach, we highly recommend *Engaging Children's Minds: The Project Approach* by Lillian Katz and Sylvia Chard.[1]

We have grouped the activities by curriculum subjects, beginning with language arts, and we strongly encourage teachers to adapt, expand, or condense the activities to meet the needs and interests of their students. We describe the first two activities in detail to provide as complete a picture as possible of the process of classroom application. Following these two activities are lots of "bare bones" that you can discard or fatten up for classroom consumption! Enjoy!

Language Arts

Quick Play

- Level: kindergarten and up
- Grouping: groups of two to five
- Time: 30 minutes (minimum)
- Supplies: space for performing and simple costumes and props (optional)
- Objective: This activity will allow students to personalize the play by placing themselves in the story. A deeper understanding of the plot and characters will result.

The group of actors led by Nick Bottom are struggling to practice their play for the duke's wedding. Give your students a chance to experience the creative energy that the "actors" must have felt by preparing and performing a short play with a small group of friends.

Children are natural performers. Given the opportunity, they will come up with wonderful dramatic presentations. This activity taps into the natural desire to "playact" that children have. There are two approaches you might take:

1. Dilemmas. Pose a playground dilemma to your students (or brainstorm them together) such as:
   - your best friend is playing with your worst enemy
   - a group of older kids is bullying your friends
   - you hear a rumor that your best friend hates you
2. Story line. Use this opportunity to make the story you are telling become real. Here's how:
   - select a scene from the play as a class
   - choose students to play the parts in front of the class
   - direct the students as they go—remember, you are modeling for the group performances
   - introduce Shakespeare's words into the scene (this would be a good time to use copies of the verses from the Will's Words section)
   - break into groups (the size depends on the scene) to practice for 10 minutes (the short time limit is essential to generate the creative energy needed for this activity)
   - gather together as a class to celebrate each group's performance
   - celebration = applause

Simile Swapping

- Level: kindergarten and up
- Grouping: whole class to groups of four
- Time: 30 minutes (minimum)
- Supplies: paper, pencil, and imagination
- Objective: This activity will add voice to your students' writing in the form of similes.

Because his plays were performed without the luxury of fancy sets to create a scene for the audience, Shakespeare used words to paint a picture in his audience's mind. The poetry in Shakespeare's plays serves as an excellent springboard to help students experiment with language.

One of the best ways to begin playing with language is to explore the descriptive power of the simile. By comparing one thing to another using the linking words *like* or *as*, your students' writing will begin to take on a new voice.

Here are some ways to get those voices going:

- Brainstorm similes as a whole class or in groups of four. Provide a sentence starter such as *The dog was as small as* ________ or *These cookies are so good, they taste like* __________ How many different descriptions can you create?
- Have your students write descriptive paragraphs either in pairs or individually. Provide a topic or choice of topics such as an elephant, a castle, or winter. Challenge your students to write descriptive paragraphs using as many similes as possible.

- Create lists of similes for use in everyday writing. Form groups of three or four. Challenge your students to make posters listing possible similes for sentence starters like these: big as, small as, beautiful like, ugly like, slow as, fast like, etc. Display these posters as reminders and references to use throughout the year.
- Using the similes your students wrote for compliments and insults (see the activities *As You Like It* and *As You Don't Like It*), enter into this friendly competition: Choose two judges who will score each simile between one and five. Form two teams and have the teams select their best 10 similes. The teams will take turns presenting them dramatically to the judges. The judges will score them and the team with the highest score wins.

Giving Life

Draw what you think Puck, Oberon, and/or Titania look like. Using the picture as the center of an idea web, surround your picture with adjectives that describe the character.

Make Demetrius Smile

Two students sit in chairs facing each other. The student playing Demetrius tries not to smile while the student playing Helena pays him compliments. The exchange could sound like this: "Do you know why I like you?" "Why?" "I like the way your eyes twinkle in the moonlight." "Well, I don't like you."

Hollywood Wannabe

The actors in the woods have trouble making their play nonviolent. You are a movie producer. Write a plot for a new movie that all kids will want to see, but it cannot have any violence.

As You Like It

Using the words *like* and *as,* write a collection of similes that would compliment a friend: "You are as nice as . . ."; "Your friendship is like . . ."

As You Don't Like It

Using the words *like* and *as*, write a collection of similes that would insult an enemy: "You are as mean as . . ."; "You are ugly like . . ."

Just a Dream

Keep a notebook by your bed and write down every dream you remember for a week. Use one of them to write a short story.

Venn Will We Meet Again

Choose two characters (one fairy and one mortal)—Puck and Bottom, for example. Draw a Venn diagram and compare and contrast the two characters.

Varying Views

Write a paragraph about what is happening in the play from the point of view of different characters. How would Egeus see the story? What about Titania?

The Dream Is Alive

Select students to portray various characters from the play and interview them in front of the class in a talk-show format. Your show topic could be, "My Best Friend Is in Love with the Man My Dad Wants Me to Marry, but I Love Someone Else" or "Fairy Slaves—The Untold Story."

Lights, Camera, Contrast

Watch a movie version of the play; create a list of differences between the story you know and the movie.

See You in the Funny Papers

Choose a scene that you like and draw a comic strip showing what is happening. Be sure to include "talking balloons" and narration where appropriate.

Social Studies/Geography/History

The Power of Choice

Hermia is bound by the law of Athens to marry whom her father chooses. List five things that you want to be able to choose in your life, and list five things that others can choose for you.

The Choice of Power

Investigate different kinds of government systems (democratic, totalitarian, communist). What are their main differences, and what would your life be like under each?

Friendly Experiment

Interview other students asking, "How can I become your best friend?" Write a summary of your findings. Is it what you do or what you say that makes a friend?

What's in a Name

In the play, the actors' names matched their jobs. What names would the people in your community have if they matched their jobs?

Can You Believe It?

People back in Shakespeare's time believed that fairies were the cause of bad luck. Investigate different superstitions (leprechauns, lucky socks, knocking on wood). What makes people superstitious? Why do people rely on superstitions so much?

Break Up

Interview students about what it would take to break a friendship. Write about your results.

Magical Map

Design your own map of Athens, Greece, showing all the important locations from the play: Theseus's palace, the woods, the path the lovers took, Titania's flowery bed, etc.

Gods Grow on Trees

Cupid's arrow is the cause of the magic in the magical flower. Where does Cupid fit on the family tree of Greek gods and goddesses? Research the relationships and draw the family tree.

Could You Be Cupid?

Who was Cupid, and what did he do? Read his myth, and make a chart showing the pros and cons of being Cupid. Write a paragraph telling why you would or would not want his job.

Pack Your Bags

Before you run away to marry the love of your life, you have to pack, but you can only take five items. What would you take and why? What makes them valuable to you?

Greetings from Greece

Research the country of Greece and prepare a list of important facts. Include a colored map showing important locations in the country.

Ancient Articles

Investigate what life was like in ancient Greece. Write three newspaper articles with headlines telling about important events of the time.

Wonderful Weddings

Three weddings at the same time: that has to be a record. Use the *Guinness Book of World Records* to collect information about record-setting weddings.

Math/Science

How Friendly Are You?

Survey a sample of students around your school to arrive at an average number of best friends. What is the range (high to low)? Graph your results.

Fairy Tag (Picking Puck)

This is a game that combines "Heads Up, Seven Up" with "Duck, Duck, Goose." You could call it "Puck, Puck, Goose." Everyone sits in a circle. Five people are chosen to be fairies. All eyes are closed as the fairies walk around on the inside of the circle and tap the head of one person each. After tapping, the fairies stand at the center of the circle. The tapped people stand and try to guess who tapped them. If they are correct, they become fairies. If they are not correct, they stay in the circle for another turn.

Guess Who?

When Titania falls in love with an ass (who is really Bottom), she isn't seeing things clearly to say the least. Choose a person to be "it." That person proceeds to describe another person in the group. The group tries to guess who is being described.

Speed of Puck

While searching for Cupid's flower, Puck made four trips around the world. How far would that be, and how fast would Puck have to fly to return in one hour?

Head in the Clouds

Demonstrate to your class how clouds and fog are formed by using a bottle and ice. Have your students replicate the demonstration with different types of containers and different amounts of ice.

Seeing with Your Ears

When your sense of sight is taken away, how sharp do your other senses become? Blindfold a student and put him or her in the center of the class. Take turns talking to that student and see if he or she can identify who is talking. Who can identify the most speakers in a row?

Amazing Mazes

Read *Theseus and the Minotaur* to learn about the labyrinth that challenged Theseus. Design your own labyrinth (maze) to challenge a friend.

Brain Drain

How do we dream? Why do we dream? Investigate how our brains work while we are sleeping, and try to satisfy your own curiosities about sleeping and dreaming.

An Ass Is a Horse, of Course

What is the difference between a donkey, an ass, a mule, and a horse? Research them to find out whether they are more alike than different.

Hee Haw Hide

The person chosen to play Bottom is "it." Bottom makes 10 *hee-haw* sounds like a donkey while covering his (or her) eyes at the base. After making the sounds, Bottom searches for the hiders. When he finds someone, the hider shouts, "What angel wakes me from my flowery bed?" and chases Bottom. If Titania (the hider) catches Bottom (the finder) before Bottom can run back to the base, they must hold hands and search for another hider. If Bottom reaches the base first, Titania is "out" and Bottom tries again. Play the game until all the Titanias (hiders) are "out" or all the hiders are found.

Fascinating Flowers

Oberon spends several lines listing the many flowers that make up Titania's "flowery bed." Investigate the names of these flowers and where you can find them. Create a "flowery bed book" that shows pictures of the flowers, some facts about them, and a map showing where to find them.

Hot Stuff

Notes

1. Lillian Katz and Sylvia Chard, *Engaging Children's Minds: The Project Approach* (Norwood, NJ: Ablex, 1989).

Annotated Bibliography and Resources

There are many excellent read-aloud versions of *A Midsummer Night's Dream.* It is worth the effort to shop around to find the version that suits your style. The following are some of our favorites, which we use in preparation for our students.

Garfield, Leon. *Shakespeare Stories*. Boston: Houghton Mifflin, 1985.
This delightful and engaging collection of 12 plays includes a creative and detailed version of *A Midsummer Night's Dream* that would be perfect in preparing for your own retelling for your class.

Nesbit, Edith. *The Children's Shakespeare: A Midsummer Night's Dream.* Los Angeles: New Star Media, 1998. Audiocassette.
Shakespeare won a Grammy Award! This collection of stories, told by a variety of famous actors, provides yet another way to share Shakespeare with children and adults.

Shakespeare. *A Midsummer Night's Dream.* Classics Illustrated edition, ed. Bruce Gassco. New York: Acclaim Books, 1997.
Here the Sunday comics meet the Bard. Shakespeare's words are found in "talking bubbles" in this comic-book version of the story. Extensive study notes, which students will find informative, follow the story.

Shakespeare. *A Midsummer Night's Dream.* Retold by Bruce Coville. New York: Dial Books, 1996.
This easily read and beautifully illustrated picture book is perfect for young children. Use the pictures while you tell the story.

Shakespeare. *A Midsummer Night's Dream for Kids.* Retold by Lois Burdett. Buffalo, NY: Firefly Books, 1997.
By a teacher, for teachers. This could be the most creative retelling yet. Complete with drawings and stories by children, Lois Burdett turns Shakespeare's plays into poetry that is accessible to anyone.

Shakespeare. *A Midsummer Night's Dream for Young People.* Shakespeare for Young People Series, ed. Diane Davidson, bk. 1. Fair Oaks, CA: Swan Books, 1986.
Here is the abridged version of the play, written as a play, complete with set and costume ideas. It is perfect for manageable performances of favorite scenes or the entire story.

Shakespeare. *Shakespeare the Animated Tales: A Midsummer Night's Dream.* Produced and directed by Dave Edwards. 30 min. New York: Random House, 1993. Videocassette.
This shortened cartoon version of the play uses narration to explain the ins and outs of the Bard's play.

Shakespeare for Children. Narrated by Jim Weiss. Benicia, CA: Greathall Productions, 1995. Audiocassette.
This audiotape contains both *A Midsummer Night's Dream* and *The Taming of the Shrew.* They are told in a way that children can understand with bits of the "real thing" sprinkled throughout.

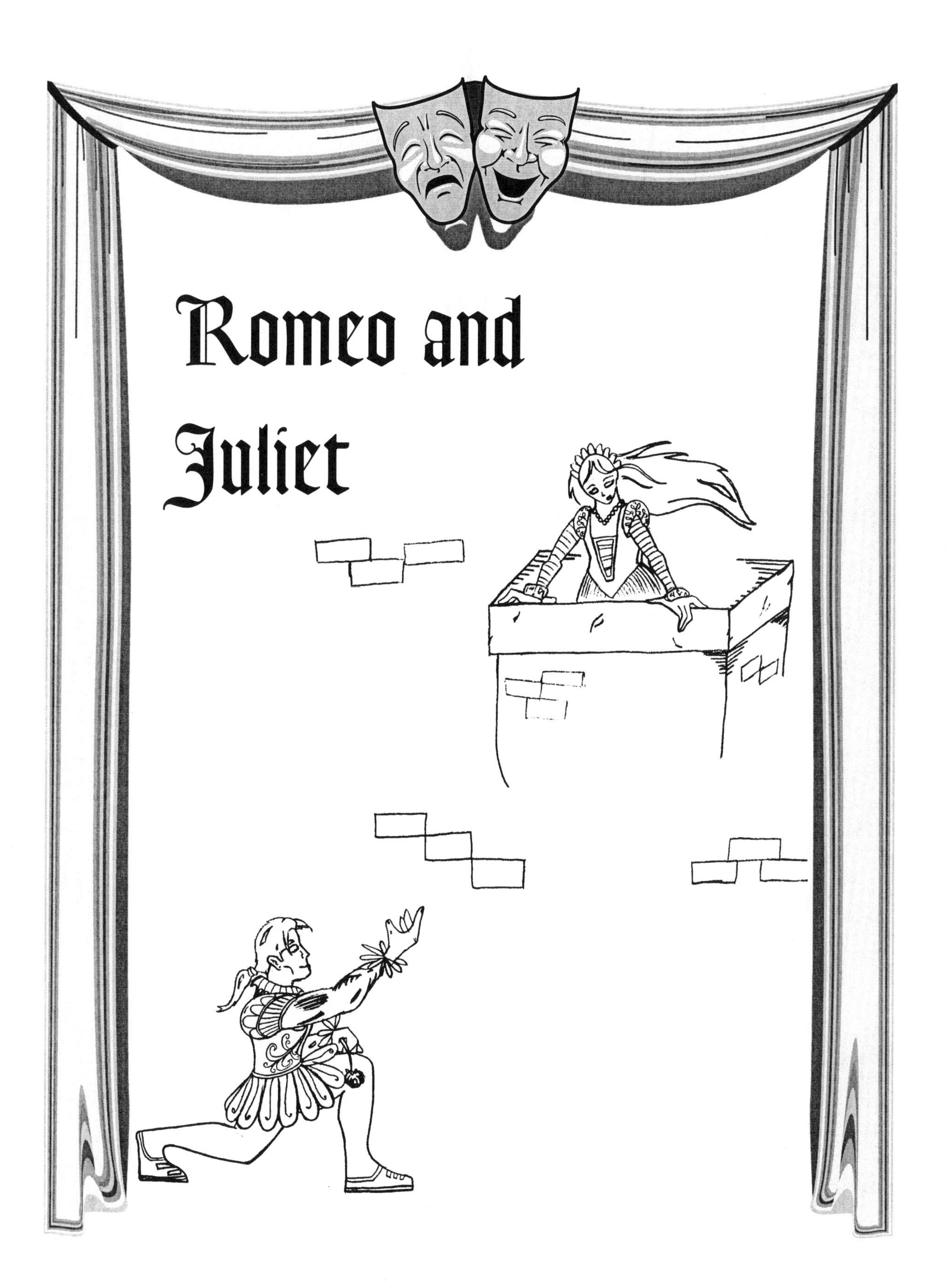
Romeo and
Juliet

What You Should Know About *Romeo and Juliet*

Who's Who

When presenting Shakespeare to young children, we believe it is necessary to simplify the plays by removing nonessential (in our opinion!) characters whose presence would contribute little to the students' understanding of the fundamental story line—but would contribute much to their confusion! If your particular favorite minor character has been axed, please keep in mind that it was for a good cause:

> *Let us from point to point this story know, to make the even truth in pleasure flow*
> *(All's Well That Ends Well, 5.3).*

The Major Characters

Romeo (RO-mee-oh)

> Did my heart love till now? forswear it, sight!
> For I ne'er saw true beauty till this night.
> **(1.5)**

The very name of this leading man is associated with romance, love, and passion. When compared to the rest of his feuding family, Romeo just doesn't fit in. While his family is fighting with swords, Romeo is serving up sonnets. He is the handsome, mild Montague. Even when he crashes the Capulets' party, his reputation as a "lover not a fighter" protects him from any harm. As a lover, however, Romeo is easily infatuated. First with Rosaline (a character we never meet), then with Juliet. It makes you wonder who would have been next had he lived long enough. However, during the five-day romance Romeo has with Juliet, he matures from a love-struck teen into a passionate young man who is willing to die to be with the woman he loves. Now that's commitment!

Juliet (joo-lee-ET)

> My only love sprung from my only hate!
> Too early seen unknown, and known too late!
> Prodigious birth of love it is to me,
> That I must love a loathed enemy.
>
> **(1.5)**

As the beautiful and young Capulet daughter, Juliet is going through her rebellious teenage years. At only 14, she defies the arranged marriage her father has planned when she falls head over heels for "lover-boy" Romeo (who was not much older). Juliet takes the idea of a "crush" a bit too far: She fakes her death to avoid her arranged marriage and to be with the man (boy) that she loves. Was it really worth it? Was it really love? Or was it merely teenage rebellion taken to the extreme?

The Major Minor Characters

The Capulets (CAP-you-lets) and the Montagues (MON-tuh-gyous)

> My sword, I say! old Montague is come,
> And flourishes his blade in spite of me.
> Thou villain Capulet!—Hold me not, let me go.
>
> **(1.1)**

Like the feuding Hatfields and McCoys, the Capulets and the Montagues have disliked and fought with one another for so long that no one remembers when or why it all started. Juliet's parents, Lord and Lady Capulet, and Romeo's parents, Lord and Lady Montague, are more interested in appearances and tradition than in a relationship with their son and daughter. The Capulets are working very hard to marry off their daughter, and in the process, alienate her. The Montagues are more interested in the feud than in their family, leaving Romeo to his own passionate interests. Only the deaths of their children bring an end to their feud. These four are sorry excuses for parents.

The Nurse

> Peace, I have done. God mark thee to his grace,
> Thou wast the prettiest babe that e'er I nursed.
> And I might live to see thee married once,
> I have my wish.
>
> **(1.3)**

In the midst of inevitable tragedy, Shakespeare provides comic relief in the character of Juliet's nurse, only known to us as the Nurse. She is actually closer and more loving to Juliet than Lady Capulet; however, it was the custom of the times for a servant to raise and care for the children in a wealthy family. The comedy of this character comes through her ability to reminisce endlessly, to involve herself in other people's conversations, and to make much ado about nothing. Her ability to annoy the jealous Lady Capulet is particularly funny.

Friar Laurence (FRY-er LOR-ens)

> Romeo, there dead, was husband to that Juliet,
> And she, there dead, that Romeo's faithful wife . . .
>
> **(5.3)**

Just as Juliet has the Nurse as her confidant, Romeo has Friar Laurence. Sympathetic to the lovers' situation and interested in bringing an end to the Capulet/Montague feud, Friar Laurence marries them secretly and devises the "fake death plan" for Juliet. This plan turns the romantic comedy into a tragedy. His intentions may have been noble at the time, but his lengthy confession at the end of the play shows just how senseless this tragedy really is. In this case, the means certainly did not justify the ends.

Mercutio (mer-KYOO-she-oh)

> If love be rough with you, be rough with love.
>
> **(1.4)**

As Romeo's friend, Mercutio tries to cheer his lovesick companion as they make their way to gate-crash the Capulet party. He is hoping that Romeo's eye will catch some new beauty. He is the type of friend who can't stand to see those around him depressed and gloomy. Mercutio is full of seemingly endless advice for the lovelorn. He uses many words to say very little. No doubt he would have had his own talk show had he survived. Ironically, it is Mercutio's death, rather than his advice, that finally motivates Romeo to act. However, Romeo's actions get him banished from the city. Sounds like a good topic for a talk show, doesn't it?

Tybalt (TI-balt)

> What, drawn, and talk of peace? I hate the word,
> As I hate hell, all Montagues, and thee:
> Have at thee, coward!
>
> **(1.1)**

Tybalt is Juliet's cousin, but that is where the similarity between the two characters ends. This belligerent hothead is always looking for a fight. He takes the family feud to heart and feels nothing but hatred for the Montagues. It is his hatred that leads him to kill Mercutio and to be killed by Romeo in turn. In this case, he who lives by the sword does indeed die by the sword.

The Minor Minor Characters

Paris

> O, I am slain! If thou be merciful,
> Open thy tomb, lay me with Juliet.
>
> **(5.3)**

From the beginning of the play to its terrible end, Paris thinks he is to be Juliet's rightful husband. Their marriage is arranged by Lord and Lady Capulet. When the wedding draws near, Friar Laurence gives Juliet the "fake death" potion. Because of Juliet's fake death, Paris confronts Romeo and is killed. What's worse than these events is that Paris doesn't have a clue about the relationship between Romeo and Juliet. He believes that Juliet is his all along. How sad!

The Capulet Servants

> Fear me not.
> No, marry, I fear thee!
> Let us take the law of our sides, let them begin.
> I will frown as I pass by, and let them take it as
> they list.
>
> **(1.1)**

The additional comic relief needed to survive this tragedy is provided by the Capulet servants. Samson and Gregory open the play by debating the best way to provoke the Montagues to a fight: "To bite my thumb or not to bite my thumb, that is the question." They are more concerned about who starts the fight than about their own well-being during the fight. Another servant, Peter, is given the dubious job of inviting people to the Capulet party; however, because he is illiterate, he cannot read any of the names. This sets up the opportunity for Romeo to invite himself and his friends to the party.

Escalus (ES-col-us), Prince of Verona

> Go hence to have more talk of these sad things;
> Some shall be pardoned, and some punished:
> For never was a story of more woe
> Than this of Juliet and her Romeo.
>
> **(5.3)**

Representing "the law," the prince spends most of his time cleaning up after the feuding Capulets and Montagues. He issues warnings and threats, but we never see him follow through on any of them. Unable to prevent the inevitable tragedy, the prince is portrayed as a powerless investigator shaking his head at the waste of young life.

What's What

A merrier hour was never wasted there.
(*A Midsummer Night's Dream*, 2.1)

Background Information

The following is not essential to the understanding of the play, so feel free to skip to The Story—but the background information on *Romeo and Juliet* is very interesting and you will be able to impress your students and colleagues if you have these little-known anecdotes at your fingertips!

Romeo and Juliet may be one of Shakespeare's most famous plays; however, as with all the plays he wrote, it is based on a familiar story or history of the times. Written around 1593, and first performed in 1594, the play is almost entirely based on an English narrative poem by Arthur Brooke called *The Tragicall History of Romeus and Juliet* (1562). Brooke's poem, in turn, it is said, was taken from Italian stories as far back as 1530. Even the two feuding families are thought to have actually existed at some time in Italian history. This borrowing of ideas to present old stories in new ways was popular with Elizabethan audiences.

Unlike today, when we only appreciate novel forms of entertainment in which we can't predict the endings, and with situations and characters that allow us to escape from the confines of our daily lives, audiences over 400 years ago found comfort in the familiar. Shakespeare took the familiar and put a new twist on it. By developing characters that were barely mentioned in Brooke's poem and by shortening the entire romance to a mere five days, Shakespeare was able to bring new drama and passion to an old story.

Shakespeare's comfort, as well as that of his audience, with this familiar story is made obvious by the opening lines of the play where the entire plot is given away:

Two households, both alike in dignity,
In fair Verona (where we lay our scene),
From ancient grudge break to new mutiny,
Where civil blood makes civil hands unclean.
From forth the fatal loins of these two foes
A pair of star-crossed lovers take their life;
Whose misadventured piteous overthrows
Doth with their death bury their parents' strife.
The fearful passage of their death-marked love,
And the continuance of their parents' rage,
Which but their children's end nought could remove,
Is now the two hours' traffic of our stage;
The which if you with patient ears attend,
What here shall miss, our toil shall strive to mend.
(Prologue)

Nearly every time one of Shakespeare's plays is performed, new twists are put on old stories in the spirit of the Bard himself; however, probably one of the most intriguing twists put on *Romeo and Juliet* came in 1956 when Jerome Robbins reinterpreted Shakespeare's play into the musical *West Side Story*. By turning the Capulet/Montague feud into a gang fight between the Jets and the Sharks, Robbins successfully made Shakespeare's 400-year-old play accessible to inner-city America.

At the same time that Shakespeare was writing and performing *Romeo and Juliet,* its comic counterpart was also in the works. *A Midsummer Night's Dream* shares the themes of forbidden love, angry parents, and teenage rebellion. Even more curious is the play within the play of *A Midsummer Night's Dream,* in which the comedic mechanicals (workers) led by Nick Bottom make their way into the woods outside Athens to practice the play *Pyramus and Thisbe*. It is thought that this play within a play intentionally pokes fun at the ludicrous lengths to which Romeo and Juliet go to "be together." Leave it to Shakespeare to weave three plays into one.

Leave it to Shakespeare also to play with words, and our modern-day understanding of them. Sexual innuendo and double meanings are at an all-time high in *Romeo and Juliet*. By today's standards, this play may receive a rating of PG-13. The character of Mercutio in particular spends much of his dialogue making sexual references. Although many of the references hold double meanings, and you may need a translator to understand the sexual meaning, it is there. Better to be forewarned than forearmed.

Probably the most famous and most familiar line Shakespeare ever wrote is also the most misinterpreted:

> O Romeo, Romeo, wherefore art thou Romeo?
> **(2.2)**

Upon hearing this line, you may have a picture of the young Juliet standing on her balcony calling for her lover, Romeo: "Where are you Romeo?" Even though Romeo was perched in the tree just outside of the balcony, he did not respond. Why? This is the love of his life calling out his name. What was he waiting for? In fact, Juliet is not asking, "Where are you Romeo? but "Why are you Romeo?" She is not calling out her lover's name; she is cursing it. Juliet is cursing because the man she loves shares the name of her family's worst enemy. She, in essence, is just talking to herself, wishing Romeo were someone else. Once again the power of Shakespeare's words is evident.

What's Happening

The Story

As described in the introductory section, introducing Shakespeare to children follows the hook, line, and sinker approach to teaching!

Activities and games for presenting the hook (a tantalizing mention of a great story waiting to be told), and the line (the introduction of the characters), can be found in the introduction and should be presented to the students before continuing the story.

While preparing to share the story of *Romeo and Juliet* with your students, you will be confronted by several choices. The most important choice is, "What will I say?" We have seen several excellent read-aloud versions of this play, and they are outlined in the resources section of this book; however, we have found that "telling" rather than "reading" the story to our students draws them deeper into the experience. What follows is our version of *Romeo and Juliet.* It is what we say when we "tell" the story to our students. We have sprinkled popular lines from the actual play throughout the story. These verses correspond with the reproducible verses in the section of this book called Will's Words. You may wish to offer the verses for memorizing and reciting to your class as you tell the story. Even better, you may want to have your students perform short scenes from the story as you tell it. We find that, by placing Shakespeare's words and actions into the mouths and bodies of the children, they understand and appreciate the play more completely. As your students settle before you in anticipation of the story of two star-crossed lovers, your challenge will be to make the play relevant to their young lives while keeping the story line intact. To do this, we have provided periodic pauses to give your class an opportunity to talk about the critical issues in the play and how they relate to their lives.

Let's Talk

We have found great success in increasing our student's connection to the play by providing frequent opportunities to discuss, debate, and just plain talk about it. Let's Talk can be done in a variety of ways:

1. Student-led discussion. Intriguing questions can be posed to the whole class; however, instead of you (the teacher) selecting the speaker, let the student who is speaking choose the next speaker.

2. Let's not talk. After asking a question to the whole class, give individual students "sticky notes" to write their responses on. After writing, students will place their responses on the chalkboard. As a whole class, group the "sticky notes" in categories and summarize the results.

3. Small group discussion. Following your question, place students in groups of two to four. In their groups, select a leader and a recorder. The leader will choose who speaks, and the recorder will write down what is said. At the end of the discussion, the recorder will report what was said to the rest of the class.

4. Debate You will need a podium (music stand) and a controversial dilemma. After posing the dilemma to the students, allow them to choose sides and move to either side of the podium. Once in place, students will take turns explaining why their point of view is "right." After each side has had a turn to state its position, students are given a chance to change sides. This will go on until there is a strong majority or you run out of time.

Look for the Let's Talk symbols for discussion and debate topics. They are located at relevant points in the story and may be used in two ways:

1. in natural breaks during your telling of the story;

2. after the entire story has been told, as a way of reviewing and solidifying the story in your students' minds.

The pace of the story and the depth of the study, through recitation, discussion, performance, and/or activities, is entirely up to you. Most of all get ready to enjoy this timeless story for yourself. If you do, then you know your students will.

The Sinker

The enthusiastic telling of the story.

Our Version

For information on some of the many excellent read-aloud versions of *Romeo and Juliet*, see the Annotated Bibliography; it is worth shopping around to find the version that suits your style. The following is the version that suits *our* style—our version!

Read it (or, preferably, loosely recite from memory) with gusto and enthusiasm—without inhibition!

Kidspeak and Shakespeak

The following story of *Romeo and Juliet* is written in simple English, Kidspeak, and at certain points in the story actual text from the play is included, Shakespeak! Don't be afraid to introduce young students to Shakespeak. The strangeness of the language is often appealing to children; when they are familiar with the story, they can relate more easily to the difficult language. The following is only one way to retell the story of *Romeo and Juliet*. You should infuse it with your personality and enthusiasm: "Here we go! Get ready to study Shakespeare!! Even though you are such itty-bitty kindies (first, second, and third graders!) Get your brains in gear 'cause here it comes! This is a really cool story all about . . ."

Romeo and Juliet

Have you ever known anyone that you just could not stand? No matter what he or she did it got on your nerves. Whether a brother or sister or a kid on the playground, you just wished that they would go away. Pause here for discussion.

Almost everybody has had those feelings at one time or another, but what if your dislike toward someone was so strong that you felt that way for your whole life? Even worse, what if your parents felt like that, too? And your grandparents? And your great-grandparents? Those are some serious negative feelings that have been around for a long, long time. Just when you think that things couldn't be much worse than that, what if nobody in your whole family could remember why he or she was angry at this person to begin with? Sound silly? Well, 600 years ago in a place called Verona, Italy, two powerful families had disliked each other so much and for so long that no one could remember how the fighting began. The families were the Capulets and the Montagues, and each blamed the other for starting the fight, but neither was willing to stop it. This is their story.

Discuss what could have happened that would have caused two families to fight for so long.

The feud between the Capulet and the Montague families has been going on longer than anyone can remember. Twice already this year fights have broken out in the streets of Verona involving members of the two feuding families. Attempting to keep peace in the city, the prince has repeatedly threatened both families to stop fighting in the streets, but to no avail. On this particular day, the sun's heat raises hatred in the Capulets and Montagues.

Two Capulet servants, Samson and Gregory, are walking down one side of the street while a group of Montagues led by Benvolio walks down the other side. There is not enough room on the entire street for the tension that is building, and after exchanging insults, the two sides draw swords.

Capulets: I will bite my thumb at them, which is disgrace to them if they bear it.

Montagues: Do you bite your thumb at us, sir?

Capulets: I do bite my thumb, sir.

Montagues: Do you bite your thumb at us, sir?

Capulets: No, sir, I do not bite my thumb at you, sir, but I bite my thumb, sir.

Montagues: Do you quarrel, sir?

Capulets: Quarrel, sir? No, sir.

Discuss the saying "Sticks and stones will break my bones, but words will never hurt me." Debate what hurts more, insult or injury.

Being able to smell a fight with a Montague from miles away, bloodthirsty Tybalt enters into the fray. Hoping to take down a few of his worst enemies, Tybalt flashes his sword and comes against Benvolio, who is trying to avoid a public confrontation: "**Put up your swords, you know not what you do**." Wanting nothing to do with peace, Tybalt attacks Benvolio, shouting, "**Peace? I hate the word, as I hate hell, all Montagues, and thee**." Obviously there is no compromising with this guy. As the fight escalates and the townspeople run for cover, the prince enters the street to bring a stop to the fighting. At the end of his rope, and sick of seeing these two families fighting, the prince announces, "**If ever you disturb our streets again, your lives shall pay the forfeit of the peace**." Something tells me that it won't be quite that simple.

After the fight breaks up, a worried Lady Montague finds Benvolio to ask if her son, Romeo, was involved. She tells Benvolio that Romeo just hasn't been himself lately, and she hopes that Benvolio can help turn Romeo's frown upside down. When he finally catches up with Romeo, Benvolio soon discovers that it is not the feud but unrequited love that has brought on Romeo's depression. Romeo laments, "**O me! What fray was here? Yet tell me not, for I have heard it all: Here's much to do with hate, but more with love: Why then, O brawling love, O loving hate, O anything of nothing first create!**" It turns out that Romeo is in love with the very beautiful Rosaline. The only problem is that she could not care less for him. Poor Romeo.

Discuss "love" and whether it is possible to really love somebody (or something) if that person or thing does not love you back. Debate whether or not Romeo is really "in love."

At the same time that Benvolio is trying to cheer up Romeo, Lord Capulet is meeting with a wealthy bachelor named Paris, who is interested in marrying Lord Capulet's daughter, Juliet. Although Juliet is only 14, Paris seems to think she would make a wonderful wife and mother. Lord Capulet, wanting his daughter to marry for love (what a concept!), proposes an alternative to Paris: "**This night I hold an old accustomed feast, whereto I have invited many a guest, such as I love, and you among the store one more, most welcome, makes my number more**." Lord Capulet hopes that, by holding a party at his mansion, Paris will be able to meet Juliet and sweep her off her feet. In a rush to get the party organized, Lord Capulet thrusts the invitations into the hands of his nearest servant, Peter, for speedy delivery. Unfortunately, had Lord Capulet taken a moment to realize that the servant he had appointed as mailman could neither read nor write, his party would have been a much greater success: "**I am sent to find those persons whose names are here writ, and can never find what names the writing person hath here writ**." Peter is beside himself with worry as to how he will deliver Lord Capulet's party invitations. Just at that moment, who should be walking down the street but Benvolio and Romeo. Still discussing Romeo's misguided love life, Peter interrupts and begs for their assistance in reading the invitations. In gratitude, Peter extends an invitation to the Capulet party, saying, "**If you be not of the house of Montagues, I pray come and crush a cup of wine**." Seeing that Rosaline would be at the party, Benvolio urges Romeo to crash the Capulet celebration in disguise. Who knows, he might even fall in love with someone else.

Little did Romeo know, that "someone else" was upstairs in the Capulet mansion about to receive news of her upcoming wedding. As Lady Capulet enters her daughter Juliet's room, her conversation is constantly challenged and interrupted by Juliet's overly talkative nurse. Filled with uncontrollable joy over Juliet's possible engagement to the very eligible Paris, her nurse says, "**Thou wast the prettiest babe that e'er I nursed. And I might live to see thee married once, I have my wish**." In those days it was the custom to have a child born into a wealthy family be raised almost entirely by a nurse; therefore, Juliet's nurse was more like a mother to her than Lady Capulet had ever begun to be. This could explain why Lady Capulet had little patience for the nurse's unbridled enthusiasm. As both Lady Capulet and the nurse encourage Juliet at least to meet Paris and consider his proposal, Juliet says, "**It is an honour that I dream not of**"; but she decides to attend the party and see what happens.

Discuss the role of servants in the Capulet mansion. Do they allow the Capulet family to avoid responsibility for themselves? Could that be why the feud keeps going? Debate the importance of doing things for yourself as opposed to having others do things for you.

As night falls on the city of Verona, a group of masked young men make their way through the streets toward the Capulet party. Benvolio and the reluctant Romeo are joined by their wild and playful friend, Mercutio. Tired of listening to Romeo's moping, Mercutio tries to cheer him up by teasing Romeo about his depressing dreams: "**True, I talk of dreams, which are the children of an idle brain, begot of nothing but vain fantasy, which is as thin of substance as the air, and more inconsistent**

than the wind." It seems that not only is Romeo spending every waking hour lamenting his love life, but he is also depressed as he dreams. Seeing this, Mercutio shares a dream of his own that predicts a new love in Romeo's future: "**O then I see Queen Mab hath been with you: She is the fairies' midwife, and she comes in shape no bigger than an agate-stone . . . Over men's noses as they lie asleep . . . And in this state she gallops night by night through lovers' brains, and then they dream of love . . .** " Maybe by some fairy queen's magic Romeo will finally find the love he is so desperately looking for.

Discuss the importance of dreams and the role that they play in students' lives. Debate whether or not dreams can be used to predict the future.

Upon arriving at the Capulet mansion, the masked Montagues join in with the dancing and festivities. All, that is, except Romeo, whose attention is focused elsewhere. No, he is not wallowing in self pity. No, he is not scanning the room for Rosaline. He is captivated by a different beauty. As if by magic (remember Queen Mab), Romeo instantly replaces his love for Rosaline with this new love at first sight. However, he is also being watched. Tybalt spots Romeo from across the ballroom and calls for his sword. He can't believe that a Montague has crashed his uncle's party. Before Tybalt can reach Romeo, he is intercepted by Lord Capulet. Not wanting his party to be spoiled by fighting, and knowing that Romeo has a reputation of being a "lover not a fighter," Lord Capulet orders Tybalt to put his sword away and leave Romeo alone. Had Lord Capulet known that Romeo had just fallen in love with his only daughter, Juliet, he might have felt differently!

Moving across the dance floor, with his eyes and heart locked on Juliet, Romeo's first words get right to the point: "**My lips, two blushing pilgrims, ready stand to smooth that rough touch with a tender kiss.**" He doesn't waste any time, does he? Unlike Rosaline, Juliet responds favorably to Romeo's words. After kissing him twice, she responds, "**You kiss by th' book.**" I guess he did it right. However, before they could even introduce themselves (which you would think would be a prerequisite to kissing), Juliet is called away by her nurse to meet with her mother. Not wanting to lose the love of his life (for the moment anyway), Romeo is determined to find out her name. Juliet is also interested in knowing who kissed her so well. Unfortunately, when they discover that the person each is in love with is also a member of the family each of them hates, Romeo and Juliet are devastated: "**My only love sprung from my only hate! Too early seen unknown, and known too late! Prodigious birth of love it is to me, that I must love a loathed enemy.**"

After leaving the Capulet party, Benvolio, Mercutio, and Romeo make their way home. Not willing just to walk away from the girl that he has just fallen in love with, Romeo leaves his friends and heads back to the Capulet estate. Not surprised by anything their friend might do for love, Benvolio and Mercutio continue home, joking about their crazed friend and saying, "**Go then, for 'tis vain to seek him here that means not to be found.**"

Romeo's love for Juliet is so strong that, after scaling a rock wall in the dark, he climbs a tree—which just happens to be growing outside the balcony of Juliet's bedroom! Perched high on a branch Romeo proclaims his love, "**But soft, what light through yonder window breaks? It is the east, and Juliet is the sun.**" Just as Romeo was getting warmed up, who should appear on the balcony but the object of his affections. Not knowing that Romeo is watching and listening, Juliet wishes out loud that they both came from different families: "**O Romeo, Romeo, wherefore art thou Romeo? Deny thy father and refuse thy name; Or if thou wilt not, be but sworn my love, and I'll no longer be a Capulet. 'Tis but thy name that is my enemy; Thou art thyself, though not a Montague. What's Montague? It is nor hand nor foot, nor arm nor face, nor any other part belonging to a man. O be some other name! What's in a name? That which we call a rose by any other word would smell as sweet**." Juliet expresses her frustration over the only thing keeping her separated from her love: his name. She wishes they could change their names and be together forever. On hearing this, Romeo makes his presence known: "**I take thee at thy word: call me but love, and I'll be new baptized; henceforth I never will be Romeo . . . With love's light wings did I o' reperch these walls, for stony limits cannot hold love out, and what love can do, that dares love attempt: therefore thy kinsmen are no stop to me**." Obviously Romeo (which we will call him until he chooses a new name) is willing to do anything for Juliet. After declaring their love for one another, Juliet tells Romeo that she'll marry him if he can find someone to do the job: "Good night, good night! Parting is such sweet sorrow, that I shall say good night till it be morrow." With stars in his eyes and love in his heart, Romeo goes in search of that someone. Romeo has his work cut out for him. He has to find someone who will perform a wedding in secret. Fortunately, he has friends in high places. Romeo's luck appears to be changing.

Discuss the importance of names. How do names influence what we eat, drink, and wear? Debate the truth of the line, "A rose by any other word would smell as sweet." Would it really?

Before Romeo arrives at the church to see his friend, Friar Laurence, the friar is working in his garden. He grows a wide variety of plants and flowers not just for their beauty but for their usefulness also. The nectar of one of his flowers is so powerful that it mimics death in the body of the person who drinks it: "**Within the infant rind of this weak flower poison hath residence, and medicine power: For this, being smelt, with that part cheers each part, being tasted, stays all senses with the heart**." Little does Romeo know the role that this lovely and dangerous flower will play in his life (or death).

When Romeo arrives, he immediately tells the friar of his newfound love for Juliet, and he asks the friar to marry them. "**Then plainly know, my heart's dear love is set on the fair daughter of rich Capulet; . . . We met, we wooed, and made exchange of vow, I'll tell thee as we pass, but this I pray, that thou consent to marry us today**." Friar Laurence is shocked at the request because just the day before, Romeo had been in love with Rosaline. The friar accuses Romeo of changing his lovers like he changes socks and starts to lecture him on the virtues of mature love and relationships. However, even as he is trying to talk Romeo out of marrying Juliet, Friar Laurence ponders the possibility of their marriage bringing an end to their families' feud. "**For this alliance may so happy prove to turn your households' rancor to pure love**." With this thought in mind, the friar comes up with a surefire plan.

Discuss whether Friar Laurence has Romeo's best interests in mind. Do you think this marriage will really bring an end to the family feud, or will it just make things worse? Debate whether or not the friar's motivation to marry Romeo and Juliet is a good one.

The next morning, Romeo gets word to Juliet's nurse that the friar will marry them secretly at the church that afternoon. To Juliet, the wait for the nurse to return with news from Romeo is agonizing. When the nurse finally shows up, she can't seem to just "spit it out." "**Lord, how my head aches! what a head have I! It beats as it would fall in twenty pieces. My back a' t'other side—ah, my back, my back!**" Finally, she shares the news of the secret wedding. As you might expect, Juliet can't wait. That afternoon, Romeo and Juliet meet Friar Laurence at the church to be married. The actual wedding ceremony, however, is not part of Shakespeare's play.

Following their secret wedding, Juliet returns to the Capulet mansion and Romeo goes into Verona to meet his friends. Before he arrives though, trouble is brewing. Benvolio and Mercutio are being taunted by the vengeful Tybalt. He wants to teach the Montagues a lesson for crashing his uncle's party—even though he was told by Lord Capulet to leave them alone. When Romeo comes on the scene, he does everything in his power to avoid fighting with Tybalt. Now that he is part of the family, Romeo even tries to make friends with Tybalt. Of course, he will have nothing to do with Romeo.

Tybalt: Romeo, the love I bear thee can afford
No better term than this: thou art a villian.

Romeo: Tybalt, the reason that I have to love thee
Doth much excuse the appertaining rage
To such a greeting. Villain am I none;
Therefore farewell, I see thou knowest me not.

Tybalt: Boy, this shall not excuse the injuries
That thou hast done me, therefore turn and draw.

Romeo: I do protest I never injured thee,
But love thee better than thou canst devise,
Till thou shalt know the reason of my love;
And so, good Capulet, which name I tender
As dearly as mine own, be satisfied.

Tybalt, tired of putting off the inevitable, draws his sword, as does Mercutio. Not wanting anyone to get hurt, Romeo tries to break up the fight. As he steps between them, Tybalt's sword slides underneath Romeo's arm and pierces Mercutio's heart. Romeo, seeing his friend dying on the ground, draws his own sword and comes at Tybalt with a vengeance. "**Now, Tybalt, take the 'villain' back again that late thou gavest me, for Mercutio's soul is but a little way above our heads, staying for thine to keep him company: Either thou or I, or both, must go with him.**"

Seeing an opportunity to do away with two pests in one day, Tybalt rushes toward Romeo. Romeo's sword finds its way into Tybalt's heart as they wrestle one another to the ground. When the prince finally comes upon the two lifeless bodies, one Montague and one Capulet, he vows that Romeo is to be banished from Verona forever.

Discuss who is at fault for the deaths of Mercutio and Tybalt. Debate whether it is justifiable to kill out of revenge or self-defense.

During the deadly street brawl, Juliet was waiting for Romeo to come for her. She sends her nurse to look for him while she waits impatiently at the mansion. Upon the nurse's return, Juliet learns about her cousin Tybalt's death and Romeo's banishment. Desperate to see her new husband before he leaves Verona, Juliet sends her nurse to find him and bring him to the Capulet mansion.

Discuss the difference between the characters of Tybalt and Romeo. What kind of reputation did they each have in Verona? How did Romeo's good reputation help him to avoid a death sentence by the prince and remain in Juliet's good graces? Debate how important a good reputation is, or if it is possible to change a bad reputation.

After Romeo finally stops running from the violence in Verona, he goes to the church to see Friar Laurence. The friar tells Romeo that he has been banished from the city because of his involvement in Tybalt's death. Romeo feels that he would rather be dead than separated from Juliet (now that's what I call foreshadowing). In the midst of his torment, Juliet's nurse arrives at the church. She explains how Juliet has forgiven him and longs to be with him. "**Here, sir, a ring she bid me give you, sir. Hie you, make haste, for it grows very late**." Hearing this, Friar Laurence devises surefire plan number two to get Romeo and Juliet back together. He suggests that Romeo remain in a town outside of Verona until the friar can tell everyone about their secret wedding. Only then would Romeo be able to return. However, before Romeo gets a chance to see Juliet one final time, another man is making his way to the Capulet mansion to pay her a visit.

The visitor is none other than Paris. He has come to plan his wedding to Juliet. Thinking that the news of her upcoming wedding would cheer her, Juliet's parents set the date for later that week. However, before her parents can come upstairs to tell Juliet, Romeo sneaks into Juliet's room through her window to be with her one last time. After telling her of the friar's plan to reunite them, Romeo flees to safety. He no sooner leaves when Lady Capulet knocks on Juliet's door. Timing is everything in this story.

Upon entering, Lady Capulet finds Juliet in tears. She thinks the tears are for Tybalt, but we know why she is really crying. Thinking that the upcoming wedding would cheer Juliet, Lady Capulet tells her the news. Juliet becomes enraged and says she refuses to marry a man that she doesn't even know or love. Of course, she neglects to inform her mother that she is already married. Hearing the commotion, Lord Capulet comes into Juliet's room, and he is shocked that his daughter is so ungrateful. With words filled with rage, Lord Capulet informs Juliet that she is getting married to Paris, and that's that. "**Thank me no thankings, nor proud me no prouds, but fettle your fine joints 'gainst Thursday next, to go with Paris to Saint Peter's Church, or I will drag thee on a hurdle thither. Out, you green-sickness carrion! Out, you baggage!**" Juliet begs him to change his mind, the nurse begs him to change his mind, even Lady Capulet begs him to change his mind, but it is no use. Either Juliet will marry Paris, or she will no longer be Lord Capulet's daughter. Devastated and completely alone, just to get her parents off her back, Juliet tells them she will consider marrying Paris, and she leaves for the church to see Friar Laurence. He seems to have a plan for everything; maybe he could help her, too.

Discuss why you think Lord Capulet has had this sudden change of heart. He began the story by insisting that Juliet marry only for love, and now he is forcing her to marry Paris, whether she wants to or not.

As Juliet reaches the church, Friar Laurence is already meeting with Paris making plans for the wedding. She pretends that all is well as she waits for Paris to leave. The plan that the friar designs to bring Romeo and Juliet back together is his most dangerous yet. "**Take thou this vial, being then in bed, and this distilling liquor drink thou off, when presently through all they veins shall run a cold and drowsy humour; for no pulse shall keep his native progress . . . Thou shalt continue two and forty hours, and then awake as from a pleasant sleep**." He combines several plant leaves with a purple flower to create a death potion. However, the potion only mimics death for a short time. After Juliet's body is laid in the family tomb, the friar will send for Romeo, and after the death potion wears off the two will be able to run away and be together forever. I sure hope this plan works better than the others have.

Juliet doesn't want anything to get in the way of her plan to be with Romeo, so she pretends to go along with her family's plan for her to marry Paris. The night before the wedding, while her family prepares for the celebration, Juliet takes the death potion and prays that when her eyes open, she will see her true love, Romeo. "**Romeo, Romeo, Romeo! Here's drink—I drink to thee**."

On the day of Juliet's marriage to Paris, the nurse discovers Juliet's lifeless body and the nurse's screams of horror fill the house. Lord and lady Capulet are shocked to find their daughter dead. When Friar Laurence arrives to perform the wedding ceremony, he proceeds to perform a funeral instead. Secretly he is pleased with the progress of his plan because earlier he sent a message to Romeo to meet Juliet at the tomb where she will be placed.

Unfortunately, the message Romeo receives first is the news of Juliet's death—not the friar's clever plan. After hearing of his true love's death, Romeo makes plans to join Juliet's body, vowing that he could never live without her. On his way to Verona, Romeo purchases a bottle of poison.

When Friar Laurence discovers that his messenger has not delivered his message, and realizing that Juliet is about to awaken alone in a tomb, he rushes toward the graveyard to rescue her. At the same time, Paris, the grieving fiancé, is standing outside Juliet's tomb when Romeo approaches. Prepared to defend Juliet's tomb from the villainous Montague who had earlier killed Tybalt, Paris draws his sword. In the dark, foggy graveyard, he challenges Romeo to a duel. In the end, only Romeo is left standing.

After prying open the tomb and seeing his beloved Juliet lying lifelessly inside, Romeo makes good on his promise to always be with her. He drinks the poison as he declares his undying love for her. "**Eyes look your last! Arms, take your last embrace! and, lips, O you the doors of breath, seal with a righteous kiss a dateless bargain to engrossing Death! . . . Thy drugs are quick. Thus with a kiss I die**." Just as life slips from Romeo's body, Juliet begins to awaken. I told you, timing is everything in this story.

News of Romeo's return and the duel in the graveyard spreads like wildfire through the streets of Verona and to the houses of the Montagues, the Capulets, and the prince. The news sends both families racing to the graveyard. Friar Laurence is the first to reach Juliet's tomb. He is hoping to reach Juliet before she awakens. Instead, he finds Romeo's dead body lying next to the awakening Juliet. When she sees the friar, she asks about Romeo, but no sooner does she get the words out when she sees her lover's dead body next to her.

In the distance Friar Laurence can hear voices nearing the graveyard. He desperately wants to get Juliet out of there and into the protective walls of the church. However, Juliet will not leave Romeo. Since the friar does not want to be caught in the tomb with his failed plan, he runs off into the night. Juliet is left alone. It does not take her long to know what she wants to do. "**O happy dagger, this is thy sheath; there rust, and let me die**." She wants to be with Romeo, so she takes his dagger and joins him in death.

Discuss the feelings that your students have surrounding the suicide of Romeo and Juliet. What alternatives did the lovers have? Debate whether Romeo and Juliet really had to die in order to be together.

When the prince, the Montagues, and the Capulets finally arrive on the tragic scene, they can't believe how all these young people could have died. It is Friar Laurence's voice that breaks the silence. He explains everything from the secret marriage to Juliet's faked death. He tells how Romeo and Juliet were happier to die together than to live apart. In the midst of all the death and sorrow, the two families that had hated one another for so long are able to come together to comfort each other, ending their feud and finally finding peace. "**A glooming peace this morning with it brings, the sun for sorrow will not show his head. Go hence to have more talk of these sad things; Some shall be pardoned, and some punished: For never was a story of more woe than this of Juliet and her Romeo**."

Discuss who your students think the prince will pardon and who he will punish. Debate the consequences that Friar Laurence should face.

Will's Words—Selections for Recitation

The Prologue Chorus

Drawn by Rachel Weintraub

Two households, both alike in dignity,
In fair Verona, where we lay our scene,
From ancient grudge break to new mutiny,
Where civil blood makes civil hands unclean.
From forth the fatal loins of these two foes
A pair of star-cross'd lovers take their life;
Whose misadventured piteous overthrows
Doth with their death bury their parents'
strife.

(Prologue)

Say What??

ancient grudge break to new mutiny—these two families have been fighting for a long time, and they still fight today
star-cross'd lovers—two people with really bad luck
misadventured piteous overthrows . . . bury their parents' strife—after all the bad things happen, the two families finally quit fighting

Kidspeak

These eight lines actually tell the whole story, in a nutshell. There are two families who live in Verona, Italy, and hate each other. They have been fighting forever. The families each have a child. After falling in love, and running into some really bad luck, their two children kill themselves. After the death of their children, the two families quit fighting.

NAME:____

Capulet and Montague Servants

Capulets: I will bite my thumb at them, which is disgrace to them if they bear it.

Montagues: Do you bite your thumb at us, sir?

Capulets: I do bite my thumb, sir.

Montagues: Do you bite your thumb at us, sir?

Capulets: (to themselves): Is the law on our side if I say ay? No.

Capulets: No, sir, I do not bite my thumb at you, sir, but I bite my thumb, sir.

Capulets: Do you quarrel, sir?

Montagues: Quarrel, sir? No, sir.

(Act 1, Scene 1)

Say What??

Capulet—pronounced CAP-you-let
Montague—pronounced MON-tuh-gyou
bite my thumb—during Elizabethan times, when this play was written, biting your thumb at someone was considered very rude and insulting

Kidspeak

The Capulet servants are trying to start a fight with the Montague servants, but they do not want to be blamed for starting it. They check with each other about the law's being on their side, and insult the Montagues without admitting that they are doing anything.

NAME:______________________________

Tybalt and Benvolio

Drawn by Jenn Rothbarth

Benvolio: Part, fools! Put up your swords, you know not what you do.

Tybalt: What, art thou drawn among these heartless hinds?
Turn thee, Benvolio, look upon thy death.

Benvolio: I do but keep the peace: put up thy sword,
Or manage it to part these men with me.

Tybalt: What, drawn, and talk of peace? I hate the word,
As I hate hell, all Montagues, and thee:
Have at thee, coward!

(Act 1, Scene 1)

Say What??

Tybalt—pronounced TI-balt
Benvolio—pronounced ben-VO-lee-oh
drawn—having your sword out and ready to fight
heartless hinds—weak servants
have at thee—come fight me

Kidspeak

Benvolio, a Montague, draws his sword to stop the fighting between the servants. When Tybalt, a Capulet, comes and sees Benvolio's sword out he wants to fight, not talk about peace.

NAME:____________________________________

Romeo (to himself)

Tybalt is fighting with Mercutio

Drawn by Jenn Rothbarth

O me! What fray was here?
Yet tell me not, for I have heard it all.
Here's much to do with hate, but more with love.
Why then, O brawling love! O loving hate!
O anything of nothing first create!

(Act 1, Scene 1)

Say What??

Romeo—pronounced RO-mee-oh
fray—fighting

Kidspeak

Romeo is witnessing his family's latest fight, and he is talking about the two opposing feelings of "love" and "hate." He is confused by how the two opposite feelings can exist together. Which comes first, love or hate (the chicken or the egg)?

NAME:____

Peter (to himself)

Drawn by Brittany Badesch

Find them out whose names are written here! It is written that the shoemaker should meddle with his yard and the tailor with his last, the fisher with his pencil and the painter with his nets; but I am sent to find those persons whose names are here writ, and can never find what names the writing person hath here writ. I must to the learned. In good time!

(Act 1, Scene 2)

Say What??

meddle—use
yard—a tailor's measuring stick
last—a shoe holder
learned—someone who can read

Kidspeak

Peter has just been given a list of names to invite to Lord Capulet's party, but he can't read. He compares the job he has been given to that of other workers (shoemaker, tailor, fisher, painter) using tools that they do not understand. Peter is looking for someone to help him read the list.

NAME:______________________________________

Mercutio (to Romeo)

O then I see Queen Mab hath been with you:
She is the fairies' midwife, and she comes
In shape no bigger than an agate-stone
On the forefinger of an alderman,
Drawn with a team of little atomi
Over men's noses as they lie asleep.
Her chariot is an empty hazel-nut,
Made by the joiner squirrel or old grub,
Time out a'mind the fairies' coachmakers:
Her wagon spokes made of long spinners' legs,
The cover of the wings of grasshoppers,
Her traces of the smallest spider web,
Her collars of the moonshine's wat'ry beams,
Her whip of cricket's bone, the lash of film,
Her wagoner a small grey-coated gnat,
Not half so big as a round little worm
Pricked from the lazy finger of a maid.
And in this state she gallops night by night
Through lovers' brains, and then they dream
of love, . . .

(Act 1, Scene 4)

Say What??

Mercutio—pronounced mer-KYOO-she-oh
Romeo—pronounced RO-mee-oh
midwife—assistant
agate-stone—pebble
alderman—judge
atomi—a small particle
long spinners—spiders
wagoner—driver

Kidspeak

Mercutio is sharing a dream that he had about a fairy named Queen Mab. He describes her in great detail although she is very small. Mercutio explains that Queen Mab is responsible for changing lovers hearts at night, and he tells Romeo about her just before Romeo falls in love with Juliet. It must have been Queen Mab that made it all happen.

NAME:____________________________________

Romeo and Juliet

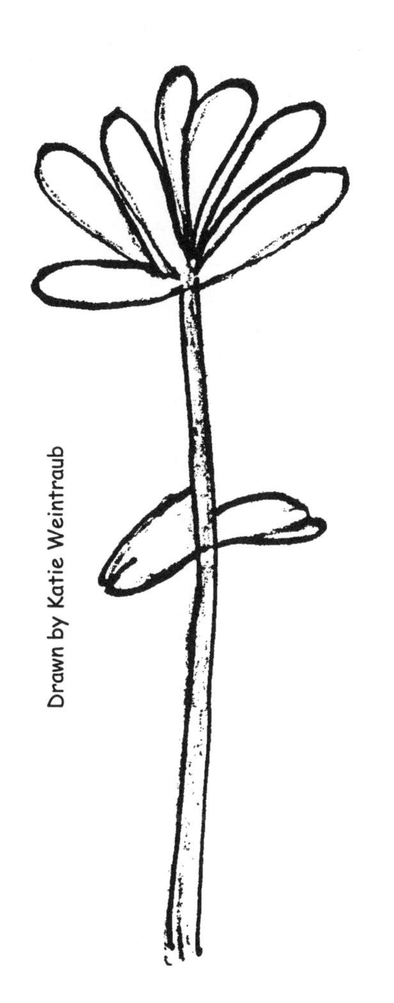

Romeo: If I profane with my unworthiest hand
This holy shrine, the gentle sin is this,
My lips, two blushing pilgrims, ready stand
To smooth that rough touch with a tender kiss.

Juliet: Good pilgrim, you do wrong your hand too much,
Which mannerly devotion shows in this,
For saints have hands that pilgrims' hands do touch,
And palm to palm is holy palmers' kiss.

Romeo: Have not saints lips, and holy palmers too?

Juliet: Ay, pilgrim, lips that they must use in prayer.

Romeo: O then, dear saint, let lips do what hands do:
They pray, grant thou, lest faith turn to despair.

(Act 1, Scene 5)

Say What??

Romeo—pronounced RO-mee-oh
profane—insult
Juliet—pronounced joo-lee-ET
pilgrims—religious people
palm—hand
palmers—pilgrims

Kidspeak

This is Romeo and Juliet's first meeting, and Romeo is trying to make a good first impression. All the talk of shrines, pilgrims, saints, faith, and praying show that Romeo is treating Juliet as a goddess. He is so deeply in love with her that he is almost worshipping her. All he is really looking for though is a kiss.

NAME:____

Juliet to (herself)

Tybalt is fighting with Mercutio

Drawn by Jenn Rothbarth

My only love sprung from my only hate!
Too early seen unknown, and known too late!
Prodigious birth of love it is to me,
That I must love a loathed enemy.

(Act 1, Scene 5)

Say What??

Juliet—pronounced joo-lee-ET
prodigious—monstrous, terrible
loathed—hated, detested

Kidspeak

After finding out that the man she just kissed is a Montague, Juliet is furious. She can't believe that she didn't find out who he was before she fell in love with him. Now it is too late. She loves her family's enemy.

NAME:_______________________________________

Romeo (to himself outside Juliet's balcony)

Drawn by Jenn Rothbarth

But soft, what light through yonder
window breaks?
It is the east, and Juliet is the sun.
Arise, fair sun, and kill the envious moon,
Who is already sick and pale with grief
That thou, her maid, art far more fair than
she.

(Act 2, Scene 2)

Say What??

Romeo—pronounced RO-mee-oh
light through yonder window breaks—look who is coming to the window
Juliet is the sun—she is the center of the universe
envious—jealous
fair—beautiful

Kidspeak

After seeing Juliet at the window, Romeo declares her to be at the center of his universe and the most beautiful thing in it. She is so beautiful, in fact, that the moon is jealous.

NAME:____

Juliet (to herself)

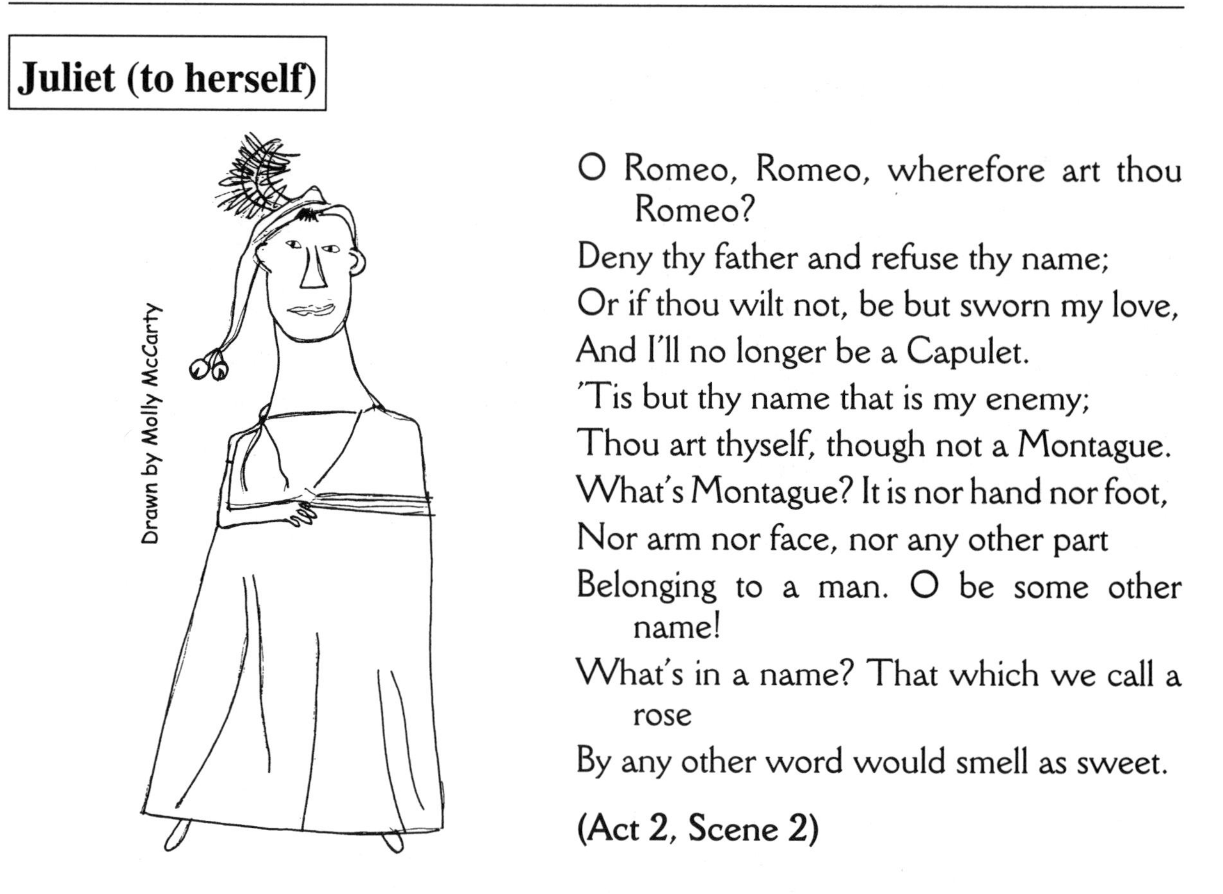

O Romeo, Romeo, wherefore art thou
Romeo?
Deny thy father and refuse thy name;
Or if thou wilt not, be but sworn my love,
And I'll no longer be a Capulet.
'Tis but thy name that is my enemy;
Thou art thyself, though not a Montague.
What's Montague? It is nor hand nor foot,
Nor arm nor face, nor any other part
Belonging to a man. O be some other
name!
What's in a name? That which we call a
rose
By any other word would smell as sweet.

(Act 2, Scene 2)

Say What??

Juliet—pronounced joo-lee-ET
Romeo—pronounced RO-mee-oh
wherefore art thou Romeo?—why are you called Romeo?

Kidspeak

Juliet is talking to herself on her balcony. She is asking why Romeo's name should be Montague. She wishes that they could change their names because names aren't that important anyway. If she changed the name *rose* to *daisy* it would still smell like a rose.

NAME:______________________________________

Friar Laurence (to himself)

Within the infant rind of this weak flower
Poison hath residence, and medicine power:
For this, being smelt, with that part cheers
each part,
Being tasted, stays all senses with the heart.
Two such opposed kings encamp them still
In man as well as herbs, grace and rude
will;
And where the worser is predominant,
Full soon the canker death eats up that
plant.

(Act 2, Scene 3)

Say What??

Friar Laurence—pronounced FRY-er LOR-ens
stays all senses—kills
opposed kings—poison versus medicine, evil versus good
grace and rude will—good and evil

Kidspeak

Friar Laurence is working in his garden at the church tending to his flowers and herbs. He is talking to himself about a flower that smells sweet and tastes deadly. It is this flower that will eventually be used to fake Juliet's death.

NAME:____________________________________

Romeo (to Friar Laurence)

Then plainly know, my heart's dear love is set
On the fair daughter of rich Capulet;
As mine on hers, so hers is set on mine,
And all combined, save what thou must combine
By holy marriage. When and where and how
We met, we wooed, and made exchange of vow,
I'll tell thee as we pass, but this I pray,
That thou consent to marry us today.

(Act 2, Scene 3)

Say What??

Romeo—pronounced RO-mee-oh
Friar Laurence—pronounced FRY-er LOR-ens
save—except for
wooed—loved
made exchange of vow—promised to marry one another

Kidspeak

Romeo is at the church asking Friar Laurence to marry him and Juliet. Romeo explains that they love each other, and they have already promised to get married. All that is left is for the friar to perform the ceremony.

NAME:______________________________________

Tybalt and Romeo

Tybalt: Romeo, the love I bear thee can afford
No better term than this: thou art a villain.

Romeo: Tybalt, the reason that I have to love thee
Doth much excuse the appertaining rage
To such a greeting. Villain am I none;
Therefore farewell, I see thou knowest me not.

Tybalt: Boy, this shall not excuse the injuries
That thou hast done me, therefore turn and draw.

Romeo: I do protest I never injured thee,
But love thee better than thou canst devise,
Till thou shalt know the reason of my love;
And so, good Capulet, which name I tender
As dearly as mine own, be satisfied.

(Act 3, Scene 1)

Say What??

Tybalt—pronounced TI-balt
Romeo—pronounced RO-mee-oh
the love I bear thee—the love I feel for you
appertaining—appropriate
turn and draw—get your sword out and fight
than thou canst devise—than you can imagine
name I tender—I like your name

Kidspeak

Tybalt wants to fight Romeo because he crashed his uncle's party. Romeo does not want to fight because he just married Tybalt's cousin, Juliet. In fact, Romeo is trying to make friends with Tybalt.

NAME:____

Lord Capulet (to Juliet)

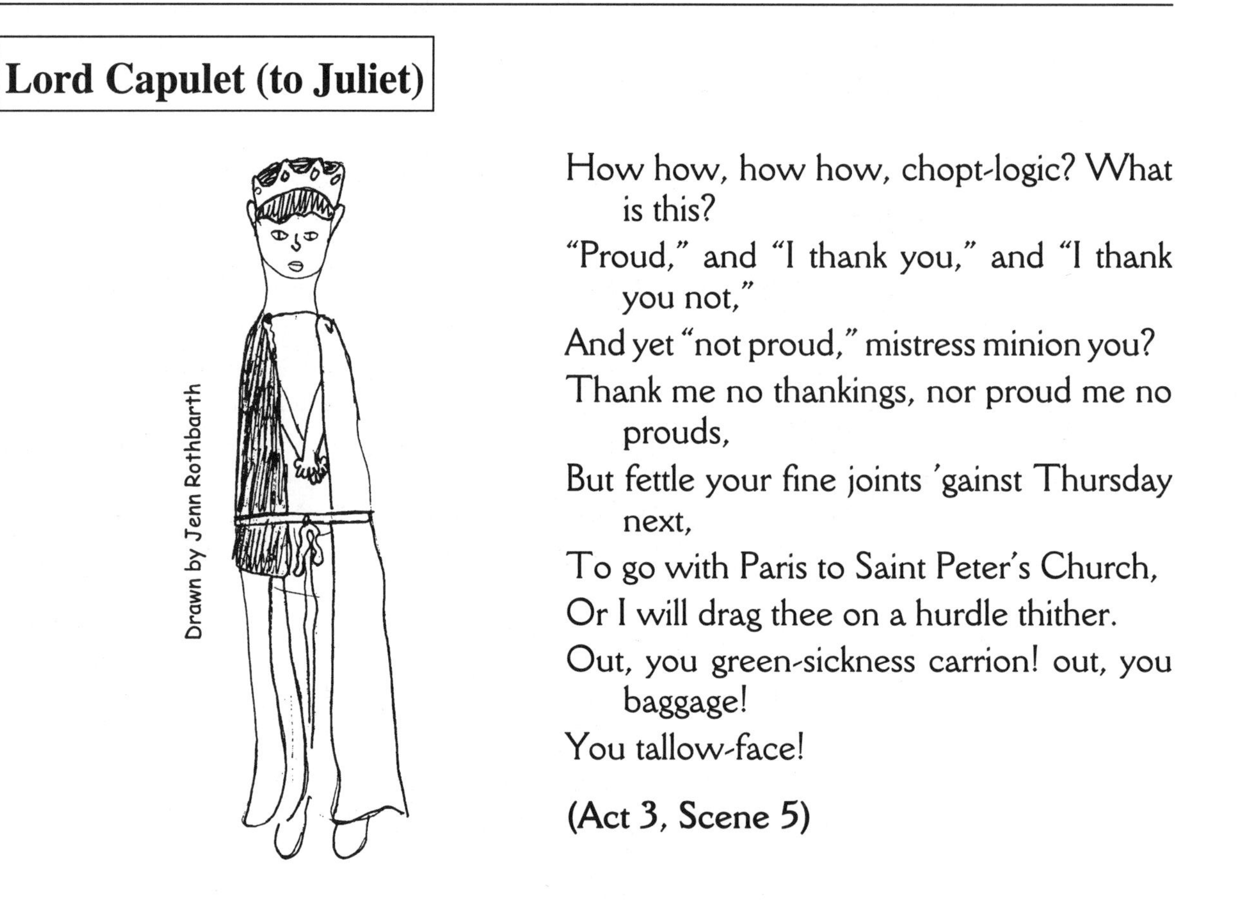

How how, how how, chopt-logic? What is this?
"Proud," and "I thank you," and "I thank you not,"
And yet "not proud," mistress minion you?
Thank me no thankings, nor proud me no prouds,
But fettle your fine joints 'gainst Thursday next,
To go with Paris to Saint Peter's Church,
Or I will drag thee on a hurdle thither.
Out, you green-sickness carrion! out, you baggage!
You tallow-face!

(Act 3, Scene 5)

Say What??

Capulet—pronounced CAP-you-let
Juliet—pronounced joo-lee-ET
chopt-logic—riddles
minion—spoiled brat
fettle your fine joints—get ready
hurdle thither—a frame that prisoners were tied to and dragged to their execution
carrion—rotting fish
tallow-face—pale face

Kidspeak

Lord Capulet has just walked into Juliet's bedroom and heard that she refuses to marry Paris. Needless to say, he is not happy about it. He orders Juliet to get to the church to marry Paris or else he will drag her there himself.

NAME:____

Friar Laurence (to Juliet)

Drawn by Jenn Rothbarth

Take thou this vial, being then in bed,
And this distilling liquor drink thou off,
When presently through all thy veins shall run
A cold and drowsy humour; for no pulse
Shall keep his native progress, but surcease;
No warmth, no breath shall testify thou livest;
The roses in thy lips and cheeks shall fade
To wanny ashes, thy eyes' windows fall,
Like Death when he shuts up the day of life;
Each part, deprived of supple government,
Shall stiff and stark and cold appear like death,
And in this borrowed likeness of shrunk death
Thou shalt continue two and forty hours,
And then wake as from a pleasant sleep.

(Act 4, Scene 1)

Say What??

vial—bottle
distilling liquor—potion
humour—liquid
no pulse shall keep his native progress, but surcease—your heart will stop beating
testify—show or tell
wanny ashes—pale
supple government—easy movement
borrowed likeness of shrunk death—state of fake death

Kidspeak

Friar Laurence is explaining to Juliet how his plan to get her back together with Romeo will work. He has made a fake death potion that will make Juliet appear dead for 42 hours.

NAME:____

Escalus, Prince of Verona (to both families)

Drawn by Rachel Weintraub

A glooming peace this morning with it brings,
The sun for sorrow will not show his head.
Go hence to have more talk of these sad things;
Some shall be pardoned, and some punished:
For never was a story of more woe
Than this of Juliet and her Romeo.

(Act 5, Scene 3)

Say What??

Escalus—pronounced ES-col-us
glooming peace—sadness
sun for sorrow wilt not show his head—the sun will not rise
pardoned—forgiven
woe—sadness
Juliet—pronounced joo-lee-ET
Romeo—pronounced RO-mee-oh

Kidspeak

These are the final lines of the play. The prince, again arriving too late, talks of the sadness felt by everyone. He does not want people to forget what happened to Romeo and Juliet.

NAME:____

Lights, Camera, Action

Movie Making

Please don't skip this section!! Movie making with elementary students will not drive you to an early retirement! Putting on a live performance is guaranteed to drive you up the nearest wall in no time flat, but, through the miracle of technology—in the shape of a camcorder—you will help your students experience the excitement of performing—and you *will* live to tell the tale!

With the complexity of Shakespeare's story lines, we have found that making a "movie" using a camcorder is much easier than preparing for a live performance "on-stage." Not only can you practice a scene immediately before you record it, but you can edit out mistakes, shoot "on location," and create special effects. Your grand performance will then become a movie premier, and copies of the video can be sent home for private viewing, or it can become part of a multimedia computer presentation. You may even decide to hold your own Oscar awards!

You are about to discover how simple the movie making process can be. All you need is a camcorder, props, simple costumes, a "castle" wall, some actors, and a little self-confidence! The question is how to get everything with a minimum of effort on your part. (You must save your energies for the creative process!)

1. Camcorder. If your school doesn't have one, send home a begging letter liberally sprinkled with veiled references as to how guilty the parents should feel if a camcorder is not forthcoming! Be sure to familiarize yourself with the camcorder before the actual filming. Nothing kills enthusiasm faster than a fumbler who misses an award-winning performance through technical ineptitude!

2. Costumes. Ask for donations and check the secondhand clothing stores. You will find a variety to choose from, at little cost.

3. Props. We have included a list of props. Dropping a few hints about what is needed usually results in instant props! Have your students make a large sign that says "ROMEO AND JULIET" for the camera to focus on as an introduction to the movie. Your students could also make a mural, or some other visual, for added effect.

4. Sets. The best thing about a camcorder, apart from the ability to edit out the disasters instantly, is its mobility. You can shoot in a variety of locations. Castle scenes require only a painted cardboard wall that can represent both indoors and out. Perhaps, the art teacher might turn his or her talented hand to this, too! Here are some location suggestions for the narrators:

    - Hallway
    - Cafeteria
    - Grassy area

Your enthusiastic students will be overflowing with ideas for locations with atmosphere. Let them have lots of input so that they feel the responsibility for the performance, as well as ownership. Remember, to have control you must give control.

5. Actors. This is the hardest part of all because everyone wants the BIG parts, and it is up to you to choose who does what. Here is an almost painless way:

   - Have students list several parts they would like to play. This gives you some leeway.
   - Have the students write down why they want to be a certain character.
   - If all else fails, flip a coin. Remember, auctioning off parts to the highest bidders is not an option!

6. Tips.

   - Slip written dialogue into books, or tape them onto props to aid the memories of nervous actors!
   - Manufacture extra parts by including lots of servants and soldiers. Shakespeare wouldn't mind—the play's the thing!
   - Your movie will take on a very professional look if you have an introduction consisting of a title, visuals, and even mood music!
   - Give the following script outline to actors and let them pad their own scenes with improvisation.
   - The key to successful improvisation is a thorough understanding of the play!
   - Hold lots of practice sessions before the film day; and for the sake of your sanity, don't try to film all the scenes in one day!
   - Insert credits at the end of the movie.

Now that you have everything you need, *go make a movie!!*

Cast of Characters

Narrator (can have more than one)
Escalus (Prince of Verona)
Lord and Lady Capulet
Lord and Lady Montague
Romeo Montague
Juliet Capulet
Benvolio (Romeo's cousin)
Mercutio (Romeo's friend)
Tybalt (Juliet's cousin)
Paris (Juliet's suitor)
The Nurse (Juliet's nurse)
Friar Laurence
Capulet servants (one named Peter)
Montague servants

Props

- costumes or distinguishable symbols for each main character (as different students will be portraying the same character, common costumes will provide continuity throughout the movie)
- sets for the streets of Verona, the Capulet mansion, the balcony, the church, and the graveyard (painted cardboard and playgrounds work great!)
- masks for crashing the party, vials for the poison, Romeo's dagger
- signs indicating locations (i.e., Welcome to the Capulet Household, No Fighting in Public, Verona, Juliet's Tomb)
- fake swords for the fights (see Management Notes)

Management Notes

The stage directions are intended to guide the students as they improvise each scene.

With so few main characters, different students can be selected to portray them for each scene. The common costumes will provide consistency for the audience.

Where appropriate, students may memorize actual dialogue from the play (see Will's Words). The Quality Quotes appear at relevant points in the text and enable students who want to recite the "real" text to do so.

At certain points during your performance there will be a fair amount of swordplay. Most of the swordplay can be merely suggested by the words of the actors; however, in the cases where characters are being killed, there are alternatives to a full-blown sword fight that you may use:

- make swords out of rolled, taped, and painted newspaper
- film the sword fight from a fighter's point of view (that way only one sword will actually be used)
- carefully plan the fight you want to film (by controlling it, you take the fighting out of the fight)

The Most Excellent and Lamentable Tragedy of Romeo and Juliet

Introduction

Narrator: Have you ever had an enemy? I mean somebody that really got on your nerves. No matter what that person did or said, you just wished that he would go away. Well, what if your hatred toward your enemy and his family was so strong that it lasted your whole life? Even worse, what if your parents hated them, too? And your grandparents? And your great-grandparents? Now that's what I call some serious negative feelings.

To make matters worse, what if nobody could remember why they started hating each other in the first place? Sound silly? Not to William Shakespeare. To him it was the making of a great story. Four hundred years ago, Shakespeare wrote a play about two fighting families from the city of Verona, Italy—the Capulets and the Montagues. Both families blamed the other for starting the fight, but neither family was willing to stop it. This is the sad story of their children, Romeo and Juliet, and how their love and death brought an end to their families' hate.

" Quality Quotes

Whole class as chorus (*introducing the play*):

Two households, both alike in dignity,
In fair Verona, where we lay our scene,
From ancient grudge break to new mutiny,
Where civil blood makes civil hands unclean.
From forth the fatal loins of these two foes
A pair of star-cross'd lovers take their life;
Whose misadventured piteous overthrows
Doth with their death bury their parents' strife.

Act 1, Scene 1

Narrator: Fights between the Capulet and Montague families have broken out twice already this year, and today, with the summer sun's heat raising even more hatred in the people below, fight number three is about to begin.

The Capulets are walking down one side of the street and the Montagues are walking down the other. Both sides want to fight, but neither wants to start it.

" Quality Quotes

(*The class can be divided in half for this scene.*)

Capulets: I will bite my thumb at them, which is disgrace to them if they bear it.

Montagues: Do you bite your thumb at us, sir?

Capulets: I do bite my thumb, sir.

Montagues: Do you bite your thumb at us, sir?

Capulets (*to themselves*)**:** Is the law on our side if I say ay?

Capulets: No, sir, I do not bite my thumb at you, sir, but I bite my thumb, sir.

Capulets: Do you quarrel, sir?

Montagues: Quarrel, sir? No, sir.

Each side tries to get the other to start the fight. After swords are drawn, Benvolio (Montague) tries to break up the fight; however, Tybalt (Capulet) wants the fight to continue.

“ Quality Quotes

Benvolio: Part, fools!
Put up your swords;
you know not what you do.

Tybalt: What, art thou drawn among these heartless hinds?
Turn thee, Benvolio, look upon thy death.

Benvolio: I do but keep the peace: put up thy sword,
Or manage it to part these men with me.

Tybalt: What, drawn, and talk of peace? I hate the word,
As I hate hell, all Montagues, and thee:
Have at thee, coward!

Benvolio is trying to stop the fight, but Tybalt wants to keep it going. Before anyone gets hurt, the prince comes in, and everyone runs off. The prince declares that the next person to fight in the streets will pay with his life.

Act 1, Scene 2

Narrator: After the fight breaks up, a worried Lady Montague finds Benvolio to ask if her son, Romeo, was involved. She is concerned because Romeo hasn't been himself lately, and she hopes that Benvolio can turn Romeo's frown upside down.

Lady Montague asks Benvolio about Romeo. Benvolio tells her that he will find Romeo and try to cheer him up. Benvolio catches up with Romeo, and they talk about the fight that happened earlier that day.

“ Quality Quotes

Romeo: O me! What fray was here?
Yet tell me not, for I have heard it all.
Here's much to do with hate, but more with love.
Why then, O brawling love! O loving hate!
O anything of nothing first create!

Romeo tells his cousin about his love for Rosaline and how she could not care less for him. Romeo is depressed. They walk away.

Act 1, Scene 3

Narrator: At the same time that Benvolio is trying to cheer up Romeo about his one-sided love for Rosaline, Lord Capulet is meeting with a wealthy bachelor named Paris who is interested in marrying his daughter, Juliet.

Paris and Lord Capulet are talking about Juliet. Lord Capulet wants her to marry for love when she is a little older, but Paris wants to marry her now. Lord Capulet decides to throw a party so that Paris and Juliet can meet. He calls over one of his servants (one that can't read) and gives him the invitations to pass out. The servant tries to explain his reading problem, but Lord Capulet has no time to listen.

" Quality Quotes

Peter (*alone on the street with a handful of invitations*)**:** Find them out whose names are written here! It is written that the shoemaker should meddle with his yard and the tailor with his last, the fisher with his pencil and the painter with his nets; but I am sent to find those persons whose names are here writ, and can never find what names the writing person hath here writ. I must to the learned. In good time!

Narrator: Peter is beside himself with worry as to how he will deliver Lord Capulet's party invitations. At that moment, who should come walking down the street but Benvolio and Romeo. Still discussing Romeo's misguided love life, Peter interrupts and begs for their assistance in reading the invitations.

Romeo and Benvolio help Peter with the invitations. Peter invites the two to the party in thanks for their help. Seeing that Rosaline will be there, Benvolio talks Romeo into crashing it.

Act 1, Scene 4

Narrator: Night falls on the city of Verona and a group of masked young men make their way through the streets to the Capulet party. Benvolio and Romeo are joined by their wild and playful friend Mercutio. He tries to cheer Romeo up by telling him about a strange dream he had the night before.

Benvolio, Romeo, and Mercutio are wearing masks as they get ready to crash the Capulet party. Mercutio talks about his Queen Mab dream.

" Quality Quotes

Mercutio: O then I see Queen Mab hath been with you:
She is the fairies' midwife, and she comes
In shape no bigger than an agate-stone
On the forefinger of an alderman,
Drawn with a team of little atomi
Over men's noses as they lie asleep.
Her chariot is an empty hazel-nut,
Made by the joiner squirrel or old grub,
Time out a'mind the fairies' coachmakers:
Her wagon spokes made of long spinners' legs,
The cover of the wings of grasshoppers,
Her traces of the smallest spider web,
Her collars of the moonshine's wat'ry beams,
Her whip of cricket's bone, the lash of film,
Her wagoner a small grey-coated gnat,
Not half so big as a round little worm
Pricked from the lazy finger of a maid.
And in this state she gallops night by night
Through lovers' brains, and then they dream of love . . .

Narrator: Maybe by some fairy queen's magic Romeo will finally find the love that he is so desperately looking for.

Act 1, Scene 5

Narrator: After arriving at the Capulet mansion, the masked Montagues join in with the dancing and festivities. All, that is, except Romeo, whose attention focuses elsewhere. No, he is not scanning the room for Rosaline. He has seen a different beauty. However, someone else has seen him first.

Benvolio and Mercutio try to get Romeo to dance, but Romeo refuses. Romeo sees Juliet across the dance floor; Tybalt sees Romeo and recognizes him as a Montague. Tybalt calls for his sword, but Lord Capulet intercepts Tybalt before he can start a fight, and he orders Tybalt to leave Romeo alone.

Narrator: Whew! That was a close one, but had Lord Capulet known that Romeo had just fallen in love with his only daughter, Juliet, he might have felt a little differently.

Romeo walks across the dance floor to meet Juliet, but they don't introduce themselves. They exchange words of love before they kiss (twice).

“ Quality Quotes

Romeo: If I profane with my unworthiest hand
This holy shrine, the gentle sin is this,
My lips, two blushing pilgrims, ready stand
To smooth that rough touch with a tender kiss.

Juliet: Good pilgrim, you do wrong your hand too much,
Which mannerly devotion shows in this,
For saints have hands that pilgrims' hands do touch,
And palm to palm is holy palmers' kiss.

Romeo: Have not saints lips, and holy palmers too?

Juliet: Ay, pilgrim, lips that they must use in prayer.

Romeo: O then, dear saint, let lips do what hands do:
They pray, grant thou, lest faith turn to despair.

Narrator: After kissing, but before introducing themselves (which you would think would come before the kissing), Juliet is called away by her nurse to meet with her mother. Not wanting to lose the love of his life, Romeo is determined to find out her name. Juliet is also interested in knowing who kissed her so well. Unfortunately, after they discover that the person they are in love with is also a member of the family that they hate, Romeo and Juliet are heartbroken.

Juliet is called away by her nurse. Romeo asks the nurse who Juliet is, and she tells him. Juliet asks her nurse to find out who Romeo is, and she does. Romeo and Juliet are heartbroken.

“ Quality Quotes

Juliet (*after hearing the nurse's news*):
My only love sprung from my only hate!
Too early seen unknown, and known too late!
Prodigious birth of love it is to me,
That I must love a loathed enemy.

Act 2, Scene 1

Narrator: Romeo's love for Juliet is so strong that after leaving the Capulet party, Romeo ditches his friends and makes his way back to the Capulet estate. In the dark, he climbs a rock wall and a tree—which just happens to be growing outside the balcony of Juliet's bedroom.

Romeo is hiding in a tree just outside Juliet's bedroom balcony. He sees her through the window and describes how beautiful she is to him.

“ Quality Quotes

Romeo (*to himself while in a tree*):
But soft, what light through yonder window breaks?
It is the east, and Juliet is the sun.
Arise, fair sun, and kill the envious moon,
Who is already sick and pale with grief
That thou, her maid, art far more fair than she.

Juliet comes out onto the balcony, not seeing Romeo in the tree, and starts talking about how names are not as important as love.

“ Quality Quotes

Juliet: O Romeo, Romeo, wherefore art thou Romeo?
Deny thy father and refuse thy name;
Or if thou wilt not, be but sworn my love,
And I'll no longer be a Capulet.
'Tis but thy name that is my enemy;
Thou art thyself, though not a Montague.
What's Montague? It is nor hand nor foot,
Nor arm nor face, nor any other part
Belonging to a man. O be some other name!
What's in a name? That which we call a rose
By any other word would smell as sweet.

After hearing Juliet, Romeo makes himself known and the two talk about getting married. Romeo leaves in search of someone to marry them.

Narrator: After declaring their love for one another, Juliet tells Romeo that she will marry him if he can find someone to do the job. With stars in his eyes and love in his heart, Romeo goes to the church the next morning to talk with his friend Friar Laurence.

Act 2, Scene 2

The friar is working in his garden talking about all the different kinds of flowers and herbs that he grows.

“ Quality Quotes

Friar Laurence: Within the infant rind of this weak flower
Poison hath residence, and medicine power:
For this, being smelt, with that part cheers each part,
Being tasted, stays all senses with the heart.
Two such opposed kings encamp them still
In man as well as herbs, grace and rude will;
And where the worser is predominant,
Full soon the canker death eats up that plant.

Romeo enters the church garden, and tells the friar about his new love for Juliet and asks him to marry them. Friar Laurence is shocked that Romeo has changed lovers so quickly. He starts to lecture him about commitment and real love. Romeo insists that his love for Juliet is real.

“ Quality Quotes

Romeo: Then plainly know, my heart’s dear love is set
On the fair daughter of rich Capulet;
As mine on hers, so hers is set on mine,
And all combined, save what thou must combine
By holy marriage. When and where and how
We met, we wooed, and made exchange of vow,
I’ll tell thee as we pass, but this I pray,
That thou consent to marry us today.

The friar thinks that a marriage between Romeo and Juliet may be just what their families need to stop their fighting, so he agrees to marry them that afternoon.

Narrator: When Romeo arrives, he immediately tells Friar Laurence of his newfound love for Juliet, and he asks him to marry them. Even as the friar tries to talk Romeo out of marrying Juliet, he considers the possibility of their marriage bringing an end to their families’ fighting. With this thought in mind, Friar Laurence agrees to the secret wedding. That afternoon, Romeo and Juliet meet at the church to be married. The actual wedding ceremony, however, is not a part of Shakespeare’s play. I wonder why?

Act 3, Scene 1

Narrator: Following their secret wedding, Juliet returns to the Capulet mansion and Romeo goes into Verona to meet up with his friends. Before he arrives though, trouble is brewing. Benvolio and Mercutio are being taunted by the vengeful Tybalt. He wants to teach these Montagues a lesson for crashing his uncle’s party.

Benvolio and Mercutio are arguing with Tybalt about crashing last night’s party. Romeo arrives and tries to break up the fight, and he even tries to make friends with Tybalt.

“ Quality Quotes

Tybalt: Romeo, the love I bear thee can afford
No better term than this: thou art a villain.

Romeo: Tybalt, the reason that I have to love thee
Doth much excuse the appertaining rage
To such a greeting. Villain am I none;
Therefore farewell, I see thou knowest me not.

Tybalt: Boy, this shall not excuse the injuries
That thou hast done me, therefore turn and draw.

Romeo: I do protest I never injured thee,
But love thee better than thou canst devise,
Till thou shalt know the reason of my love;
And so, good Capulet, which name I tender
As dearly as mine own, be satisfied.

Tybalt draws his sword, not listening to a word Romeo has said. Mercutio draws his sword in defense of Romeo. Romeo steps between them to break up the fight, and Tybalt's sword slides under Romeo's arm and kills Mercutio. A furious Romeo then attacks Tybalt, wrestles him to the ground, and kills him with his sword. Seeing that Mercutio and Tybalt are dead, Romeo runs away. The prince comes on the scene and banishes Romeo from Verona forever.

Narrator: During the deadly street brawl, Juliet was waiting for Romeo to come for her. She sends her nurse to look for him while she waits impatiently at the mansion. Upon the nurse's return, Juliet learns about her cousin Tybalt's death and Romeo's banishment. She desperately wants to see her new husband before he has to leave Verona forever. However, before Romeo gets a chance to see Juliet one last time, another man is making his way to the Capulet mansion to pay her a visit.

Act 3, Scene 2

Paris comes to the Capulet mansion to plan for his upcoming marriage to Juliet. Lord and Lady Capulet set the wedding for later that week, thinking that it will cheer their daughter. Lady Capulet comes to Juliet's room to tell her about the wedding, but Juliet is very upset. Lord Capulet can't believe his daughter's reaction, and loses his temper with her.

“ Quality Quotes

Lord Capulet: How how, how how, chopt-logic? What is this?
“Proud,” and “I thank you,” and “I thank you not,”
And yet “not proud,” mistress minion you?
Thank me no thankings, nor proud me no prouds,
But fettle your fine joints 'gainst Thursday next,
To go with Paris to Saint Peter's Church,
Or I will drag thee on a hurdle thither.
Out, you green-sickness carrion! out, you baggage!
You tallow-face!

Lord Capulet will force Juliet to marry Paris. Juliet, the nurse, and Lady Capulet all beg Lord Capulet to change his mind. Because Juliet needs help, she tells her family that she will consider the marriage to Paris. Juliet leaves for the church.

Narrator: Juliet begs Lord Capulet to change his mind, the nurse begs him to change his mind, even Lady Capulet begs him to change his mind, but it is no use. Either Juliet will marry Paris or she will no longer be his daughter. Devastated and completely alone, Juliet tells her family that she will consider marrying Paris just to get them off her back, and she leaves for the church to see Friar Laurence. He seems to have a plan for everything; maybe he could help her.

Act 4, Scene 1

Narrator: As Juliet reaches the church, Friar Laurence is already meeting with Paris making plans for the wedding. She pretends that all is well as she waits for Paris to leave. The plan that the friar designs to bring Romeo and Juliet back together is his most dangerous yet.

Juliet enters the church and finds Paris and the friar talking. She pretends that all is well. After Paris leaves, Juliet tells Friar Laurence of her father's plans and asks for help. The friar tells her about the fake death plan.

“ Quality Quotes

Friar Laurence: Take thou this vial, being then in bed,
And this distilling liquor drink thou off,
When presently through all thy veins shall run
A cold and drowsy humour; for no pulse
Shall keep his native progress, but surcease;
No warmth, no breath shall testify thou livest;
The roses in thy lips and cheeks shall fade
To wanny ashes, thy eyes' windows fall,
Like Death when he shuts up the day of life;
Each part, deprived of supple government,
Shall stiff and stark and cold appear like death,
And in this borrowed likeness of shrunk death
Thou shalt continue two and forty hours,
And then wake as from a pleasant sleep.

Juliet takes the fake death potion and leaves for the Capulet mansion.

Act 4, Scene 2

Narrator: Because Juliet doesn't want anything to get in the way of her plan to be with Romeo, she pretends to go along with her family's plans for her to marry Paris. The night before the wedding, while her family prepares for the celebration, Juliet takes the death potion and prays that when her eyes open again she will see her truelove, Romeo.

Juliet is alone in her room reminding herself about the friar's plan. Juliet drinks the potion, and her body is discovered by the nurse. Instead of a wedding, the Capulets have a funeral performed by Friar Laurence. Juliet is placed in the tomb. The plan has begun.

Act 5, Scene 1

Narrator: Unfortunately, the message Romeo receives first is the news of Juliet's death—not the friar's clever plan. After hearing of his truelove's death, Romeo makes plans to join Juliet, vowing that he could never live without her. He purchases a bottle of poison and heads for Verona.

Friar Laurence gets word that Romeo has not received his message about Juliet's fake death and rushes to the graveyard to save Juliet before she awakens. Paris is outside Juliet's tomb, sad about her death, when Romeo arrives. Paris draws his sword to defend Juliet's tomb against the evil Montague that killed Juliet's cousin. Romeo kills Paris, and opens the tomb. After seeing Juliet lying dead in the tomb, Romeo drinks his poison and dies. Right after Romeo dies, Juliet starts to wake up.

Narrator: News of Romeo's return and the duel in the graveyard spreads like wildfire through the streets of Verona and to the houses of the Montagues, the Capulets, and the prince. The news sends both families racing to the graveyard. Friar Laurence is the first to reach Juliet's tomb. He is hoping to reach Juliet before she comes to. What he finds is Romeo's dead body lying next to the awakening Juliet. When she sees the friar, she asks about Romeo, but no sooner does she get the words out of her mouth when she sees his body next to her.

The friar tries to persuade Juliet to leave the tomb before the families arrive. Juliet refuses. The friar runs from the tomb to save himself from being caught with this failed plan. Seeing her truelove dead, Juliet takes Romeo's dagger and kills herself.

Act 5, Scene 2

Narrator: When the Prince, the Montagues, and the Capulets finally arrive on the tragic scene, they can't believe how all these young people could have died. It is Friar Laurence's voice that breaks the silence. He explains everything from the secret marriage to the secret death plan. He tells the families how Romeo and Juliet were happier to die together than to live apart.

The Capulets, the Montagues, and the prince arrive at the tomb: They can't believe their eyes. Friar Laurence comes back and tells them everything. The two families begin to comfort each other, and make up for all the years of fighting. The prince hopes that with the deaths of their children, the Capulets and Montagues will stop fighting.

“ Quality Quotes

Escalus: A glooming peace this morning with it brings,
The sun for sorrow will not show his head.
Go hence to have more talk of these sad things;
Some shall be pardoned, and some punished:
For never was a story of more woe
Than this of Juliet and her Romeo.

Narrator: In the midst of all the death and sorrow, the two families that had hated each another for so long were able to come together and comfort each other, ending their fighting, and finally finding peace.

Don't Just Sit There!

Knowledge, the wing wherewith we fly to heaven.
(*Henry VI*, 4.7)

The following activities are intended to bring the play into all curriculum areas and thus enhance students' understanding and interest. The teacher may select several activities to deepen students' understanding of a certain aspect of the play, or only one or two, merely as fun breaks during rehearsals. On a grander scale, the teacher may decide to use *Romeo and Juliet* as the core of a thematic study. In brief, the thematic, or project, approach to learning involves an extended study of a topic that crosses all curricula areas. The benefits of this approach lie in the total immersion of students in the topic and the learning that occurs from connections students make between their lives and experiences and the topic. For a more detailed look at thematic learning and the aims of this approach, we highly recommend *Engaging Children's Minds: The Project Approach* by Lillian Katz and Sylvia Chard.[1]

We have grouped the activities by curriculum subjects, beginning with language arts, and we strongly encourage teachers to adapt, expand, or condense the activities to meet the needs and interests of the students. We have described the first two activities in detail to provide as complete a picture as possible of the process of classroom application. Following these two activities are lots of "bare bones" that you can discard or fatten up for classroom consumption! Enjoy!

Language Arts

Pretend Pen Pals

- Level: 2 and up
- Grouping: pairs or individually
- Time: a one-time activity or used throughout the study of the play
- Supplies: paper, pencil, and imagination
- Objectives: This activity will not only reinforce your students' letter-writing skills, but it will help them practice character development and writing from different points of view.

In order for your students to appreciate and understand the plot and characters in *Romeo and Juliet,* it is essential that they be able to live in the skin of the characters and relate to them as real people. Being able to act out a scene using either Shakespeak or Kidspeak is the best way for your students to put themselves in the characters' shoes; however, an equally powerful way to live in the skin of the characters is through writing.

Using the format of a friendly letter, a student can take on the voice of one character from the play and write to another character in order to ask questions and give advice. That same student can then write a response back to himself or herself as a different character (or a partner could serve in that role) and become a dramatic pen pal.

Some ideas for imaginary pen pals are:

- Juliet to Romeo
- Friar to Romeo
- Nurse to Juliet
- Friar to Montagues and Capulets

The combinations are as broad as your imagination.

Once students have exchanged letters several times, you can collect them into a class book for everyone to enjoy.

Say What?

- Level: kindergarten and up
- Grouping: whole class to individual
- Time: 45 minutes (minimum)
- Supplies: paper, pencil, and creativity
- Objective: This activity involves creatively retelling a portion of the play. The skills being developed are comprehension, retelling, and sequencing.

If anything scares people away from Shakespeare, it has to be the language. "People just don't talk that way anymore; how am I supposed to figure it out!?" is a common complaint and excuse heard from high school and college students. However, surprisingly, young children embrace the language, rhyme, and rhythm of Shakespeare without complaint or excuse. Indeed, they are intrigued with the puzzle within the words and feel extremely successful when they break the code and make the words their own. "But how do young children accomplish what adults find difficult?" you may be asking yourself. First, if you follow our hints and suggestions throughout this book, you will brim with confidence, as will your students. Second, by putting Shakespeare into the mouths and pencils of your students, you present them the gift of owning the Bard for themselves.

By sharing a modern (Kidspeak) retelling of the play with your students, you make the story accessible to them. If you take the time to discuss and debate the critical issues in the play, your students will start to relate the characters and their problems to their own lives. At this point, the responsibility shifts to the students for telling the play. Once they know the story and the characters, you can begin to introduce the "real" language. It is amazing how clear Shakespearean English can become if you know first what the words are supposed to mean. In fact, you may discover that your students prefer the Shakespeak to the Kidspeak when they begin to understand it.

Here are several ways to help your students own the Bard:

- Before you start Shakespeare each day, have your students retell what has happened so far in the play. You can even make a game out of it by playing Add On. One student starts the retelling, and (in mid-sentence) you select another student to add on to what the first student said, and so on and so on and so on, until the retelling is complete.

- You can assign scenes to small groups. With the expectation that everyone has a part, each group will do a mini-presentation retelling the scene. It may be helpful for the group to make posters illustrating the action that takes place within its scene. You might even challenge the groups to include lines from the real play.
- Individuals or pairs can rewrite scenes. By explaining that another class (possibly kindergartners) is interested in learning about *Romeo and Juliet* and that they would like a book that they can understand, your students can collaborate on a class book to share with them. This places your students in an "expert" role and motivates them to be clear and detailed. You may even challenge your students to include some Shakespeak within their retelling of the play.

There may be some students in your class that really want to personalize *Romeo and Juliet* in a creative way. Either in the form of a poem, a song, a rap, a comic strip, a puppet show, or a pantomime we have seen students convert the play into a variety of creative formats.

Will's Words

Use the Will's Words pages we have provided to spark your acting career. Explanations of the verses are given. Draw and color an illustration that goes with your verse, practice your lines, and recite them for your class.

Being the Bard

Choose your favorite or most memorable scene from the play. Write what happens in your own words and design an illustration that will bring the scene to life.

Who's Who? You!

Choose your favorite or most memorable character from the play. Describe what the character looks like and acts like. Include a full-color picture of your character as you see him or her in your mind.

Venn in Verona

Select two characters from the play and describe their similarities and differences using a Venn diagram.

Playground Problems

Think of a situation that happened at home or school where you were not allowed to play with someone or do something for some reason, and write your own story about your experience.

Trash the Tragedy

Instead of everyone getting killed, what if they would have lived? Write a new ending for this play turning the tragedy into a comedy.

Rappin' Rhymin' Romeo

Are you a poet and you know it? Here's your chance to prove it! Write a summary of the play as a poem and present it as a song or a rap.

Love Is . . .

People love chocolate, parents, toys, cars, friends, and many other things. The word *love* is used all the time by people, but what does it really mean? Write what it means to you.

Bard's-Eye View

How different would this story be if it were told by Paris, or the friar, or the prince? Write a new version of this play from a different point of view.

Social Studies/Geography/History

On This Day . . .

Juliet's nurse was able to recall all of the events during the year that Juliet was born. Investigate your birth year and make a newspaper with articles highlighting important events that occurred.

Venn in Europe

Compare maps of modern-day Europe with Renaissance Europe on a Venn diagram. My, how things change.

Just the Facts

Research the country of Italy. Outline all the important facts that you find. Include a model of Italy's flag using cut paper.

Renaissance Research

Write a report explaining life during the time of Romeo and Juliet. Be sure to include customs and clothing that was different from today.

Life After Death?

Romeo thinks that he and Juliet will be together in death. Interview your family and write what you believe happens after death.

Who Do You Trust?

Romeo had the Friar and Juliet had her nurse. Who do you trust with your secrets and problems? List two people and explain why they are trustworthy.

Vacation in Verona

Do some research on Italy and design a travel brochure for the city of Verona. What can you say that would make people want to visit?

Romeo's Rivals

Write short biographies for other famous lovers in history. See what you can find on people like Don Juan, St. Valentine, or Casanova.

Finding Feuds

Like the feud between the Capulets and Montagues, there have been other feuds throughout history such as the North versus the South (the Civil War) and England versus America (Revolutionary War). Research them and write a report about how they began. Someone must know.

Cupid's Arrow

Read about the story of Cupid in Greek mythology and retell it in your own words. Include a picture of what you think Cupid looks like.

Suicide Survival

The problems that Romeo and Juliet face are problems that people have to deal with. What could they have done differently to solve their problems? Write a letter of advice to Romeo and Juliet telling them what other choices they could make.

Math/Science

Don't Break My Heart

Many people attribute love with the heart. Is there a connection? Research the function of the human heart and write a report complete with diagram explaining how it works.

To Die or Not to Die

Does the fake death potion that Juliet used really exist? Some people say that a substance called *curare* mimics death. Visit the library and look for information on *curare*. Write a report on what you find.

What's Happenin'

The entire play *Romeo and Juliet* takes a total of five days. Create a time line that shows the time that certain events in the play occurred. Write sentences that tell how much time has elapsed or how much time is left until the end.

Pesky Potions

Create your own concoction by choosing an experiment and following the directions carefully.

You Got a Problem?

Use characters and events from the play to write your own story problems using addition, subtraction, multiplication, or division.

Getting Board?

Use the plot of the play to design a board game. Be sure to include spaces that send you forward, backward, and make you stay put. You may use dice or a spinner to determine the number of spaces moved.

Survey Says . . .

Who do people prefer? Romeo or Juliet? Is there a difference between boys and girls? Design a survey and graph the results. Try it with other characters as well.

Poison Patrol

Keep you and your family safe by drawing a map of your house and counting the number of poisons found in each room (with an adult). Are all the poisons out of the reach of children? Make a Poison Patrol poster listing rules to keep kids safe; include the poison control phone number.

Venn Are You Safe?

When is something a poison and when is it not? Make a Venn diagram by listing items that are always poisonous, sometimes poisonous, and never poisonous. Write a sentence telling what you discover.

Hot Stuff

Notes

1. Lillian Katz and Sylvia Chard, *Engaging Children's Minds: The Project Approach* (Norwood, NJ: Ablex, 1989).

Annotated Bibliography and Resources

There are many excellent read-aloud versions of *Romeo and Juliet*. It is worth the effort of shopping around to find the version that suits your style. The following are some of our favorites that we used in preparation for our students:

Garfield, Leon. *Shakespeare Stories*. Boston: Houghton Mifflin, 1985.

This collection of stories makes the plays of Shakespeare accessible to students. Using today's language with some of Shakespearean English sprinkled in, the author makes the characters and stories come to life in an entertaining way.

McCaughrean, Geraldine. *Stories from Shakespeare*. New York: Margaret K. McElderry Books, 1995.

Geraldine McCaughrean offers an alternative to Shakespeare's iambic pentameter. These stories have all the entertainment value of the original but are more accessible to students.

Nesbit, Edith. *The Best of Shakespeare*. New York: Oxford University Press, 1997.

Edith Nesbit retells classic Shakespeare by integrating the original verse with today's language.

———. *The Children's Shakespeare: Romeo and Juliet*. Los Angeles: New Star Media, 1998. Audiocassette.

Shakespeare won a Grammy Award! This collection of stories, told by a variety of famous actors, provides yet another way to share Shakespeare with children and adults.

Ronnie and Julie. VHS, 99 min. Hallmark Entertainment, Los Angeles: 1997.

Your students will really be able to identify with the characters in this modern day retelling of the classic play. He is a hockey player and she is a figure skater. Their families are running against each other in a political campaign for mayor. The many references to *Romeo and Juliet* throughout the movie will keep your students watching; there is even a happy ending.

Shakespeare. *Romeo and Juliet*. Classics Illustrated edition, ed. Susan Shwartz. New York: Acclaim Books, 1996.

Here the Sunday comics meet the Bard. Shakespeare's words are found in "talking bubbles" in this comic-book version of the story. Extensive study notes, which students will find informative, follow the story.

Shakespeare. *Romeo and Juliet.* Retold by Andrea Hopkins. New York: Barnes and Noble Books, 1998.

This picture book will allow you to read the story while you help your students visualize the characters and action. The illustrations can also be used to stimulate discussions.

Shakespeare. *Romeo and Juliet.* Retold by Billy Aronson. New York: Harper Paperbacks, 1996.

In chapter book form, a cute little dog, Wishbone, guides you through the tragic story of Romeo and Juliet with just the right amount of humor. The fourth-grade reading level makes this a perfect book to use with a reading group.

Shakespeare. *Romeo and Juliet.* Retold by Margaret Early. New York: Harry N. Abrams, 1998.

This gorgeous picture book allow you to read the story while helping your students visualize the characters and action. The detailed illustrations provide a launching point for discussion and retelling.

Shakespeare. *Romeo and Juliet for Kids (Shakespeare Can Be Fun).* Retold by Lois Burdett. Buffalo, NY: Firefly Books, 1998.

By a teacher, for teachers. This could be the most creative retelling yet. Complete with drawings and stories by children, Lois Burdett turns Shakespeare's plays into poetry that is accessible to anyone.

Shakespeare. *Romeo and Juliet for Young People.* Shakespeare for Young People Series, ed. Diane Davidson, bk. 2. Fair Oaks, CA: Swan Books, 1986.

The author abridges Shakespeare's plays and puts them in dialogue form (with stage directions) to make them manageable for your students.

Shakespeare. *Shakespeare the Animated Tales: Romeo and Juliet.* Produced and directed by Dave Edwards. 30 min. New York: Random House, 1993. Videocassette.

This shortened cartoon version of the play uses narration to explain the ins and outs of the Bard's play.

West Side Story. VHS, 151 min. MGM/United Artists Studios, Los Angeles, 1961.

This classic musical is based on the classic Shakespearean play. Your students will be able to watch the parallels unfold before their eyes, and they will experience a very creative and popular retelling of the tragic play.

Conclusion

We hope, now that you have reached this point in the book, that you are convinced of the value of introducing Shakespeare to young children, and have the tools and enthusiasm to get started.

The following section should dispel any lingering doubts about teaching Shakespeare by giving you an insight into an added bonus that we have not mentioned previously. As we all know, appreciation for teachers is often slow in coming, unlike criticism, and education has a tarnished image in the public's eye. It has been our experience that the study of Shakespeare with young children makes parents sit up and take notice in a very positive way. They see their children's enthusiasm and excitement, as well as their increasing knowledge and understanding of a subject that probably was extremely difficult for them in high school, or even in college. The parents hear about the reasons for our class study of Shakespeare, the goals we hope to achieve, the regular updates on the progress being made, and the skills being covered. Through this ambitious project, the parents see the high expectations their school had for their children, and perhaps they reach a better understanding of how education can look different from when they were at school without sacrificing the basics.

The following are excerpts from a survey of parents that we send home after the completion of our Shakespeare projects. They illustrate the support we receive from our community and show that parents do appreciate the time, effort, and energy creative teachers put into their work.

Parent Responses

I am amazed at what I have seen Danny do and learn with Shakespeare as the vehicle. Here is what I have noticed:

- (It has) placed him on a "level playing field" with other readers and given him increased confidence.
- (It has) shown him a different side to reading and literature. Positive!
- (It has) tricked him into not realizing that he was reading and actually enjoying himself.
- (It has) empowered him with what he has learned—he can quote Shakespeare!
- He knows that he is special with his knowledge of Shakespeare.

Ms. S. Stotz

Although children may not understand all of what they read by Shakespeare, they come away with an enhanced view of the world. They are also stimulated to learn more.

Mrs. S. Levine

The recitations from Shakespeare have captured Mamie's imagination! Exposure to Shakespeare has been a great introduction to classical literature that will fire her imagination to persevere. Bravo!

Mrs. M. Stevenson

I can't tell you enough how impressed I am that the kids are learning and studying Shakespeare at such an early age. I know she will continue to appreciate Shakespeare far into the future! Who knows what it will lead to for her?

Mrs. J. Potts

It's amazing to me that a kindergartner is conversant [with] Shakespeare. She has been able to carry on conversations with adults about *A Midsummer Night's Dream* and *Twelfth Night* and actually correct them on pronunciation of names and sequence of events.

Ms. M. Romer

It has amazed us that, at such a young age, Katie has enjoyed the humor of Shakespeare. Introducing her to Shakespeare now establishes an appreciation and excitement [for] Shakespeare in the future.

Mrs. H. Kucera

Shakespeare and his plays have become part of our family's dinner conversation. To listen to a five-year-old explaining *A Midsummer Night's Dream* to his older brother is priceless! Many thanks to both of you for your enthusiasm and all your hard work that made this possible for all the children.

Mrs. P. Eby

It is very rewarding as a parent to have your six-year-old tell you about *A Midsummer Night's Dream.* He also entertained our whole family by acting out *Twelfth Night.*

Mrs. S. Clark

It has broadened his horizon to different types of literature . . . We heard a lot about Hermia.

Mrs. L. Yurglich

Jessie has never been as "turned on" to any unit in school as she has been since the Shakespeare unit was introduced. Not only does she come home quoting passages from *A Midsummer Night's Dream,* but she expresses herself with emotion and interprets meanings correctly.

In addition, Jessie's attitude and motivation toward all her schoolwork has greatly improved since the inception of Shakespeare.

Mrs. J. Jacobson

What a surprise to have my children study Shakespeare in second grade and kindergarten! It is still amazing to hear my second-grader quoting entire excerpts of *A Midsummer Night's Dream* from memory!

Mrs. C. Leonard

I think this introduction to Shakespeare will make all future study of his works non threatening. I'm amazed at how easily young children accept Shakespearean English; they are not at all intimidated by it.

Ms. D. Hodgeson

Without even knowing it, my child is extremely excited about literature and history. He thinks nothing of learning and understanding Shakespeare's language, and he has gained even more confidence in speaking and acting in front of others. Thank you for introducing Shakespeare to my child.

Mrs. C. Kiffor

I believe that the presentation of a complex story with multiple characters is quite a challenge to kindergartners; I believe that when these stories were placed on a level that he could follow, he felt a sense of accomplishment [through being] able to understand them.

Mrs. T. Sachen

It's been great fun having Jamie, our eight-year-old, coming home reciting lines from *A Midsummer Night's Dream.* I waited until my thirties to get the courage to delve into Shakespeare, and he's inspiring me. It's contagious.

Ms. K McClintock

Student Responses

Finally, in case you still need one more little push to get started, we have included the following comments from eighth-grade students who studied Shakespeare with us in third grade. Their comments present a powerful case for elementary school Shakespeare:

Studying Shakespeare in third grade expanded my understanding of other kinds of literature. Studying Shakespeare made me be able to better understand and make analogies to other subjects and other books and stories. I remember most our acting out of *The Merchant of Venice.* This type of learning helped me understand and remember Shakespeare.

Kazy Ferguson

Shakespeare has opened many new doors to my learning abilities. The literature has increased my vocabulary and writing ability. I remember many things about our study of Shakespeare. What I loved most about it was our reading out loud in class and our costume party. I was Juliet. Shakespeare was a great influence on my education. It should be used in early education for years to come.

Penny Wyman

I remember the plays the most because it was fun and educational . . . now I have some background.

Tommy Brainard

> I remember lots about studying Shakespeare. First, I remember performing. Getting costumes and using props was really fun! Also, being filmed was neat. Second, I never thought I would have so much fun in learning Shakespeare. I always thought Shakespeare was boring until we acted it out. At the time, it made me feel older because I was reading Shakespeare. At the same time, there was something weird—I really understood it! I wasn't just pretending; I really got it. Now, when I go to high school in a year, I will already have knowledge of Shakespeare. Clearly, it was awesome!
>
> **Kim Hess**

The study of Shakespeare in elementary school is a great exercise in public relations, but it is much more than that. Besides making parents aware of the abilities of the students, the dedication and skills of the teachers, and the diversity and quality of education today, this project gives so much to all the students who participate. Students who are gifted can be challenged and enriched; students who struggle can find an area of strength and achieve success in this unconventional approach to learning; and all students can develop an appreciation for, instead of a fear of, the amazing works of Shakespeare.

Beguile the time and feed your knowledge . . .
(*Twelfth Night*, 3.3)

Index

Activities, xiii-xv, 6-9, 15
    Art, 56-57, 104-105
    Creative thinking, 106
    Hamlet, 50-59
    Language Arts, 50-55, 96-102, 149-152, 203-206
    Macbeth, 96-106
    Math, 57-58, 105, 153-154, 207-208
    Midsummer Night's Dream, 149-154
    Romeo and Juliet, 203-208
    Science, 58-59, 106, 153-154, 207-208
    Social Studies, 55-56, 102-104, 152-153, 206-207

Characters, xiii, 12-14,
    Hamlet, 23-25, 45
    Macbeth, 63-64, 89
    Midsummer Night's Dream, 111-115, 140
    Romeo and Juliet, 159-162, 193
Cooperative groups, 16-17

Globe Theatre, 7, 65, 116

Hamlet, 23-60
Hathaway, Anne, 3, 4

Macbeth, 63-108
Midsummer Night's Dream, 111-155

Plot, *see* story
Props
    Hamlet, 45
    Macbeth, 89
    Midsummer Night's Dream, 140
    Romeo and Juliet, 193
Pyramus and Thisbe, 115, 123, 164

Recitation, xiv-xv
Romeo and Juliet, 159-210
Rubrics, 16, 18

Shakespeare, Hamnet, 4
Shakespeare, Susanna, 4
Shakespeare, William, biography, 3-5
Story, xiii, 15
Stratford-on-Avon, 3

West Side Story, 164